Privacy and Data Protection Law in Japan

Privacy and Data Protection Law in Japan

Fumio Shimpo

This book was originally published as a monograph in the International Encyclopaedia of Laws/Privacy and Technology Law.

Founding Editor: Roger Blanpain
General Editor: Frank Hendrickx
Volume Editors: Jos Dumortier, Pieter Gryffroy, Ruben Roex &
Yung Shin Van Der Sype

Wolters Kluwer

Published by:
Kluwer Law International B.V.
PO Box 316
2400 AH Alphen aan den Rijn
The Netherlands
E-mail: lrs-sales@wolterskluwer.com
Website: www.wolterskluwer.com/en/solutions/kluwerlawinternational

Sold and distributed by:
Wolters Kluwer Legal & Regulatory U.S.
920 Links Avenue
Landisville, PA 17538
United States of America
E-mail: customer.service@wolterskluwer.com

ISBN 978-94-035-2867-0

e-Book: ISBN 978-94-035-2877-9
web-PDF: ISBN 978-94-035-2887-8

The Author

Professor of Faculty of Policy Management at Keio University, PhD in Law: the area of academic expertise is Constitutional Law, Cyber-Law and Robot Law.

The previous Commissioner for International Academic Exchange at the Personal Information Protection Commission of Japan, (2018–2023), the former Vice-Chair of the OECD Working Party on Security and Privacy in the Digital Economy, (SPDE), (2009–2016), the Chair of the Board of Directors of the Association of Law and Information Systems, the Executive Director of the Japanese Constitutional Law Society, the Vice-Chair of the Board of Directors of the Japan Society of Information and Communication Research, the Director of the Law and Computer Society, and Senior Research Fellow at the Institute for Information and Communications Policy of the Ministry of Internal Affairs and Communications.

The Author

Table of Contents

List of Abbreviations

AA	Accountability Agents
AI	Artificial Intelligence
APEC	Asia-Pacific Economic Cooperation
API	Anonymously Processed Information
APPA	Asia-Pacific Privacy Agencies
APPI	Act on the Protection of Personal Information
CBPR	Cross-Border Privacy Rules
CIO	Chief Information Officer
CPEA	Cross-Border Privacy Enforcement Arrangement
CPTPP	Comprehensive and Progressive Agreement on Trans-Pacific Partnership
DFFT	Data Free Flow with Trust
DMP	Data Management Platform
DPA	Data Protection Act
DPS	Data Privacy Subgroup
ECSG	Electronic Commerce Steering Group
EPA	Economic Partnership Agreement
EU	European Union
GDPR	General Data Protection Regulation
ICT	Information and Communications Technology
IWGDPT	International Working Group on Data Protection in Telecommunications
JIPDEC	Japan Institute for Promotion of Digital Economy and Community
JIS	Japanese Industrial Standard
METI	Ministry of Economy, Trade and Industry
MIC	Ministry of Internal Affairs and Communications
MITI	Ministry of International Trade and Industry, (re-named METI)
OECD	Organisation for Economic Co-operation and Development
PIA	Privacy Impact Assessment
PPC	Personal Information Protection Commission

List of Abbreviations

PPI	Pseudonymously Processed Information
PRI	Personally Referable Information
SNS	Social Networking Services

Preface

The Japanese personal information protection legal system and the protection of the right to privacy have been mainly developed based on tort law privacy. In particular, Japanese judicial precedents protecting the right to privacy have been influenced by the four common law privacy torts categorised by Dean William Prosser.[1] Prosser restructured all invasions of privacy into four categories of torts and implanted his own taxonomy directly into the American Law Institute's Restatement 2nd of Torts.

Regarding data protection law in general, the Organisation for Economic Co-operation and Development (OECD) established privacy guidelines in 1980, and the first Japanese personal information protection act for administrative organs was enacted eight years after the adoption of the OECD guidelines. However, it was not until 2003 that legislation was also developed to cover businesses which handle personal information in the private sector. Until then, voluntary efforts to protect personal information were made as a part of compliance. Throughout this period, efforts to protect personal information based on guidelines had been implemented before the enactment of the Act on the Protection of Personal Information .

In understanding the Japanese legal system, it should be noted that various guidelines have been established together with the law. These guidelines, which can be divided into those enacted by administrative organs and those enacted by private organisations, function as a set of rules for interpreting the law and also as an indicator for administrative organs to make decisions when enforcing the law. It is, therefore, necessary to understand that the guidelines are not merely standards to encourage purely voluntary efforts on the part of businesses and individuals, but also set out specific criteria for compliance with the law. Hence, in this manuscript, the guidelines are quoted in detail and specific standards are provided in order to clarify the specific criteria for interpretation of the commentary on the Act on the Protection of Personal Information in Japan.

This monograph was supported by JST Moonshot R&D Grant Number JPMJMS2215.

I would like to thank Devereux Education, (Southport Language Services) and Editage (www.editage.com) for English language editing.

October 2022

1. William Prosser, *Privacy*, 48 CAL. L. REV. 383, 423 (1960).

General Background of the Country

§1. GEOGRAPHY AND POPULATION

1. Japan is an island nation located in East Asia, bordered by the Pacific Ocean to the east and the Sea of Japan to the west.[2] Japan is known for its diverse geography, with mountains, forests, beaches, and plains. Japan's highest mountain is Mount Fuji, which is an active volcano and a popular tourist destination.

2. The country has a population of 124.49 million people,[3] making it the eleventh most populous country in the world. Tokyo is the capital city. Japan's economy is the third-largest in the world, behind the United States and China, in terms of nominal GDP JPY 555 trillion.[4]

§2. POLITICAL SYSTEM

3. The political system of Japan is a parliamentary democracy with a constitutional monarchy. The Emperor is the symbolic head of state, while the Prime Minister is the head of government and holds administrative power.

4. Japan has a centralised government structure, with forty-seven prefectures which are governed by elected governors and assemblies.

5. Overall, the Japanese political system is characterised by a stable parliamentary democracy, with a strong emphasis on consensus-building and compromise. The government is committed to promoting economic growth and maintaining a high standard of living for its citizens, while also maintaining strong ties with the international community.

---

2. Geospatial Information Authority of Japan, Number of islands in Japan https://www.gsi.go.jp/kihonjohochousa/pressrelease20230228.html> gt; (accessed 1 Mar. 2023).
3. Statistics Bureau of the Ministry of Internal Affairs and Communications (MIC), Population Estimates (finalised October 2022) (published 20 Mar. 2023) & https://www.stat.go.jp/data/jinsui/new.html.
4. Cabinet Office, Government of Japan, Quarterly Estimates of GDP October–December 2022 (The 2nd preliminary) https://www.esri.cao.go.jp/en/sna/ menu.html.

I. Principle of Separation of Powers

6. The Constitution of Japan adopts the principle of separation of powers as a system in which the Diet is responsible for 'legislative power,' such as enacting and amending laws, the Cabinet is responsible for 'executive power' to carry out actual administration based on laws and budgets decided by the Diet, and the courts are responsible for 'judicial power' to judge people's disputes and crimes in accordance with the Constitution and laws.

7. In Japan, the separation of powers is based on the parliamentary cabinet system, in which the Diet appoints the prime minister and the Cabinet is formed on the basis of the confidence of the Diet.

II. National Diet

8. The Japanese parliament is known as the National Diet and consists of two chambers: the House of Representatives and the House of Councillors. Members of the House of Representatives are elected by popular vote every four years, while members of the House of Councillors are elected every six years. Ministers of Japan are appointed by the Diet.

9. The composition of the House of Representatives and the House of Councillors is shown in the table below:

	House of Representatives	*House of Councillors*
Fixed number of members of parliament	465 constituencies, 289 primary constituencies, and 176 proportional representation.	248 electoral districts with 148 members and 100 proportional representatives.
Term of office	Four years (if disbanded, position is lost even mid-term).	Six years (half elected every three years)
Suffrage	18 years of age or older	18 years of age or older
Eligibility for election	25 years of age or older	Over 30 years of age
Electoral district	Primary election: 289 constituencies nationwide Proportional representation: 11 constituencies nationwide	Electoral districts: 45 prefectural constituencies in principle (Tottori and Shimane prefectures and Tokushima and Kochi

	House of Representatives	*House of Councillors*
		prefectures each have one electoral district in the area of two prefectures) Proportional representation: one district for the whole country.
Dissolution	Existence (at the present moment)	Without

10. The National Diet holds a 'regular session' (ordinary Diet) in January each year, but also holds 'extraordinary sessions' (extraordinary Diet) and 'special sessions' (special Diet) when necessary. In addition, there is an emergency meeting of the House of Councillors, when the House of Representatives is dissolved and an urgent national issue arises:

Type	*Convocation and Timing*	*Session (of a Legislature)*
Ordinary Diet session	Convened once a year, in January	150 days (with one extension)
Extraordinary meeting	When the Cabinet considers it necessary; When one quarter or more of the total members of either House demand it; When a general election of the House of Representatives or a regular election of the House of Councillors is held due to the expiry of the term of office, the House is convened within thirty days from the beginning of the term of office.	Decided by a parliamentary resolution (up to two extensions).
Special Diet session	. Convened within thirty days of the date of the general election of the House of Representatives due to dissolution.	
Emergency meeting of the House of Councillors	During the dissolution of the House of Representatives, the Cabinet calls for a meeting in the event of an urgent national issue.	Ends when all urgent matters have been voted on.

§3. JUDICIAL SYSTEM

11. The Japanese judicial system is based on the principles of due process and the protection of individual rights. It consists of a combination of public prosecutors, judges, and lawyers, and emphasises the importance of evidence-based decision-making.

I. Court System

12. An overview of Japanese courts is presented based on the Supreme Court commentary.[5]

13. Article 76(1) of the Constitution provides that 'all judicial power shall be vested in the Supreme Court and in such subordinate courts as may be established by law'. Based on this provision, the Courts Act (Act No. 59 of 1947) establishes four types of courts as lower courts: High Courts, District Courts, Family Courts and Summary Courts, and defines the cases to be heard by each court. The Act on the Establishment and Jurisdiction of Subordinate Courts (Act No. 63 of 1947) provides for the specific establishment and jurisdiction of the courts.

II. The Trial Level System

14. The Japanese court system is based on a three-trial system (three-trial system), with three levels of court – first, second and third instance – where parties can, in principle, have up to three repeated hearings if they wish.

15. A party who is dissatisfied with the judgment of the Court of First Instance may appeal to the Court of Second Instance (appeal), and a party who is also dissatisfied with the judgment of the Court of Second Instance may further appeal to the Court of Third Instance (appeal).

III. Supreme Court

16. The Supreme Court is the sole and highest court in Japan, established by the Constitution, and consists of the President and fourteen Supreme Court Justices. The Chief Justice of the Supreme Court is appointed by the Emperor on the basis of a nomination by the Cabinet. The fourteen Supreme Court Justices are also appointed by the Cabinet and certified by the Emperor.

17. Trials before the Supreme Court take place in one Grand Chamber (quorum 9) consisting of all members and in three smaller Chambers (quorum 3), each consisting of five members.

---

5. Supreme Court, 'Overview of the Courts' https://www.courts.go.jp/about/sosiki/gaiyo/index.html.

18. The Supreme Court has jurisdiction to hear and determine appeals and appeals specifically provided for in the Code of Procedure, as well as first and final instance jurisdiction in cases of impeachment of personnel officers.

19. Appeals include (1) appeals against judgments of the second or first instance of a higher court, which account for the majority of appeal cases; (2) leapfrog appeals against judgments of the first instance of a district or family court or criminal first instance of a summary court; (3) appeals or appeals to a higher court which are transferred on certain grounds; (4) special appeals against judgments of the final civil appeal instance of a higher court; and (5) extraordinary appeals against a final criminal judgment. The grounds for an appeal to the Supreme Court are limited to constitutional violations and serious procedural violations enumerated by law in civil and administrative cases. However, the Supreme Court may, upon request, accept a case as an appeal if the original judgment is considered to contain important questions of legal interpretation. In criminal cases, this is limited to violations of the Constitution or judicial precedents. Appeals specifically provided for in the Code of Procedure include appeals for violation of the Constitution in civil cases and appeals with the permission of the higher court in cases involving important questions of interpretation of laws and regulations, and appeals for violation of the Constitution or judicial precedents in criminal, juvenile, court order maintenance and other cases.

20. The Supreme Court, as the only Supreme Court in our country, is vested with judicial jurisdiction. Furthermore, in order to ensure the full independence of the judiciary, the Constitution provides for the power to make rules on matters relating to procedure, lawyers, internal court discipline and the administration of judicial affairs. In addition, the Supreme Court is vested with the so-called judicial executive power to appoint persons to be appointed as judges of lower courts, to appoint and fill court officials other than judges, and to participate in and implement the establishment of the budget relating to the courts. For the exercise of these powers of the Supreme Court, the General Secretariat, the Judicial Training Institute, the General Training Institute for Court Officials and the Supreme Court Library have been established as attached bodies.

21. The Supreme Court is thus free from interference by the executive and the legislature and is autonomous in the administration of the courts.

IV. High Court

22. The High Court is located in eight major Japanese cities (Tokyo, Osaka, Nagoya, Hiroshima, Fukuoka, Sendai, Sapporo and Takamatsu) and has branches in six other cities. In addition, a special branch, the Intellectual Property High Court, has been established in the Tokyo High Court.

23. The High Court is organised by the Chief Judge of the High Court and the judges. The Chief Judge of the High Court is appointed by the Cabinet and certified by the Emperor.

24. The High Court has jurisdiction to hear appeals from judgments of the District or Family Courts or from criminal decisions of Summary Courts, appeals from second-instance civil judgments of the District Courts and leapfrog appeals from civil judgments of the Summary Courts, and appeals from Judgements of the District or Family Courts. In addition, the High Court has first-instance jurisdiction over administrative disputes relating to elections and criminal cases regarding offences such as domestic disturbance, etc. The Tokyo High Court also has first-instance jurisdiction to hear appeals against decisions of quasi-judicial bodies such as the Fair Trade Commission and the Patent Office.

25. The Intellectual Property High Court trials certain intellectual property cases which fall under the jurisdiction of the Tokyo High Court, such as appeals from district court, decisions on patent rights and actions to annul decisions of the Patent Office.

26. Cases before the High Court are usually heard by a panel of three judges. Internal offences and cases before the Fair Trade Commission are heard by a panel of five judges.

V. District Court

27. There are fifty district courts throughout the country, whose jurisdiction corresponds to that of the various prefectures, with the exception of Hokkaido, which is divided into four. The district courts have branches, of which there are 203 in total.

28. The district court is the principal Court of First Instance and has jurisdiction to hear all cases of first instance, except for special cases where another court has exclusive jurisdiction of first instance. District courts also have jurisdiction to hear appeals from civil judgments of Summary courts.

29. Cases in the District courts are heard either by a single judge or by a panel of judges, usually three in number. The majority of cases are heard by a single judge. However, there are exceptions to this rule for (i) cases where the panel has decided to 'hear and try the case in a panel'; (ii) cases involving offences punishable by death or life imprisonment or short-term imprisonment of one year or more or imprisonment without labour (except for robbery, quasi-burglary, attempts to commit these offences and cases involving habitual burglary as defined in the Anti-Burglary Act); (iii) appeal cases; (iv) other cases designated by law as joint cases, which require a trial by a joint panel.

VI. Family Court

30. There are fifty family courts throughout Japan, with jurisdiction over the same areas as the prefectures, except for Hokkaido, which is divided into four. In addition, there are 203 branches and seventy-seven family court sub-branches.

31. If domestic disputes are dealt with through the normal litigation process, spouses, parents, children and other relatives will be litigated in an open courtroom, and legal decisions will take centre stage, with the risk that mutual emotional conflicts may end up not being adequately resolved. Therefore, in domestic disputes, it is considered appropriate to first of all try to resolve the dispute on the basis of the circumstances in an appropriate closed procedure, rather than in a court case.

32. Furthermore, imposing punishment on delinquent juveniles in open court proceedings, as is the case with adults, does not always lead to a favourable outcome for juveniles. For juveniles who are immature and have a high potential for improvement through education, it is often more appropriate to decide on the punishment after educational encouragement to prevent them from re-offending in an appropriate closed procedure.

33. The Family Court was established on the basis of the principle that the court should not only make legal decisions but also investigate the causes of disputes and delinquent behaviour and, upon considering how various problems in the family and among relatives can be resolved amicably and how delinquent juveniles can be prevented from committing delinquent acts again, take appropriate and reasonable measures according to each case and solve the problem with a view to the future. The Family Court was established on the basis of the principle of taking appropriate and reasonable measures according to each case and trying to find a solution with a view to the future. In order to implement this philosophy, family court investigators are appointed to investigate and coordinate the facts of the case using specialist knowledge and techniques from psychology, sociology, social welfare, education and other behavioural sciences. For example, family courts use mediation to discuss disputes such as marital and parent-child relationships, conduct litigation and trials related to these disputes, and adjudicate cases involving juvenile delinquents.

VII. Summary Court

34. There are 438 summary courts throughout the country.

35. Summary courts have first-instance jurisdiction in civil cases where the value of the subject matter of the proceedings does not exceed JPY 1.4 million, and in criminal cases, including cases involving offences punishable by a fine or less and relatively minor offences such as theft and embezzlement.

36. Summary courts can only impose a sentence of up to a fine or up to three years' imprisonment for cases under their jurisdiction. If it is considered appropriate to impose a sentence exceeding this limit, the case must be referred to the District Court.

37. In summary courts, special procedures are available for the simplified handling of civil or criminal cases. In civil cases, at the request of the plaintiff and if the defendant does not object, the court may, in principle, conclude the hearing on a single day and issue a judgment for payment in instalments, etc., in cases where the plaintiff requests payment of money up to JPY 600,000, and the court clerk may, at the request of the creditor, order payment of money without examining the debtor. The court clerk may also order the payment of money without examining the debtor at the request of the creditor. In criminal cases, a fine of up to JPY 1 million or a fine of up to JPY 1 million in a case under the jurisdiction of the public prosecutor may be imposed at the request of the public prosecutor only by examining the documentary evidence, provided that the defendant does not object. The above-simplified procedure does not deprive the debtor or the accused of the right to a trial by ordinary procedure.

38. The summary court also has a system of mediation for resolving common civil disputes through discussion. Civil mediation is inexpensive and a mediation committee, consisting of a judge or civil mediator and two or more civil mediators, listens to the arguments of both parties and tries to reach an agreement. If an agreement is reached in mediation and the content of the agreement is recorded in the minutes, the statement in the minutes has the same effect as a final and binding judgment of the court.

39. Civil cases before the Summary Court may also be heard orally. Depending on the nature of the dispute, standard forms for civil litigation and civil mediation are available at the counter for easy filing. All summary court cases are heard and decided by a single summary court judge.

§4. Judicial System Reform

I. Overview of Judicial Reform

40. Judicial reform has been implemented according to the Judicial Reform Act passed in 2001, and by 2009 several new systems had been introduced and existing systems improved.

41. The reform of the Japanese judicial system is based on the idea that the role of the judiciary will become even more important as society undergoes various changes, such as a shift from an '*ex ante* regulatory type' to an '*ex post* monitoring and remedial type' due to deregulation and other reforms, in addition to the complexity, diversification and internationalisation of society, and that the functions of the judiciary should be improved and strengthened so that the public can have access to the judicial system.[6]

42. In July 1999, the Act on the Establishment of the Council for the Reform of the Judicial System (Act No. 68 of 1999)(Hereinafter referred to as the 'Council Act'). After two years of deliberations, the Opinion of the Judicial System Reform Council was compiled in June 2001. In the Opinion, in order to enhance and strengthen the functions of the judicial system and contribute to the formation of a free and fair society: (1) the construction of a judicial system that meets the expectations of the public; (2) the way of being of legal professionals who support the judicial system; and (3) the establishment of a national infrastructure were set as the three pillars, and studies were conducted to reform the judicial system and to improve its infrastructure.[7]

43. In March 2002, the Cabinet adopted the Plan for the Promotion of the Reform of the Judicial System based on the Law for the Promotion of the Reform of the Judicial System, and on the basis of the Plan, the Headquarters for the Promotion of the Reform of the Judicial System proceeded with the drafting of related bills and other work, and by December 2004, twenty-four bills had been passed and enacted in each Diet session. In May 2009, the jury system was introduced and all laws related to the reform of the judicial system came into force.

II. Building a Judicial System Which Meets the Public's Expectations

44. Building a judicial system which meets the expectations of the public (developing the institutional infrastructure) means widening public access to justice and establishing a system that provides for fairer, more appropriate and speedy hearings and effective resolution of cases in order to make justice more accessible, understandable and reliable for the public. The system is designed to enable the effective resolution of cases through fairer, more appropriate and speedier hearings.

45. The institutional infrastructure consists of 'Civil Justice Reform', 'Criminal Justice Reform' and 'Responding to Internationalisation'.

46. Specifically, the Houterasu (officially known as the Japan Legal Support Centre: JLSC) has been established. It was established in 2006 as a 'legal general

6. Ministry of Justice, 'On Judicial System Reform' https://www.moj.go.jp/housei/servicer/kanbou_housei_chousa18.html; Supreme Court, 'Judicial System Reform: the Judicial System in the 21st Century' https://www.courts.go.jp/about/sihou/kaikaku_sihou_21/index.html.
7. Supreme Court, 'The Government's Plan to Promote Reform of the Judicial System' https://www.courts.go.jp/about/sihou/kaikaku_keikaku/seihu_suisin/index.html.

information centre' where people can seek legal advice on legal problems, even if they do not have a lawyer or other legal professional nearby and do not know where and how to go for advice.

47. Houterasu's services include 'Information Provision Services' (providing information on the legal system and advice institutions (bar associations, etc.) for legal problems), 'Civil Law Services' (providing legal advice and information on the legal system and advice institutions (bar associations, etc.) for legal problems) for legal problems, 'Civil Legal Aid Services' (free consultations for those who cannot afford them and payment of legal fees), 'Crime Victim Support Services' (legal support for victims of crime and their families), 'Services for Measures against Judicial Underpopulation' (establishment of regional offices staffed by Houterasu lawyers in 'judicially underpopulated areas' where there is a shortage of lawyers, such as rural areas), 'Court Appointed Defence Counsel Services' (providing legal aid to suspects in criminal cases and their families), 'Work against Depopulation' (providing legal aid to suspects in criminal cases and their families), 'work against depopulation of the judiciary' (setting up regional offices staffed by Houterasu lawyers in 'depopulated areas' where there is a shortage of lawyers, such as rural areas), 'court-appointed defence counsel and other related work' (appointing and contracting court-appointed defence counsel for those who are suspects or accused in criminal cases but cannot appoint a defence counsel for financial reasons), and so on.

48. There has also been the establishment of the High Court of Intellectual Property. The High Court of Intellectual Property is a specialised court that deals with disputes relating to intellectual property rights such as patents and trademarks. It hears appeals against decisions of the Patent Office (actions for annulment of court decisions) as well as appeals against first-instance appeals in district courts in intellectual property cases.

III. The Legal Profession in Support of the Judicial System

49. With regard to the 'Legal Professionals Supporting the Judicial System (Expanding the Human Resource Base)', systemic reforms are being implemented with the aim of producing legal professionals who not only have a high degree of specialised legal knowledge, but also have acquired sufficient professional ethics based on a broad education and rich humanity, and who are active in various areas of society as members of a thick layer of the legal profession.

50. The development of the human infrastructure includes the development of the legal profession, the reform of the legal education system, the reform of the lawyer system, the reform of the procurator system, the reform of the judiciary system and the nature of the mutual exchange of legal professionals.

51. Specifically, the law schools and the new bar examinations are in place. Law schools are professional graduate schools established with the aim of improving legal education in order to improve the human system in the judiciary. It is also called the 'Japanese version of law school', derived from the American system. There are two types of courses, the 'untrained course (three years)' and the 'learned course (two years)', depending on whether the student has previously studied law or not.

52. Since 2004, a total of sixty-eight law schools have opened at national, public and private universities; from 2005 to 2010, seventy-four; as of January 2023, there were twenty-one national law schools (six of which have suspended or stopped recruitment), two public and forty-six private schools (twenty-eight of which have suspended or stopped recruitment).

IV. Building a National Infrastructure Citizen Participation in Justice

53. With regard to the 'Establishment of a national infrastructure (public participation in the judiciary)', institutional reforms have been implemented to deepen and support the public's understanding of the judiciary through various forms of participation, including participation in certain legal proceedings. Public participation in the judiciary consists of 'building the national infrastructure (public participation in the judiciary)' and 'creating the conditions for building the national infrastructure'.

54. Specifically, 'jury trials' have been introduced. Jury trials are a system in which citizens without legal rights participate in criminal trials and began in 2009.

55. In the first instance of criminal cases of a certain degree of seriousness (e.g., murder, robbery and manslaughter), 'judges', chosen by a lot from among citizens with the right to vote, participate in the trial together with the judge. For each trial, three judges, including the presiding judge, and six judges from the public deliberate. The purpose of the deliberation is to decide whether the person is guilty or not guilty and, if guilty, what sentence he or she should receive.

56. As mentioned above, the reform of Japan's judicial system was decided and implemented as part of Japan's structural reform. The structural reform path itself is currently being evaluated in various ways in light of the ensuing social and economic situation in Japan, and its modification is often discussed in various quarters.

Part I. Privacy Protection in Japan

Chapter 1. Privacy Protection in the Constitution

57. The Constitution of Japan does not explicitly provide for the right to privacy because, since the 1946 amendment, the Constitution has not been amended again.

58. Nevertheless, the Constitution still protects the right to privacy as a fundamental human right. In judicial decisions, the right to privacy has historically been remedied in court. In the *Utage-No-Ato ('After the Banquet')* case (Tokyo District Court, 28 September 1964), the court defined the right to privacy as 'the legal right not to have one's private life exposed to the public'. The requirements for the establishment of a tort of invasion of privacy are as follows: (1) the disclosed content must be a fact of private life or a matter which may be perceived as such; (2) it must be recognised that the public would not want the content disclosed from the standpoint of the private individual concerned based on the sensitivity of the general public; and (3) the content must be a matter which is not yet known to the general public.

59. Additionally, the right to privacy was practically recognised as a constitutional right in the case of the *Kyoto Federation of Students' Associations*, where the Constitution guaranteed 'the freedom not to be photographed without consent of the person' as 'freedom in private life'. In the *Kyoto-Fugakuren* case, the Supreme Court ruled that 'the freedom not to be photographed without permission' is protected by the Constitution (24 December 1969).

60. The above-mentioned Supreme Court case was the first case to set out clear standards for the relationship between photography as a means of investigation and the right of portrait, showing that Article 13 of the Constitution guarantees rights not explicitly stipulated in the Constitution and that the article has a concrete judicial normative nature. This case was also the first to recognise that Article 13 guarantees rights not expressly provided in the Constitution. The case was evaluated as having constitutional significance in that it recognised the right of portrait, but it was also shown that Article 13 of the Constitution guaranteed a protected legal interest equivalent to the right to privacy, which, in effect, means recognition of the right to privacy in the Constitution. Hence, the decision has been considered an endorsement of the constitutional right to privacy.

61. The judgment states that:

> Article 13 of the Constitution stipulates that the private liberties of citizens should be protected against the exercise of state power, such as police power, and as one of the freedoms of private life of individuals, everyone should have the freedom not to be photographed in his or her appearance without his or her consent. Whether or not this is called the right of portrait, at the very least, it must be said that it is against the purpose of Article 13 of the Constitution and impermissible for police officers to photograph the appearance of individuals without a legitimate reason.

62. The Court stated that 'freedom from having one's appearance and demeanour photographed without consent' is recognised as 'freedom in one's private life' on the basis of Article 13 of the Constitution.

63. Thus, the right to privacy, which was recognised as a right under the law of torts in the wake of the *'After the Banquet'* case (1964), is not limited to infringement of privacy between private individuals but rather has become a matter of infringement by public authorities and is now also recognised as a constitutional right.

64. Furthermore, as a case in which the Supreme Court squarely discussed the right to privacy as an infringement of privacy rather than as a right of portrait, the *Kyoto City Criminal Record Inquiry* case (Supreme Court, 14 April 1981, Minshu (Supreme Court Civil Casebook), vol. 35, no. 3, p. 620) involved a person's previous convictions and the fact that he or she had been convicted of a criminal offence. The case concerned whether an enquiry into a person's criminal record and criminal history constituted an infringement of privacy.

65. The judgment states that:

> [C]riminal convictions and criminal history (criminal records) are matters directly related to a person's honour and credibility, and persons with criminal records have a legally protected interest in not having them disclosed to the public unnecessarily. It goes without saying that the mayor of a municipality must not divulge the criminal record and other information contained in the register of offenders, which is originally prepared and kept for the purpose of investigating electoral eligibility.

66. The court also held that, with regard to criminal records, it is necessary to avoid the disclosure of criminal convictions that were entered in the criminal register prepared for the investigation of the original electoral qualifications. The judgment states that not having the facts relating to a previous conviction published without reason is an interest that deserves legal protection and goes on to say that:

> [A]fter a person has been convicted or served his or her sentence, he or she is expected to return to society as a citizen. Therefore, the person should have the

interest that his/her rehabilitation will not be disturbed by the publication of the facts relating to the conviction, and that the peace of his/her newly formed social life will not be disturbed.

67. The Supreme Court ruled that the act of publishing facts relating to a person's criminal record by using the person's real name in a work constitutes an infringement of his or her privacy. Although the term 'privacy' is not used in any of these Supreme Court judgments, it is recognised that the right to privacy has been guaranteed on the basis of Article 13 of the Constitution.

68. The concept of the right to privacy in academic theory was proposed in the early stages as 'the right to be let alone',[8] and the Warren and Brandeis approach was also referred to when discussing the Japanese concept of the right to privacy. In Japan, the concept of the right to privacy has been proposed as 'the right to control information about oneself',[9] based on the idea that it is necessary to actively guarantee rights from the perspective of the protection and management of information in line with the development of computerised information processing and databases. This concept of rights aims to protect the privacy of the individual in an information society. However, the fact that it must be difficult to practically control personal information under circumstances where individual information is combined to generate a new set of personal information in a dimension completely unrecognisable to the individual is acknowledged. In fact, the Act on the Protection of Personal Information (hereinafter 'APPI') does not explicitly provide for the guarantee of the right to privacy.

69. The APPI distinguishes 'personal data', 'special care-required personal information', and 'retained personal data', but these distinctions are not made from the perspective of privacy protection. The term 'personal data' refers to personal information that is searchable and systematic. 'Retained personal data' makes a distinction based on the external criterion of the retention period (i.e., the data are not erased within six months). Additionally, 'special care-required personal information' is defined as related to avoiding discrimination and prejudice. It should be noted that this latter category contributes to the protection of personal privacy, as it is information that the individual does not want to be known to others and must be obtained based on the consent of the person concerned.

8. Samuel D. Warren & Louis D. Brandeis, *The Right to Privacy*, 4 HARV. L. REV.193, 1890.
9. Koji Sato, *A Constitutional Theory of the Right to Privacy (Its Public Law Aspects)*, 86(5) KYOTO L. REV. (1970).

Chapter 2. Regional/International Conventions: National Application

§1. International Framework & Japanese Information Protection Legal System

70. International privacy agreements in which Japan is involved include the Organisation for Economic Co-operation and Development (OECD) 1980 Privacy Guidelines (revised 2013), the Asia-Pacific Economic Cooperation (APEC) Privacy Framework, Cross-border Privacy Enforcement Arrangement (CPEA), and the Council of Europe Convention No. 108 (1981) on the Protection of Individuals with Regard to Automatic Processing of Personal Data.

71. Japan is a member of the OECD, and its legislation is influenced by the OECD's Privacy Guidelines. After the OECD Privacy Guidelines were introduced in 1980, they became the model for regulations in Japan.

§2. International Commitment of the Personal Information Protection Commission

72. The Personal Information Protection Commission (PPC) participates in international cooperation frameworks consisting of national data protection bodies and other organisations to establish cooperation and exchange information. For detailed information about participation in international cooperation frameworks, *see* the PPC's website.[10]

73. The PPC has participated in meetings with the G7 countries' commissioner-level data protection and privacy agencies to discuss collaboration between national enforcement agencies to promote Data Free Flow with Trust (DFFT), with the participation of the commissioner-level G7 Data Protection and Privacy Agency Roundtable.

74. The Asia-Pacific Privacy Agencies (APPA) Forum is a biannual meeting of privacy-related enforcement agencies in the Asia-Pacific region for the purpose of building cooperation and exchanging information. The PPC has participated in the APPA Forum as an observer since 2014 and became an official member in June 2016.[11]

---

10. Personal Information Protection Commission, 'International Relations' https://www.ppc.go.jp/enforcement/cooperation/international_conference/.
11. Asia Pacific Privacy Authorities welcome new member Japan, 29 Jun. 2016 http://www.appaforum.org/resources/media_release/asia-pacific-privacy-authorities-welcome-new-member-japan/.

75. The Global Privacy Assembly (GPA) brings together national data protection agencies, government agencies, operators, and researchers to discuss and exchange information about the promotion and strengthening of international personal data protection.

76. The International Working Group on Data Protection in Telecommunications (IWGDPT) discusses and adopts recommendations on privacy protection in the field of information and communications within the framework of the Data Protection Privacy Commissioner's Conference and on the initiative of the Data Protection Commissioner of the State of Berlin, Germany, with the participation of national personal information protection agencies, representatives of international organisations, researchers, and others.

§3. Revision of the 1980 OECD Privacy Guidelines

77. In 1980, the OECD published the OECD Council Recommendations on Guidelines for the Protection of Privacy and the International Distribution of Personal Data (eight Principles), and the OECD member countries, including Japan, have developed legislation for the protection of personal data based on the said Guidelines. As thirty years have passed since then, a study was initiated to revise the Guidelines, and on 11 July 2013, a draft proposal to revise the Guidelines was published as a Council Recommendation. A draft amendment was adopted as a Council Recommendation on 11 July 2013 and published on 9 September of the same year.

78. Japan's Act on the Protection of Personal Information (APPI) was amended in 2015, making Japan the first OECD Member State to amend its domestic law after the 2013 revision of the OECD Guidelines.

79. Trends and changes in the course of the revision of the OECD Guidelines have resulted in the following four trends and changes in personal data protection: (1) issues associated with technological advances; (2) international data distribution; (3) changes in the activities of organisations; and (4) changes in the activities of individuals. The issue was examined as a problem that has undergone a major transformation. In the revision of Japan's Personal Data Protection Law, consideration was also given to revising the law in light of these issues.

§4. APEC Privacy Framework

80. The APEC Privacy Framework[12] aims at promoting electronic commerce throughout the Asia-Pacific region with due consideration for the different legal features and contexts of the APEC region. The Framework is consistent with the core

12. APEC Privacy Framework (2015) https://www.apec.org/publications/2017/08/apec-privacy-framework-(2015).

values of the OECD Privacy Guidelines, and it reaffirms the value of privacy to individuals in the information society. The first version of the Framework was enacted in 2005, modelled upon the OECD 1980 Privacy Guidelines. The updated 2015 Framework draws upon concepts introduced into the OECD 2013 amended Guidelines.

81. APEC is a framework for economic cooperation involving twenty-one countries and regions in the Asia-Pacific region. APEC is committed to sustainable growth and prosperity in the Asia-Pacific region through trade and investment liberalisation, business facilitation, human security, economic and technical cooperation, and other activities.

82. The APEC Privacy Framework (adopted on 29 October 2004, with international implementation approved on 16 November 2005) is a set of regulations designed to promote consistent personal information protection practices in APEC member economies and remove unnecessary barriers to the flow of information. This scheme has been encouraging economies to develop national personal data protection systems based on the framework. The purpose of this framework was to promote efforts in APEC member economies and serves to remove unnecessary obstacles to the distribution of information. The target economies are APEC member economies, including Japan, which are required to establish a system that enables them to request cooperation through the Data Protection Act (DPA) of other economies when enforcing laws based on domestic laws and regulations in cases of cross-border personal information leaks.

83. With regard to the handling of personal information circulating across borders in APEC member economies, the APEC Electronic Commerce Steering Group (ECSG) was considering establishing a system for protection based on the Privacy Framework. The Data Privacy Subgroup (DPS) established in the ECSG has been studying the issue since February 2008 and has developed the APEC Cross-Border Privacy Rules (CBPR) and the APEC Data Privacy Pathfinder project, while also attempting to establish the CPEA.

84. With the globalisation of business, it has become common for personal information to frequently move across borders, and the protection of cross-border personal information has become a major issue. The CPEA was established in 2009 to ensure that when personal data are entrusted, transferred, and shared across borders, in the event of a breach at the cross-border destination, enforcement authorities at the source have recourse. The CPEA is a framework for requesting information, investigations, and other cooperation from enforcement agencies in the destination country for the enforcement of the DPA in each country.

85. The purpose of the CPEA is information sharing among DPA in APEC economies, specifically effective cross-border cooperation between DPA in the enforcement of data protection laws, including case enquiries, joint investigations, and enforcement activities; cooperation between DPA in enforcing the CBPR; and information sharing with DPA outside the APEC region, ensuring close cooperation with the OECD Privacy Recommendations.

86. APEC has established further rules based on the APEC Privacy Framework, and in November 2011, the CBPR system was established to certify businesses that comply with the rules for handling personal information across borders within the APEC region. The CBPR aims to ensure that personal information is appropriately protected, even when it is transferred across borders, by requiring companies to self-assess their personal information rules and systems and seek certification from an accredited personal information protection organisation. In other words, the CBPR is a system whereby companies self-assess their rules and systems relating to personal information and are audited and certified by accredited certification bodies (Accountability Agents [AA]).

87. Japan's participation in the CBPR was approved on 28 April 2014, after Japan applied for participation on 7 June 2013. Japan's approval made it the second country to join the CBPR system, after the United States and Mexico. The Japan Institute for Promotion of Digital Economy and Community (JIPDEC) was accredited as an AA in January 2016. This allows APEC to grant CBPR certification to Japanese companies for their cross-border personal information initiatives.

88. Furthermore, in April 2022, a forum consisting of Japan, the United States, Canada, South Korea, the Philippines, Singapore, and Taiwan was established to expand the APEC CBPR.[13]

§5. Data Free Flow with Trust

89. Article 1 of the APPI states that:

> [T]he purpose of this Act is to protect the rights and interests of individuals, while giving due consideration to the usefulness of personal information, including the fact that the appropriate and effective use of personal information contributes to the creation of new industries and the realisation of a dynamically economic society and an affluent national life.

90. Further, it sets out the obligations to be observed by business operators who handle personal information, based on a balance between the appropriate 'use' and 'protection' of personal information. The development of a data protection system based on the free flow and protection of information has been fostered by the OECD Privacy Guidelines, which were established in 1980 and share the basic principles of the free flow and protection of personal data between OECD countries.

13. Global Cross-Border Privacy Rules (CBPR) Declaration, 21 Apr. 2022 https://www.meti.go.jp/press/2022/04/20220421001/20220421001-1.pdf.

91. Now that large volumes of data are being handled, this principle has been continued in the IT Strategic Headquarters' New IT Policy Framework for the Digital Age[14] (decided on 7 June 2019) as DFFT. This IT Policy Framework sets out the concept of 'promoting the free-flow of data internationally, where data useful for solving business and social issues can freely come and go without regard to national borders, while ensuring trust in privacy, security and intellectual property rights'. To achieve this objective, the Declaration on the Creation of the World's Most Advanced Digital Nation and the Basic Plan for the Promotion of Public–Private Data Utilisation was approved by the Japanese Cabinet on 14 June 2019.

92. As for measures aiming at promoting the formation of multi-lateral digital trade rules with the goal of expanding the 'international data distribution network' based on DFFT, DFFT-related disciplines are included in e-commerce arrangements and form part of bilateral and multilateral trade agreements, such as the Japan–US Digital Trade Agreement,[15] the UK–Japan EPA,[16] and the TPP11.[17]

93. Furthermore, as a result of the 27th EU–Japan Summit (held on 27 May 2021), the Japan–EU Summit 2021 Joint Statement (paragraph 11) stated that continued cooperation on DFFT should be based on the recognition of the importance of data and digital transformation for the benefit of society, the environment, and the economy while upholding fundamental rights and encouraging an innovative environment, particularly in the areas of cyber security, secure 5G and beyond 5G/6G technologies, blockchain, and the safe and ethical use of Artificial Intelligence (AI). Such goals should be pursued simultaneously with working together to promote a comprehensive approach, including global standards and regulations for digital policies and technologies, stressing our joint commitment to a high level of personal data protection based on the already high degree of alignment between the European Union (EU) and Japan and promoting safe and secure cross-border data flows through enhanced security and privacy.[18]

94. Subsequently, at the G7 Summit held in Cornwall, United Kingdom, in June 2021, a communique was published on 13 June endorsing the G7 Roadmap for Co-operation on DFFT[19] (adopted at the Digital and Technology Ministers' Meeting at the end of April 2021).

---

14. New IT Policy Framework for the Digital Age' (decided on 7 Jun. 2019) https://warp.ndl.go.jp/info:ndljp/pid/12187388/www.kantei.go.jp/jp/singi/it2/kettei/pdf/20190607/siryou1.pdf.
15. Agreement between Japan and the United States of America on Digital Trade (abbreviated as US-Japan Digital Trade Agreement), 1 Jan. 2020.
16. The UK-Japan Comprehensive Economic Partnership Agreement (EPA) (26 Mar. 2021).
17. TPP11 Agreement (Comprehensive and Progressive Agreement on Trans-Pacific Partnership), signed by twelve countries in February 2016. The TPP Agreement was signed by twelve countries in February 2016; the US declared its withdrawal in January 2017 and the TPP Ministerial Meeting was held in Vietnam in November 2017. The TPP11 agreement (Comprehensive and Progressive Agreement on Trans-Pacific Partnership: the (CPTPP)) was agreed and signed by ministers from eleven countries, including Japan, in March 2018.
18. Ministry of Foreign Affairs, 'The 27th EU-Japan Summit' (27 May 2021), https://www.mofa.go.jp/mofaj/erp/ep/page6_000563.html.
19. G7 Leaders' Communiqué, G7 Summit (Cornwall, 11–13 Jun. 2021).

95. To bolster international efforts based on the free flow and protection of personal data, the Government of Japan proposed DFFT at the G20 Ibaraki Tsukuba Trade and Digital Economy Ministerial Meeting (8–9 June 2019). At a subsequent G20 Ibaraki Tsukuba Trade and Digital Economy Ministerial Meeting (8–9 June 2022), the DFFT concept was agreed upon by the entire G20, and it was confirmed that to establish trust, the countries' legal frameworks should be interconnected.

96. As opportunities for the cross-border transfer of personal data expand, differences in national and regional systems for the protection of personal data make the predictability of individuals and data-handling operators precarious and raise concerns in terms of the protection of individual rights and interests. For example, excessive governmental access by foreign governments may lead to the use of personal data acquired in a country and transferred across borders in a way that the concerned person is not aware of or cannot foresee, such as through contact, surveillance, or unauthorised investigation of the person, or through a chain of third-party provision for transborder distribution. In the context of data localisation policies, such state control of data may pose an unacceptable risk in terms of the protection of the rights and interests of individuals, where the operator of a cross-border transfer may be unable to respond to a request for erasure of personal data by the principals.

97. In the context of such international trends, the Government of Japan is committed to 'promoting the free flow of data internationally, where data beneficial to business and the resolution of social issues can come and go freely without regard to national borders, while ensuring trust in privacy, security and intellectual property rights' (Growth Strategy Follow-up, Cabinet Decision of 18 June 2021). To achieve this, it is necessary to promote the free flow of data between countries where mutual trust is ensured, while simultaneously ensuring that data transfers to countries with state-controlled regulations that could undermine the trust that supports the free flow of personal data, such as those mentioned above, are properly managed. Efforts are underway to ensure that transfers are appropriately controlled.

Chapter 3. Privacy in Electronic Communications

§1. Protection of Personal Information in the Telecommunications Sector

98. The protection of personal data and privacy in the telecommunications sector including electronic communications has been safeguarded on the basis of the constitutional guarantee of secrecy of communications.

99. Article 21, paragraph 2 of the Constitution of Japan provides the 'secrecy of communications' as one of the fundamental human rights. The constitutionally protected secrecy of communications is meant to complement the protection of freedom of expression by guaranteeing communications as an essential means of communication in social life and also has a character as part of the protection of privacy.

100. Presently, all telecommunications operators in Japan are private operators, but prior to the establishment of NTT (Nippon Telegraph and Telephone Corporation), telecommunications were managed by the Nippon Telegraph and Telephone Public Corporation as a public corporate body. At that time, there was no question of the 'secrecy of communications' of the Constitution being directly applicable to this corporation as an organisation under public law. The Public Telecommunications Act (Act No. 97 of 1953) also stipulated the protection of the secrecy of communications.

101. In April 1985, the Nippon Telegraph and Telephone Public Corporation was privatised, and NTT was established, introducing the principle of competition into the telecommunications market. In line with this liberalisation of telecommunications, the Telecommunications Business Act (Act No. 86 of 1984) was enacted in 1984, together with the Nippon Telegraph and Telephone Corporation Act (Act No. 85 of 1984), which also contains provisions on the protection of the secrecy of communications.

102. The protection of personal data in the telecommunications sector is set out in detailed procedures in the Guidelines for Protection of Personal Information in Telecommunications Businesses (MIC Public Notice),[20] together with obligations under the APPI.

103. These guidelines are based not only on the APPI but also on the Basic Policy on the Protection of Personal Data (approved by Cabinet in April 2004 and partially amended in June 2008). Based on Article 4 of the Telecommunications

20. Guidelines for Protection of Personal Information in Telecommunications Business(MIC Public Notice No. 152 of 18 Apr. 2017) https://www.soumu.go.jp/main_content/000744054.pdf. In details of this guideline, please refer to Commentary for Guidelines for Protection of Personal Information in Telecommunications Business (MIC Public Notice No. 297 of 14 Sep. 2017 (Updated in February 2021)) https://www.soumu.go.jp/main_content/000744055.pdf.

Business Act (Act No. 86 of 1984) and other relevant provisions pertaining to the secrecy of communications, and considering the perspective of privacy protection, these guidelines provide telecommunications carriers with as much specific guidance as possible on the proper handling of personal information, including procedures pertinent to the secrecy of communications, in order to improve the convenience of telecommunications services by ensuring the free distribution of information and to protect the rights and interests of users of electronic communication.

§2. Cookies and Their Applicability to Personal Information

104. The APPI defines information related to an individual, such as an identifier, as falling under the category of personal information when it can be readily collated with other information and thereby identify a specific individual. Therefore, cookies fall under the category of personal information when they can be readily collated with other information. Furthermore, Article 7 of the APPI provides the term 'personally referable information', which means information relating to a living individual that does not fall under personal information, pseudonymously processed information, or anonymously processed information.

105. When it is assumed that the third party to which the personally referable information is provided will acquire the personally referable information as personal data, the entity handling the personally referable information must not, in principle, provide the personally referable information without confirming in advance that the consent of the individual to whom the personally referable information refers has been obtained.

106. The entity that obtains the consent of the individual is, in principle, the third party to whom the information is provided, and the business operator handling the personally referable information shall confirm that the consent of the individual has been obtained by receiving a declaration from the third party or by other appropriate methods. When receiving a declaration from a third party to whom the information is provided, it is sufficient for the business operator handling the personally referable information to confirm the contents of the declaration 'with caution'.

107. If the third party to whom the information is provided obtains consent from multiple individuals using the same method, the provider will need to confirm that consent has been obtained from each individual. However, it is not necessary to receive individual declarations from each person regarding the method of obtaining consent.

108. Additionally, the act of a third party providing an ID, for which the third party has already obtained the consent set out in Article 31(1)(i) of the APPI, may fall under the provision of personal data to a third party when the third party provides the report to the provider of personal data. However, the act of providing only the information required for the confirmation act under Article 31(1) of the APPI falls under the case based on laws and regulations (Article 27(1)(i) of the Act).

109. Additionally, in the case where the business operator handling the personally referable information, from which the information is provided, obtains consent on behalf of the business operator, the method of confirming such consent by itself also falls under the category of confirmation by '[an]other appropriate method'.

110. Thus, cookies do not directly constitute personal information under Japan's APPI as long as they can be readily collated with other information and thereby identify a specific individual. However, the amended APPI introduced new obligations regarding 'Personally Referable Information'. This is due to the proliferation of Data Management Platforms (DMPs), which collect, store, integrate, and analyse Internet user data. DMPs include private DMPs, which companies employ to utilise their own accumulated data, while public DMPs are non-private and also collect, integrate, and analyse data. Unlike targeted advertising that only uses non-personal information, these businesses are becoming more widespread in that they provide personally referable information linked to cookie identifiers to other businesses, knowing in advance that such information will be considered personal information when a third party matches it with other information.

111. In light of these problems, in October 2018, the PPC issued administrative guidance to Facebook Inc. regarding (1) social plug-ins; (2) the Cambridge Analytica scandal; and (3) unauthorised access to personal data. Furthermore, the PPC issued a recommendation based on the APPI to Recruit Carrier, which operated a job-hunting information website called Riku Navi DMP Follow and acquired and provided students' personal information. For details about the law enforcement for the PPC's address of such issues, *see* 'Part 8: Enforcement, Chapter 3: Competence, Duty, and Authority – Four Examples of Enforcement against Foreign Business Operators'.

Chapter 4. Other Relevant National Legal Provisions

112. The right to privacy is guaranteed separately in relation to the protection of fundamental human rights provided by the Constitution. For example, Article 35 of the Constitution, which guarantees the inviolability of dwellings, is considered to have as its objective the protection of privacy within an individual's dwelling, while the Criminal Code makes trespassing into a dwelling punishable under Article 130. Article 235 of the Civil Code provides for the observation of neighbouring residential premises, while Article 1, Item 23 of the Misdemeanour Act (Act No. 39 of 1948) prohibits peeping.

113. In relation to the guarantee of secrecy of communications as stipulated in Article 21(2) of the Constitution, Article 133 of the Criminal Code punishes the act of opening a letter without reason. Similarly, Article 8 of the Postal Code prohibits censorship of mail, Article 9(1) guarantees the secrecy of letters, and Article 9(2) stipulates the duty of confidentiality of postal workers. Those who open mail without a reason can be punished according to Article 77 of the Postal Code.

114. Furthermore, Article 4 of the Telecommunications Business Act stipulates that the secrecy of communications handled by telecommunications carriers must not be violated, and Article 104 of the same law stipulates that violation of secrecy is punishable; that is, infringement of secrets is subject to punishment. Articles 9 and 14 of the Wire Telecommunications Act also contain provisions to the same effect. Moreover, Article 59 of the Radio Act provides that interception of communications itself is not a punishable offence due to the nature of radio communications, but if communications are leaked, this act is punishable under Article 109 of the same law. Article 9 makes it a punishable offence to divulge such information, and there are legal provisions in which personal privacy is considered to be a protected legal interest on the basis of Article 21 of the Constitution.

Part II. National Data Protection Law

Chapter 1. National Data Protection Law: General Description

§1. Structure of the Japanese Personal Information Protection Legal System

115. Japan's personal information protection legal system consists of (1) laws; (2) basic policies; (3) Cabinet orders; (4) regulations; (5) supplementary rules; (6) basic principles; and (7) guidelines; as well as (8) protection of personal information based on related provisions in individual laws and regulations (e.g., the Act on Securing the Proper Operation of Worker Dispatching Businesses and Protecting Dispatched Workers (Law Number: Act No. 88 of 1985) and the Employment Security Act (Law Number: Order of the Ministry of Labour (Act No. 12 of 1947)); (9) professional confidentiality obligation provisions stipulated by laws and regulations (e.g., the Civil Service Act (Act No. 120 of 1947) and various professional business laws); (10) laws and regulations pursuing legal responsibility for acts such as leakage or misuse of personal information (e.g., the Unfair Competition Prevention Act (Act No. 47 of 1993)); (11) standards and guidelines based on other laws and regulations (e.g., the Industrial Standardisation Unfair Competition Prevention Act (Act No. 185 of 1949), the Act on the Limitation of Liability for Damages of Specified Telecommunications Service Providers and the Right to Demand Disclosure of Identification Information of the Sender (Act No. 137 of 2001), and guidelines based on the Act on Electronic Signatures and Certification Business (Act No. 102 of 2000)); and (12) guidelines established by authorised personal data protection organisations and other private bodies:

Japan's Personal Information Protection Legal System	
Law	
	Act on the Protection of Personal Information (Act No. 57 of 30 May 2003) (APPI)
Basic Policy	
	Basic Policy on the Protection of Personal Information (Cabinet Decision of 2 April 2004, partially amended on 1 April 2022)

Cabinet Orders	
	Order for Enforcement of the Act on the Protection of Personal Information (Cabinet Order No. 507 of 10 December 2003)
Regulations	
	Regulations for Enforcement of the Act on the Protection of Personal Information (Regulation No. 3 of the Personal Information Protection Commission, 5 October 2008)
Basic Principles	
	Basic Principles of Policy Relating to the Proper Handling of Personal Information
Supplementary Rules	
	Supplementary Rules under the Act on the Protection of Personal Information for the Handling of Personal Data Transferred from within the EU and the UK
Guidelines	
	Guidelines and Q&As for Personal Information Handling Business Operators (relating to the General Provisions of the Act on the Protection of Personal Information, Chapter 4, etc.)
	Guidelines on the Act on the Protection of Personal Information (General Guidelines) (updated 8 September 2022)
	Guidelines on the Act of the Protection of Personal Information (Provision to Third Parties in Foreign Countries) (updated 17 November 2021)
	Guidelines on the Act on the Protection of Personal Information (Obligation to Verify and Record regarding Third Party Provision) (updated 29 October 2021)
	Guidelines on the Act on the Protection of Personal Information (Pseudonymously Processed Information and Anonymously Processed Information) (updated 29 October 2021)
	Guidelines on the Act on the Protection of Personal Information (Accredited Personal Information Protection Organisations) (29 October 2021)

	Foreign Countries which have Systems for the Protection of Personal Information which are Recognised as Being at the Same Level as Japan in Protecting the Rights and Interests of Individuals (Personal Information Protection Commission Notice No. 1 of 2019)
	Q&As on the Guidelines to the Act on the Protection of Personal Information (Q&As added and updated May 2022)
	Notice for Handling Health Information among Personal Information in the Field of Employment Management
	Guidelines Pertaining to Administrative Organs (related to Chapter 5, etc., of the Act on the Protection of Personal Information)
	Guidelines on the Act on the Protection of Personal Information (administrative organs, etc.) (effective 1 April 2023)
	Administrative Guide to the Act on the Protection of Personal Information (for administrative organs, etc.) (effective 1 April 2023)
	Q&A on the Act of the Protection of Personal Information (for administrative organs, etc.) (addition to and update of Q&A, effective 1 April 2023) (enacted on 1 April 2023)

Guidelines for Specific Sectors	
Financial Sector	
	Guidelines for the Protection of Personal Information in the Financial Sector
	Practical Guidelines on Safeguards and Other Measures in the Guidelines for the Protection of Personal information in the Financial Sector
	Q&A on Personal information Protection in Financial Institutions
	Guidelines for the Protection of Personal Information in the Credit Sector
	Guidelines for the Protection of Personal Information in the Debt Management and Collection Sector

Healthcare Sector	
	Guidance on the Proper Handling of Personal information by Medical and Nursing Care Providers
	Q&As (Case Studies) on the Guidance for the Appropriate Handling of Personal Information by Medical and Nursing Care-Related Businesses
	Guidance for the Appropriate Handling of Personal information in Health Insurance Associations
	Q&As on Case Studies to Supplement the Guidance for the Appropriate Handling of Personal Information in Health Insurance Associations
	Guidance for the Appropriate Handling of Personal information in National Health Insurance Associations
	Guidance for the Appropriate Handling of Personal Information in National Health Insurance Federations
	Guidelines for the Protection of Personal Information in the Economic and Industrial Sector in the Business Sector Using Personal Genetic information
Guidelines for the Information and Telecommunications Sector	
	Guidelines for the Protection of Personal Information in the Telecommunications Business Sector
	Explanation of the Guidelines on the Protection of Personal Information in the Telecommunications Sector
	Guidelines for the Protection of Personal Information of Broadcast Recipients
	Explanation of the Guidelines for the Protection of Personal Information of Broadcast Recipients
	Guidelines for the Protection of Personal Information in the Postal Services
	Commentary on the Guidelines for the Protection of Personal Information in the Postal Services Sector
	Guidelines on the Protection of Personal Information in the Field of Letter Delivery Services
	Explanation of the Guidelines for the Protection of Personal Information in the Field of Letter Services

Report

116. Pseudonymously Processed Information/Anonymised Processed Information: Towards the Trustworthy Utilisation of Personal Information – System (11 May 2022).

117. Pseudonymously Processed Information/Anonymised Processed Information Towards the Trustworthy Utilisation of Personal Information – Case Studies (11 May 2022).

118. Report of the Expert Committee on the Use of Camera Images for Crime Prevention and Security (March 2023).

§2. Overview of the Act on the Protection of Personal Information

119. The purpose of the APPI is to 'protect the rights and interests of individuals' while 'taking into account the usefulness of personal information', as the use of personal information has expanded significantly with the development of an advanced information and communications society. The main objective of this Act is to require the state and local authorities, as well as private business entities, to handle personal information appropriately.

120. The Obligations of a Personal Information Handling Business Operator are divided into those applicable to 'personal information' (Article 2(1)), 'personal data' (Article 16(3)), and 'retained personal data' (Article 16(4)). In addition to these three definitions, the obligations to handle individual identification codes (Article 2(2)), special care-required personal information (Article 2(3)), pseudonymously processed information (Article 2(5)), anonymously processed information (Article 2(6)), and personally referable information (Article 2(7)) are defined.

121. Personal information handling business operators (Article 16(2)) are obliged to specify the purpose of use of personal information and use it within that scope (Article 17(1)). The consent of the person concerned is required if the information is to be used beyond the scope of the specified purposes of use (Article 16(1)). The purpose of use may change but only to the extent that it is reasonably related to the purpose of use before the change (Articles 17(2) and 21(3)).

122. The acquisition of 'personal information' is subject to proper acquisition (Article 20(1)). If the information is obtained directly from the concerned person in writing or otherwise through electronic means, the purpose of use must be clearly stated (Article 21(2)). If the information is acquired by other means, the purpose of use must be notified or made public (Article 21(1)). Acquisition of 'special care-required personal information' requires the consent of the person concerned (Article 20(2)).

123. Obligations in relation to 'personal data' require that accuracy is ensured (Article 22). In principle, personal data cannot be provided to third parties without the consent of the individual (Articles 27–30). However, if certain exemptions apply, such as opting out, the consent of the person is not required (Article 27(2)–(5)). Provision to contractors and in cases of business succession and joint use does not fall under the category of third parties and can be provided without the consent of the individual (Article 27(5)(i)–(iii)). There are additional restrictions on provision if provision to a third party is to a foreign third party (Article 28). In view of the continuing number of large-scale personal data leaks, there is also an obligation to record the provision of personal data to a third party (Articles 29 and 30). Furthermore, personal information handling business operators are obliged to report to the PPC and notify the concerned individual of any leakage, loss, or damage of personal data they handle or any other situation relating to the security of personal data that is highly likely to harm the rights and interests of individuals (Article 26).

124. Additionally, to ensure that personal data are securely managed, the obligation to take security control measures (Article 23) is imposed pertaining to personal data, and the obligation to supervise employees (Article 24) and contractors (Article 25) is incurred.

125. Furthermore, if the information cannot identify a specific individual at the source of the data but is acquired as personally identifiable data by a third party to whom the data are provided, the obligations relating to restrictions on the provision of 'personally referable information' to third parties apply (Article 31).

126. With regard to obligations concerning 'retained personal data', business entities are obliged to publish matters relating to retained personal data (Article 32). To comply with this obligation, business entities often publish such matters as a personal information protection policy or privacy policy. The right of the individual to disclose, correct, or suspend the use of retained personal data is stipulated (Articles 33–39). Additionally, personal information handling business operators must endeavour to appropriately and promptly handle complaints about the handling of personal information (Article 40).

127. Other provisions include the Obligations of a Pseudonymously Processed Information Handling Business Operator (Articles 41 and 42) and the Obligations of an Anonymously Processed Information Handling Business Operator (Articles 43–46) for the handling of 'anonymously processed information' that is not obliged to be handled as personal information.

128. The Obligations of a Personal Information Handling Business Operator are not applicable to mass media, the literary profession, religious organisations, and political organisations that handle personal information for the purpose of using it for news reporting, writing, religious activities, and political activities, respectively. With regard to academic research institutions, the 2021 Amendment to the APPI abolished the uniform exemption from the Obligations of a Personal Information

Handling Business Operator and the obligations of (i) restriction based on the purpose of use (Article 18); (ii) restriction on the acquisition of special care-required personal information (Article 20, paragraph 2); and (iii) restriction on the use of personal information for the purpose of providing information to the media (Article 20, paragraph 1), as these do not apply except in cases where there is a risk of unjustified infringement of the rights and interests of individuals.

§3. Background to the Enactment of the APPI

129. After adopting the OECD Guidelines in 1980, the Administrative Management Agency established a Privacy Protection Research Group to investigate the domestic legislation of the OECD Guidelines. In July 1982, this research group compiled a report titled 'Personal Data Management and Privacy Protection Measures' and proposed legislation on the grounds that it was necessary to establish a new law based on the basic principles of privacy protection. This was also the foundation of the OECD Privacy Guidelines.

130. The Japanese considered an omnibus formula of personal data protection laws, but the Management and Coordination Agency subsequently examined and legislated the retaining of personal data within administrative agencies. That led to the establishment of the Law Relating to the Protection of Personal Data Stored on Administrative Agency Computers in 1988.

131. Based on the recommendation, there were deliberations on private sector legislation, but no laws were enacted, so protection measures based on the Guidelines were introduced. Personal data protection guidelines in the financial sector were put in place in 1987, using the basic principles of the jurisdiction of the Ministry of Finance. The private sector, under the jurisdiction of the former Ministry of International Trade and Industry (MITI), adopted these guidelines in 1989, followed by the telecommunications industry, also under the watch of the MITI and the former Ministry of Posts and Telecommunications, in 1991. These guidelines were all based on the OECD Privacy Guidelines and are representative of Japan's personal data protection policies.

132. In Japan, the government has considered personal data protection laws in the private sector on a national level since July 1999. At that time, a personal data protection investigation unit was established in the High-Tech Telecommunications Society Promotion Department. Taking advantage of these investigations, a personal data protection law was finally enacted in May 2003. At the same time, an administrative agency personal data protection law and independent administrative corporation personal data protection law took effect. This new administrative agency personal data protection law was a complete overhaul of the 1988 Protection of Personal Data Stored on Administrative Agency Computers Law.

133. All of these personal data protection laws have been shaped around the main points of the OECD Privacy Guidelines. Using the personal data protection laws applicable to the private sector as an example, I would like to refer to the eight OECD principles and Japanese personal data protection laws and present the specific regulations that correspond to the eight privacy guideline principles.

§4. Act on the Protection of Personal Information Covering Administrative Organs (1988 Law)

134. The first personal information protection law in Japan was the Act on the Protection of Personal Information Pertaining to Computer Processing Held by Administrative Organs (Act No. 95 of 16 December 1988), which covers the handling of personal information by national administrative organs for computer processing.

135. This Act was enacted in response to the OECD's Council Recommendation on Guidelines for the Protection of Privacy and Personal Data, which set out the measures necessary to protect personal data while ensuring the free flow of information between countries to develop their own domestic legislation.

§5. Act on the Protection of Personal Information (Act No.57 of 2003)

136. The Act on the Protection of Personal Information (APPI) (Act No. 57 of 2003), which also covers the private sector, was enacted on 30 May 2003 and came into force on 1 April 2005.

137. Along with the enactment of the APPI, the Act on the Protection of Personal Information Held by Administrative Organs (Act No. 58 of 30 May 2003) and the Act on the Protection of Personal Information Held by Independent Administrative Agencies (Act No. 59 of 30 May 2003) were also enacted for the public sector, covering administrative organs and independent administrative agencies.

138. In addition to the five Acts on the Protection of Personal Information, the Basic Policy on the Protection of Personal Information (Cabinet Decision of 2 April 2004), regulations, Cabinet orders, enforcement orders, and guidelines have been enacted.

139. In the period before the APPI was enacted for the private sector, in order to promote voluntary initiatives in the handling of personal information, in 1999, based on the Industrial Standardisation Act, a Japanese Industrial Standard for the protection of personal information, known as JIS Q 15001 was established and subsequently revised in line with the enactment of the APPI, at which point it became JIS Q 15001: 2006 Personal Information Protection Management Systems – Requirements, published on 23 May 2006.

§6. 2015 Amendments of the Act on the Protection of Personal Information

I. Summary of Legislative Amendments

140. The Bill for Amendment of the Act on the Protection of Personal Information and the Act on the Use of Numbers to Identify Specific Individuals in Administrative Procedures (189th Diet session: Cabinet Act No. 34) was passed on 3 September 2015 and promulgated as Act No. 65 on 9 September of the same year.

141. The APPI was amended together with the Law on the Use of Personal Numbers because, although the Specified Personal Information Protection Commission has been in place since 1 January 2014 as the body to supervise the handling of national identification personal numbers (My Number), the Commission was reorganised as a new body, the PPC. My Number notification began in October 2015, and the system became operational on 1 January 2016.

142. With regard to the changes in the means of communication in the 2000s, such as social networking services (SNS) and smartphones, it was anticipated that the environment for handling personal information would be affected by the use of SNS and smartphones, resulting in the handling of so-called big data. However, a grey-zone problem has arisen, where it is difficult to determine whether the information is 'personal information'. The APPI was amended to address these issues.

143. JIS Q 15001 has also been amended to Personal Information Protection Management System – Requirements (JIS Q 15001:2017) and was notified on 20 December 2017 (amended on 14 March 2018) after deliberations by the Japan Industrial Standards Committee based on the Industrial Standardisation Act.

II. Reason for the 2015 Amendments

144. The reason for the 2015 amendments to the Act was to contribute to the realisation of a vibrant economic society and a prosperous life for the people by actively promoting the proper and effective use of personal information and My Number, while protecting personal information in response to the dramatic development of Information and Communications Technology (ICT), and to make the necessary legislative changes with regard to the proper handling and procedures necessary for the protection of personal information. Furthermore, the PPC has been established to supervise and ensure the proper handling and protection of personal information.

III. Outline of the 2015 Amendments

145. The main issues pertaining to the 2015 amendments reflected in the revised APPI are (i) clarification of the definition of 'personal information'; (ii) the development of provisions to ensure the usefulness of personal information and other information under the appropriate discipline; (iii) the development of provisions to strengthen the protection of personal information; (iv) the establishment of a new PPC and provisions regarding its powers; and v) the development of provisions to cope with the globalisation of the handling of personal information.

146. First, to clarify the scope of personal information, the Act places personal information in the category of information that includes codes that convert some physical characteristics of a specific individual, codes that appear on a document issued to an individual, and other codes that are specified by a Cabinet order.

147. Second, to prevent unjustified discrimination or prejudice against individuals, provisions should be established for the handling of personal information, including race, creed, social status, and medical history.

148. Third, to promote the safe and secure use of personal data, 'anonymously processed information' is defined as personal information that has been processed in such a way that a specific individual cannot be identified and such that the personal information cannot be restored, and regulations on the handling of such information, as well as the processing method, have been established.

149. Fourth, as a response to personal information leaks, which have become increasingly serious in recent years, when personal information is provided to a third party, it should be mandatory to confirm the circumstances of acquisition and prepare records, etc., and penalties should be established for the provision of personal information databases for the purpose of gaining unfair profit.

150. Fifth, to establish a system to centrally monitor and supervise businesses that handle personal information in order to ensure the proper handling of personal information, the PPC, which is based on the Act on the Use of a Number to Identify a Specific Individual in Administrative Procedures, has been reorganised to establish and develop regulations on its organisation and affairs under its jurisdiction.

151. Sixth, to ensure the proper and smooth distribution of personal data in the context of the globalisation of business activities, provisions should be developed for cases where personal data are provided to third parties located in foreign countries, and provisions should be developed for cases where personal information is acquired by foreign business operators, in relation to the provision of goods or services to persons in Japan.

IV. Main Aspects of the 2015 Amendments

(1) Revision of Definitions

152. Although the scope of personal information has not changed as a result of the amendments to the Act, new definitions for the following terms have been added for clarity: individual identification code, special care-required personal information, anonymously processed information, anonymously processed information handling business operator, and anonymously processed information database.

(2) Re-Definition of Personal Information

153. 'Personal information' is defined as information relating to a living individual that falls under any of the following items: (i) those containing a name, date of birth, or other descriptions, etc., meaning any and all matters, excluding an individual identification code, stated, recorded, or otherwise expressed using voice, movement, or other methods in a document, drawing, or electromagnetic record (i.e., a record kept in an electromagnetic form, i.e., an electronic, magnetic, or other forms that cannot be recognised through the human senses (the same applies in item (ii) and hereinafter) whereby a specific individual can be identified, including those that can be readily collated with other information and thereby identify a specific individual); (ii) those containing an individual identification code.

(3) Newly Added Definition

154. The term 'special care-required personal information' means personal information comprising a principal's race, creed, social status, medical history, criminal record, the fact of having suffered damage by a crime, or other descriptions, etc., prescribed by Cabinet Order as information of which the handling requires special care so as not to cause unfair discrimination, prejudice, or other disadvantages to the principal(s).

(4) Revised Obligations of a Personal Information Handling Business Operator

155. The Obligations of a Personal Information Handling Business Operator have been amended with regard to (i) specifying the purpose of use; (ii) proper acquisition; (iii) ensuring the accuracy of data content; (iv) limiting provision to third parties; (v) limiting provision to third parties located abroad; (vi) creating records relating to provision to third parties; (vii) checking when receiving from third parties; and (viii) disclosure. Each of these will be elaborated sequentially in the following paragraphs:

(i) With regard to specifying the purpose of use, the provisions have been amended so that when the purpose of use changes, the change must not exceed the extent to which it is reasonably deemed to be related to the original purpose of use. The word 'reasonable' has been deleted.

(ii) With regard to appropriate acquisition, it is prohibited to acquire special care-required personal information without obtaining the prior consent of the individual, except in certain cases.

(iii) With regard to ensuring the accuracy of data content, the obligation to make efforts to erase personal data without delay is stipulated when there is no longer a need to use the personal data.

(iv) With regard to restrictions on provision to third parties, the opt-out provisions have been reviewed. In the procedures relating to opt-out to the effect that personal data identifying the person concerned may be provided to a third party without the prior consent of the person in certain cases, special care-required personal information is excluded from the personal principals to the said discipline. To provide personal data without the consent of the individual by opting out, a new procedure has been established whereby certain matters must be notified to the individual or made readily available to the individual and notified to the PPC in advance, in accordance with the rules of the PPC. When the PPC is notified of matters pertaining to the opt-out, it shall make public the matters pertaining to the notification in accordance with the PPC Regulations.

(v) With regard to restrictions on the provision of personal data to third parties located in a foreign country, the consent of the individual must be obtained in advance to allow the provision of personal data to third parties located in a foreign country, except in certain cases. In this case, even joint use and provision to contractors, which are exempted from provision to third parties, are not exempted from the principle of consent of the individual when providing personal data to third parties in foreign countries.

(vi) With regard to maintaining records relating to the provision of personal data to third parties, when personal data are provided to a third party, a record of the date of provision of the personal data in question and the name of the third party in question must be made and stored for a certain period of time, in accordance with the rules of the PPC.

(vii) With regard to confirmation when receiving personal data from a third party, a record of the circumstances of the acquisition of the relevant personal data by the third party must be confirmed, and a record of the date of the provision of the relevant personal data must be prepared and maintained for a certain period of time, as prescribed by the Rules of the Personal Information Protection Commission.

(viii) With regard to disclosure, the individual may request that a personal information handling business operator disclose retained personal data that identify the individual and, in certain cases, correct, add to, or delete the content of such retained personal data, stop its use, or erase it, or stop its provision to a third party. The law has been amended to define the procedure more clearly.

§7. 2020 AND 2021 AMENDMENTS OF THE APPI

I. Summary of Legislative Amendments

156. The challenges in the research, development, and use of AI and the personal data protection system are the increasing sophistication of machine learning methods, as typified by deep learning, and the need to consider the proper handling and protection of big data for the realisation of such methods. The issue of the handling of personal information in relation to AI requires consideration of the handling and protection of personal information under the APPI, the guarantee of the right to privacy, and the protection of personal interests, such as portrait and honour.

157. The issues relating to AI and personal information protection are not necessarily that problems arise with regard to the handling of personal information as a result of AI's autonomous acquisition and use of personal information; rather, the essence of the issue is whether personal information handling business operators using AI are able to handle personal information appropriately in conjunction with AI's use.

158. Given the wide variety and enormous amount of so-called big data,[21] the volume of information handled will increase dramatically in the future due to the evolution of AI, as it will become possible to collect and analyse the data, which will further spur the creation of new industries and services. At the same time, information about individuals, as represented by information about their behaviour and condition, can now be utilised for the public good as well as for their own benefit by means of advanced ICT.

159. With the spread of the Internet of Things (IoT) and 5G, the volume of information is expected to increase dramatically compared to the volume of information handled in the past. Further, such information will be instantaneously available without time lag, anytime and anywhere. Considering the anticipated future changes in the situation of personal information handling, it is likely that (i) ubiquity, (ii) immediacy, and (iii) enormity will increase dramatically.

160. Thus, the situation regarding the handling of personal information has undergone a significant transformation compared to when the APPI was enacted in 2003. In particular, ICT has developed remarkably, and the 2015 amendments to the Act take such environmental changes into account, specifically 'taking into account international trends on the Protection of Personal Information, developments in information and communication technology and the accompanying creation and development of new industries utilising personal information' (Article 12, paragraph 3 of the Supplementary Provisions of the 2015 Revised Act on the Protection of Personal Information).

---

21. Fumio Shimpo, *Big Data as Cliche*, Electronic Intellectual Property and Social Infrastructure (EIP) 2012-EIP-55(7) (2012), pp. 1-6.

161. In light of such environmental dynamism, there is a new provision stipulating that a review shall be conducted every three years. The so-called Triennial Review of the Act, the Outline of Revision, published on 13 December 2019, sets out five focal points for the review, which can be summarised as follows: (1) improving measures to protect the rights and interests of individuals in response to growing interest in the handling of personal information; (2) ensuring a balance between protection and utilisation in terms of both economic growth and the protection of the rights and interests of individuals; (3) the need for international institutional harmonisation and collaboration; (4) addressing risks associated with the growing business of handling personal information across borders; and (5) addressing accountability in the handling of personal information and the development of an appropriate environment for its use within predictable limits. These are the specific viewpoints of the amendments.

162. The APPI (Act No. 44 of 2020) was promulgated on 12 June 2020. To consolidate provisions on the protection of personal information pertaining to the private sector, administrative organs, and incorporated administrative agencies and to review the personal information protection system of local governments, the Disciplinary Approach to the Protection of Personal Information in the Public Sector (national administrative agencies, local government agencies, etc., related to the 2021 amendment of the APPI) and the Disciplinary Approach to the Protection of Personal Information in the Academic Research Sector (related to the 2021 revision of the APPI) were decided upon by the PPC. Based on these, the APPI was amended in the Act on the Development of Relevant Acts for the Formation of a Digital Society (Act No. 37 of 19 May 2021), which was promulgated on 19 May 2020. As two amendments were made in a short period of time, the former is referred to as the '2020 amendment' and the latter as the '2021 amendment'.

II. Enforcement Date of the 2020 and 2021 Amendments

163. The 2020 Amendment Act came into force on 1 April 2022. However, the transitional measures for the provision of personal data to third parties pursuant to Article 23(2) of the amended Act came into force on 1 October 2021, and an increase in the statutory penalty (Articles 83–87) came into force on 12 December 2020.

164. The 2021 Amendment Act came into force on 1 April 2022 with regard to the provisions on administrative organs and independent administrative agencies and the revision of the exemption provisions for academic research institutions (amendment in accordance with Article 50 of the Digital Society Formation and Development Act) and will come into force on 1 April 2023 with regard to the provisions on local governments (amendment in accordance with Article 51 of the Digital Society Formation and Development Act).

III. Outline of the 2020 Amendments

165. The main 2020 amendments to the APPI concern (1) the nature of individual rights; (2) the nature of the responsibilities of business operators to protect; (3) the nature of the mechanism to encourage voluntary efforts by business operators; (4) the nature of measures for data utilisation; (5) the nature of penalties; and (6) the nature of the extra-territorial application and cross-border transfer of the Act.

(i) Individual Rights

166. The right of an individual to request the suspension of use or erasure of a principal's personal information was limited to cases of procedural violations, such as unauthorised acquisition or provision to a third party. With this amendment, the requirements for the right to request have been relaxed to cases where there is a risk of harm to the rights or legitimate interests of the individual, in addition to some violations of the Act, such as, as abovementioned, unauthorised acquisition, etc.

167. Furthermore, retained personal data which are erased within six months were not included in the coverage of the suspension of use or erasure. The amended Act covers personal data which are erased within six months through the inclusion of such data in 'retained personal data'.

168. With regard to the method of disclosure, Article 9 of the Enforcement Order of the APPI provides that the method by which retained personal data are disclosed by personal information handling business operators is 'by way of delivery of a written document (if there is a method to which the person making the request for disclosure has agreed, such method)'. In other words, the Act has been amended to allow the person to instruct the method of disclosure of retained personal data, including the provision of electromagnetic records, as written delivery was the principle for requests for disclosure.

169. Although, in principle, the provision of personal data was subject to the consent of the individual, even if the individual had given consent to the provision, there was no way to confirm to whom the personal data had been provided. Therefore, the Act has been amended to allow the individual to request disclosure of third-party provision records relating to the transfer of personal data.

170. With regard to personal data provided to third parties, such as data brokers' sale of lists of names, even if the data were acquired illegally, the data can still be provided legitimately by opting out. Furthermore, it was possible to acquire personal data that had been opted out and provided and to provide personal data that were circulated in turn by opting out further. Therefore, the scope of personal data that can be provided to third parties through opt-out provisions was limited, and (i) personal data acquired illegally and (ii) personal data provided through opt-out provisions were also excluded.

(ii) The Nature of the Responsibilities Businesses Should Uphold

171. Leakages of personal data are often reported in the daily news. On the other hand, there is a problem that even after being exposed to such reports, it is unknown whether the individual is affected or not until the damage is actually caused. The amended Act has made it mandatory to report to the PPC and notify the individual when a personal data leakage has occurred and there is a risk of harm to the individual's rights and interests. It has also been clarified that personal information must not be inappropriately used, such as by encouraging illegal or unjustified acts.

(iii) Mechanisms to Promote Businesses' Voluntary Initiatives

172. The Accredited Personal Information Protection Organisation system has been established to promote initiatives for the protection of personal information. However, this system was only designed with the industry associations to which businesses belong in mind, and as businesses diversify, there are more and more cases where businesses are engaged in activities that do not conform to the jurisdiction of the industry associations to which they belong. Therefore, the existing Accredited Personal Information Protection Organisation system is expected to promote personal information protection initiatives in line with the content of individual businesses by enabling this organisation to accredit organisations that target specific fields (sectors) of companies in addition to the current system.

(iv) The State of Measures for Data Utilisation

173. With the aim of realising more active handling of personal information within the business and utilising it in the business, a new definition of 'pseudonymously processed information' has been added, in which names and other information that can identify specific individuals have been deleted from the perspective of promoting innovation, for example, by relaxing restrictions on the purpose of use. Pseudonymously processed information may not be provided to third parties, but the obligation to respond to requests for disclosure and suspension of use has been relaxed, provided that it is limited to internal analysis.

174. A new procedure for personally referable information has also been added. The background to the addition of this procedure is that an inappropriate service involving the use of data providing information about job offer decline rates became problematic as a violation of the APPI. The problem, in this case, was that the unofficial job offer rejection rate was calculated using cookies instead of names, which constitute personal information, to ensure that specific individuals are not identified, and this information was provided to the companies using the service without obtaining the consent of the principals. Additionally, while the companies that received the unofficial job offer refusal rates knew that they could identify specific individuals, the companies that provided the rates to the users avoided acquiring consent for the provision of personal data to a third party, on the grounds that they could not identify specific individuals. The PPC issued a recommendation as a violation of the APPI on 4 December 2019. In light of these cases, a new definition of 'personally referable information' has been added.

(v) Penalties

175. The statutory penalties for violation of an order issued by the PPC and false reporting to the PPC have been increased. For violation of an order, the penalty of imprisonment for not more than six months or a fine of not more than JPY 300,000 has become imprisonment for not more than one year or a fine of not more than JPY 1 million, and for false reporting, the penalty of a fine of not more than JPY 300,000 has become a fine of not more than JPY 500,000.

176. Additionally, with regard to the offence of illicit provision of personal information databases and fines for violations of orders issued by the PPC, the maximum amount of fines for legal entities has increased compared to that for the offender, taking into account the disparity in financial resources between legal entities and individuals, and the maximum fine for a legal entity has increased from the same amount as for an individual (a fine of up to JPY 500,000 or JPY 300,000) such that the maximum fine is now up to JPY 100 million.

(vi) Extraterritorial Application of the Act and Cross-Border Transfers

177. Personal information is handled across national borders on a daily basis, and foreign business operators handling personal information pertaining to persons in Japan are now also subject to the collection of reports and orders secured by penalties. Additionally, when personal data are provided to a third party in a foreign country, the amendment requires the provision of enhanced information to the individual regarding the handling of personal information by the transferring entity.

IV. Outline of the 2021 Amendments

178. The overall purpose of the 2021 amendments to the APPI was to review the personal information protection legal system with respect to the public and private sectors. In response to the inevitable qualitative and quantitative increase in the data volume handled by the public sector in line with the promotion of national and local digital business reforms, a major structural change was made to the legal framework of Japan's personal information protection legal system, consisting of the following two points:

(1) The PPC, an independent administrative commission, has established a system to centrally supervise the handling of personal information in the public sector as well as in the private sector.
(2) To respond to the active use of data across public-private and regional boundaries, the imbalances and inconsistencies in the former legislation caused by separate laws and regulations have been corrected.

179. The specific amendment items of the 2021 Amendment Act are as follows: (1) the Act on the Protection of Personal Information Held by Administrative Organs (Act No. 58 of 2003) and the Act on the Protection of Personal Information

Held by Incorporated Administrative Agencies (Act No. 59 of 2003) are integrated into the APPI, and the overall jurisdiction is centralised in the PPC, while definitions and basic concepts are unified into disciplines for private entities; (2) the Ordinances on the Protection of Personal Information of Local Government Agencies, previously regulated by individual local government ordinances, will be applied as a nationwide common rule based on the integrated APPI, with the same rules as those newly applied to administrative agencies and incorporated administrative agencies; (3) upon the integration of the laws, the rules for administrative organs and incorporated administrative agencies will be enhanced with reference to the rules for private entities, including the rules established by the 2020 legal reform, while maintaining the mechanism for the protection of rights that should be ensured as public institutions; and (4) disciplinary rules applicable to public institutions related to the medical and academic fields are unified with those applicable to private operators in order to realise smooth public–private partnerships by correcting disciplinary imbalances, based on the need to solve social problems through public-private partnerships.

Chapter 2. Scope of the National Law

180. The APPI in Japan applies to the handling of personal information in Japan as a general rule. Furthermore, Article 171 of the APPI provides that:

> [T]his Act also applies in those cases where a personal information handling business operator, a pseudonymously processed information handling business operator, an anonymously processed information handling business operator, or a personally referable information handling business operator, in relation to supplying a good or service to a person in Japan, handles the personal information which has a person in Japan as the principal, personally referable information which is to be acquired as that personal information, pseudonymously processed information or anonymously processed information produced by using that personal information, in a foreign country.

181. The Guidelines on the Act on the Protection of Personal Information [updated 17 November 2021] (hereinafter referred to as the 'General Guidelines') issued by the PPC stipulate[22] that a personal information handling business operator in a foreign country may, in relation to the provision of goods or services to a person in Japan, such as a resident of Japan, handle personal information of which a person in Japan is the principal, personally referable information which is to be acquired as such personal information, or pseudonymously processed information or anonymously processed information created by using such personal information in a foreign country. Extraterritorial application is not limited to cases where a personal information handling business operator in a foreign country acquires such information directly from the individual concerned and handles it; it also includes cases where the information is provided by a third party other than the individual concerned.

182. Personal information handling business operators located in foreign countries are not limited to business operators that have a base of activity exclusively in a foreign country (including those that have moved their base of activity from Japan to a foreign country). For example, a personal information handling business operator with a head office in a foreign country and a branch or sales office in Japan or a personal information handling business operator with a branch or sales office in a foreign country and a head office in Japan are also included.

183. A person in Japan, such as a resident of Japan, does not necessarily have to be the same as a 'person in Japan' who is the subject of the 'provision of goods or services' and a 'person in Japan' whom the 'personal information' may identify. For example, if a personal information handling business operator in a foreign country

22. The Personal Information Protection Commission, *Guidelines on the Act on the Protection of Personal Information* (updated 17 Nov. 2021)(hereinafter referred to as the 'General Guidelines')p. 161.

handles personally referable information in relation to selling a list of names containing the personal information of a person A in Japan to a person B in Japan, the personal information is subject to extraterritorial application.[23]

184. The provision of 'goods or services' is defined as the provision of goods or services, regardless of whether or not the person has paid compensation for the 'provision of goods or services'.[24]

185. If a foreign operator to which the Act applies according to Article 171 of the Act violates the APPI, the PPC may give guidance, advice, recommendations, or orders based on the APPI enforcement scheme.[25]

186. For a subsidiary in Japan to provide the personal data of its employees to its parent company in a foreign country, it is necessary to take measures to provide personal data to a third party in a foreign country, such as acquiring the consent of the individual, in accordance with Article 28 of the Act. For more information, it is necessary to refer to the Guidelines for the Provision of Personal Data to Third Parties in Foreign Countries.[26]

187. 'Personal information' subject to the APPI is not only limited to Japanese citizens but also includes foreign nationals (Guidelines – General Rules – Part 2. Definitions – 2-1. Personal Information; related to Article 2.1 of the Act).

188. On the acquisition of special care-required personal information (related to Article 20, paragraph 2 of the Act), Item 7 states that '[w]hen such special care-required personal information is disclosed by the person in question, a state organ, a local government agency, an academic research institution, a person listed in each item of Article 57, paragraph 1, or any other person specified by the Rules of the Personal Information Protection Commission', it is stipulated that this does not apply.

189. Article 6 of the Regulations stipulates that the persons specified by the Regulations of the Personal Information Protection Commission under Article 20(2)(vii) of the Act shall be those falling under any of the following items:

(1) Foreign governments, foreign government agencies, foreign local government agencies, or international organisations.
(2) A person who is equivalent to an academic research institution, etc., provided for in Article 16(8) of the Act in a foreign country.
(3) Persons equivalent to those listed in each item of Article 57(1) of the Act in a foreign country.

---

23. General Guidelines, p. 66.
24. General Guidelines, p. 166.
25. *Ibid.*
26. General Guidelines, p. 161.

190. With regard to the notification of opt-out, Article 12 of the Regulations provides that:

> A Personal Information Handling Business Operator in a foreign country shall, when making a notification pursuant to Article 27, paragraph 2 or 3 of the Act, appoint a person having an address in Japan who has the authority to represent said Personal Information Handling Business Operator in all acts concerning said notification. In this case, a person who has an address in Japan and is authorised to act on behalf of said business operator handling personal information shall be designated. In this case, said Personal Information Handling Business Operator shall, at the same time as said notification, submit to the Personal Information Protection Commission a document (including a translation in Japanese) certifying that said Personal Information Handling Business Operator has authorised a person having an address in Japan to represent said Personal Information Handling Business Operator with regard to all acts concerning said notification.

191. Additionally, in the opt-out procedure, the 'method of accepting the request of the person' includes the contact details (name of the business, name of the contact person, mailing address or e-mail address to which the request is sent, etc.; the same shall apply hereinafter). If the personal information handling business operator concerned is based in a foreign country, the name and contact details of the domestic representative, etc., shall be provided.

192. As an increasing number of foreign business operators are handling personal information in Japan, extraterritorial application (Article 75) has recently been established. However, even if extraterritorial application is made possible, it is difficult to impose criminal penalties under the APPI on foreign operators.

193. First, there is the issue of whether criminal penalties (foreign criminal penalties) or surcharge payment orders can be imposed on foreign operators (the issue of extraterritorial application), but even if each of these is cleared, the issue of enforcement remains, and when considering the possibility of sanctions against foreign operators, the enforceability of criminal penalties and surcharges is completely different.

194. Imposing criminal penalties on foreign-based operators involves considerable practical difficulties. Putting aside the issue of the difficulty of investigative activities, even if some offence can be clarified, if the offender is not located in Japan, it is not possible to conduct a criminal trial in Japan. Therefore, it is necessary to first secure the extradition of the offender through an extradition treaty, but Japan has concluded extradition treaties with only two countries, namely the United States and South Korea.

Chapter 3. Concepts and Definitions

§1. Definition of Personal Information

(i) Definition of Personal Information

195. The APPI defines 'personal information' as follows:

Article 2 (1):

The term 'personal information' as used in this Act means information relating to a living individual which falls under any of each following item:
(i) those containing a name, date of birth, or other descriptions, etc., (meaning any and all matters, excluding an individual identification code, stated, recorded, or otherwise expressed using voice, movement, or other methods in a document, drawing, or electromagnetic record (i.e., a record kept in an electromagnetic form, i.e., electronic, magnetic, or other forms that cannot be recognised through the human senses; the same applies in item (ii) of the following paragraph; the same applies hereinafter) whereby a specific individual can be identified, including those which can be readily collated with other information and thereby identify a specific individual;
(ii) those containing an individual identification code.

(2) The term 'individual identification code' as used in this Act means those prescribed by Cabinet order, which are any character, letter, number, symbol, or other codes falling under any of each following items:
(i) those able to identify a specific individual that are characters, letters, numbers, symbols, or other codes into which a bodily partial feature of the specific individual has been converted in order to be provided for use by computers;
(ii) those characters, letters, numbers, symbols, or other codes which are assigned in regard to the use of services provided to an individual or to the purchase of goods sold to an individual, or which are stated or electromagnetically recorded in a card or other document issued to an individual so as to be able to identify a specific user or purchaser, or recipient of issuance by having made the said codes differently assigned or stated or recoded for the said user or purchaser or recipient of issuance.

(ii) Retained Personal Information (Definition for Administrative Organs Only)

196. The definition of 'personal information' is the same as that in the Obligations of a Personal Information Handling Business Operator, but for administrative organs, a separate definition of 'retained personal information' is provided, that is, 'retained personal information' (definition only for administrative organs) recorded in the following documents (Article 60(1) of the Act):

(1) Administrative documents (i.e., those recorded in the Act on Access to Information Held by Administrative Organs, Act No. 42 of 1999, hereinafter referred to as the 'Administrative Organs Information Access Act') and administrative documents as defined in Article 2, paragraph 2 of the Administrative Organs Information Access Act.
(2) Corporate documents (referring to administrative documents stipulated in Article 2, paragraph 2 of the Act on Access to Information Held by Independent Administrative Institutions, Act No. 140 of 2001, hereinafter referred to as the 'Act on Access to Information Held by Independent Administrative Institutions').

197. Personal information may be recorded on paper or other media or not (e.g., orally), but for the stable operation of the disciplines of the Act, the media on which personal information is recorded, such as documents, drawings, and electromagnetic records, must be fixed to some extent. Therefore, the 'retained personal information' to which the main disciplines of this Act apply is limited to that recorded in administrative documents.

198. The disciplines covered by 'retained personal information' in the Act are security control measures (Article 66(1) of the Act), restrictions on use and provision (Article 69 of the Act), and requests for disclosure from the individual concerned.

199. A definition of a 'personal information file' is also provided. A 'personal information file' is a collection of information containing retained personal information that is (i) systematically structured so that specific retained personal information can be retrieved using a computer to achieve a certain administrative purpose (a personal information file pertaining to computer processing); or (ii) systematically structured so that specific retained personal information can be retrieved using a computer to achieve a certain administrative purpose (a personal information file pertaining to computer processing).

§2. Special Care-Required Personal Information (Related to Article 2(3) of the Act)

200. The APPI provides a definition regarding certain sensitive personal information as 'special care-required personal information' as follows. Article 2(3) of the APPI provides that:

> The term 'special care-required personal information' as used in this Act means personal information comprising a principal's race, creed, social status, medical history, criminal record, the fact of having suffered damage by a crime, or

other descriptions, etc. prescribed by Cabinet order as those of which the handling requires special care so as not to cause unfair discrimination, prejudice, or other disadvantages to the principals.

201. 'Special care-required personal information' specifies information that may be a source of discrimination on the grounds of, according to the PPC Guidelines,[27] (1) race (which broadly means race, lineage, or ethnic or tribal origin; note that simple nationality or 'foreigner' information is a legal status and does not by itself constitute race. Skin colour is also not included in race, as it is merely information from which race can be inferred); (2) creeds (i.e., an individual's basic way of seeing and thinking, which includes both ideas and beliefs); (3) social status (i.e., a status that is attached to an individual as a condition and from which he or she cannot easily and readily extricate himself or herself for the rest of his or her life, not including mere occupational status or educational background); and (4) medical history (i.e., a history of illness, which is part of the history that indicates a specific medical condition, e.g., a particular individual has cancer, suffers from schizophrenia, etc.).

§3. Personal Information Databases, Etc., (Article 16 of the Act)

202. The APPI defines 'personal information database, etc.' as follows:

Article 16 (1)

The term 'personal information database, etc.' as used in this chapter and Chapter VIII means those set forth in the following which are a collective body of information comprising personal information (excluding those prescribed by Cabinet order as having little possibility of harming an individual's rights and interests considering their utilisation method):

(i) those systematically organised so as to be able to search for particular personal information using a computer;
(ii) beyond what is set forth in the preceding item, those prescribed by Cabinet order as having been systematically organised so as to be able to easily search for particular personal information.

203. 'Personal information database, etc.' means a collection of information containing personal information that is systematically structured so that specific personal information can be retrieved using a computer. Even if a computer is not used, the term also applies to personal information that has been processed on paper, organised and classified according to certain rules (e.g., in alphabetical order), and placed in a state where it can be easily retrieved by others by attaching table of contents, index, or code to facilitate the easy retrieval of specific personal information.

27. General Guideline, pp. 17–18.

204. However, the following do not fall under the category of 'personal information databases' as there is little risk of harm to the rights and interests of individuals in view of the method of use:

(1) The information has been issued for the purpose of selling to an unspecified and large number of persons, and the issuance has not been made in violation of the provisions of the Act or an order based on the Act.
(2) It can or could have been purchased at any time by an unspecified and large number of persons.
(3) It is used for its intended purpose without the addition of any other personal information about living individuals.

205. The PPC Guidelines provide the following specific examples:[28]

[Cases falling under personal information databases]:

(Case 1) Email address stored in email software (when information combining email addresses and names is entered).
(Case 2) An electronic file in which log information relating to the services used by a user in an Internet service is organised and stored according to the user ID (when the user ID and personal information can be easily matched).
(Case 3) When information on business cards is entered and organised by an employee using spreadsheet software on a work computer (regardless of the owner).
(Case 4) When a staffing agency organises registration cards in alphabetical order by name and files them with an index in alphabetical order.

[Cases that do not fall under the category of personal information databases]:

(Case 1) Where an employee has classified their business cards according to a unique classification method which is not easily searchable by others, even if the employee has placed such business card case in a situation where others can freely view it.
(Case 2) When return postcards from questionnaires are not classified and organised according to name and address.
(Case 3) Commercially available telephone directories, residential maps, staff records, and car navigation systems.

28. General Guidelines, p. 17.

§4. Personal Information File (Definition Applies Only to Administrative Organs)

206. Article 60(2) of the APPI provides a definition of a 'personal information file' that applies only to administrative organs:

> Article 60(2)
>
> The term 'personal information file' as used in this chapter and Chapter VIII means a collection of information including retained personal information, as set forth below:
>
> (i) a collection of information systematically arranged in such a way that specific retained personal information can be retrieved by a computer for achieving the purpose of certain processes;
> (ii) beyond what is set forth in the preceding item, a collection of information systematically arranged in such a way that specific retained personal information can be easily retrieved by using a name, date of birth, or other description for achieving the purpose of certain processes.

207. Additionally, Article 74(1) provides that:

> If an administrative organ (excluding the Board of Audit; hereinafter the same applies in this Article) intends to retain a personal information file, the head of that administrative organ must notify the PPC of the following particulars in advance. The same applies to cases where an administrative organ intends to change any particular for which notification has already been given.

208. This obligation to notify the PPC in advance is not imposed on any personal information handling business operator but only on state administrative organs excluding incorporated administrative agencies, as the purpose is to ensure uniformity and legal compliance in the operation of the Act among administrative organs.

§5. Personal Information Handling Business Operator (in Relation to Article 16(2) of the Act)

209. Article 16(2) of the APPI provides the following definition of 'personal information handling business operator':

> (2) The term 'personal information handling business operator' as used in this chapter and Chapters VI through VIII means a person providing a personal information database, etc., for use in business, provided, however, that a person set forth in the following is excluded:

(i) a national government organ;
(ii) a local government;
(iii) an incorporated administrative agency, etc.;
(iv) a local incorporated administrative agency.

210. 'Personal information handling business operator' means a person who uses personal information databases for business purposes, excluding national administrative organs, local government agencies, incorporated administrative agencies stipulated in Article 2(9) of the Act (excluding the corporations listed in Annex 2), and local incorporated administrative agencies provided for in Article 2(10) of the Act. The term 'business' in 'utilising for business' means the same kind of activities carried out repeatedly and continuously for a certain purpose, which are regarded as a business in the common sense of society, regardless of whether they are for-profit or not-for-profit.

211. Any person who uses personal information databases for business purposes is a personal information handling business operator, irrespective of the number of specific individuals identified by the personal information comprising the personal information databases in question.

212. Even unincorporated associations (private organisations) or individuals without juridical personality and without the capacity to exercise rights fall under the category of personal information handling business operators if they use personal information databases for their business.

§6. Personal Data (in Relation to Article 16(3) of the Act)

213. Article 16(3) of the APPI provides the following definition of 'personal data':

> Article 16(3)
>
> The term 'personal data' as used in this chapter means personal information constituting a personal information database, etc.
>
> 'Personal data' means personal information comprising 'personal information databases' managed by personal information handling business operators.

214. In accordance with Article 16(1) of the Act and Article 4(1) of the Cabinet order, personal data comprising personal information that is excluded from personal information databases (e.g., commercially available telephone directories, residential maps, etc.) because there is little risk of harm to the rights and interests of individuals in view of the manner of use does not constitute personal data.

215. The General Guidelines[29] of the PPC provide the following examples of what constitutes personal data.

[Cases falling under personal data]:

> (Case 1) Personal information stored on external storage media from personal information databases.
> (Case 2) Personal information printed on paper output from personal information databases.

[Cases that do not fall under personal data]:

> (Example) Personal information printed on forms, etc., for input before constituting personal information databases.

§7. Retained Personal Data (in Relation to Article 16(4) of the Act)

216. Article 16(4) of the APPI provides the following definition of 'retained personal data':

> Article 16(4)
>
> The term 'retained personal data' as used in this chapter means personal data in regard to which a personal information handling business operator has the authority to disclose, correct, add or delete the contents of, cease the utilisation of, erase, and cease the third party provision of, and which are not to be those prescribed by Cabinet order given the likelihood of harming the public or other interests if their presence or absence is made known.

217. 'Retained personal data' means 'personal data' regarding which the personal information handling business operator is authorised to respond to all requests from the individual or representative of the individual for disclosure, correction, addition or deletion of content, suspension of use, erasure, and suspension of provision to third parties.

218. The General Guidelines of the PPC provide the following examples of cases that fall under retained personal data:[30]

219. The following types of personal data are not 'retained personal data':

(1) Personal data that are likely to cause harm to the life, body, or property of the person concerned or a third party if their existence or non-existence is revealed:

29. General Guidelines, p. 19.
30. General Guidelines, pp. 20–21.

(Case) Retained personal data of the perpetrator (spouse or person with parental authority) and the victim (spouse or child) as the principals, which are held by a support group for victims of domestic violence or child abuse.

(2) Personal data which may encourage or induce illegal or unjust acts if the existence or non-existence of such personal data is revealed:

(Case 1) Retained personal data of a person who falls under the category of an anti-social organisation in order to prevent damage from unjustified demands by anti-social organisations such as crime syndicates.
(Case 2) Personal data retained by a business operator to prevent damage from unreasonable demands by suspicious persons [or] malicious claimants, that identify the person who has committed the act in question.

(3) Personal data which, if revealed, may cause harm to national security, damage the relationship of trust with other countries or international organisations, or may be detrimental to negotiations with other countries or international organisations:

(Case 1) Personal data retained by manufacturers [or] information service providers, in which the name of the person in charge of the design or development of defence-related weapons, facilities, equipment, [or] software is recorded, and the person in charge is identified as the person in question.
(Case 2) Retained personal data held by visiting dignitaries or their security companies, such as schedules of activities, which identify such dignitaries as the principal persons concerned.

(4) Personal data which could hinder the prevention, suppression, or investigation of crimes, or the maintenance of other public safety and order if the existence or non-existence of such personal data were to become known:

(Case 1) Personal data acquired for the first time as a result of an investigation-related enquiry from the police.
(Case 2) Personal data such as enquiry reception and response transmission lists, lists of persons subject to enquiries, etc., prepared by a business operator that has received an investigation-related enquiry, etc., from the police with regard to subscriber information (the subscriber information itself falls under the category of 'retained personal data').
(Case 3) Suspicious transactions based on Article 8(1) of the Act on Prevention of Transfer of Criminal Proceeds (Act No. 22 of 2007).
(Case 4) Personal data contained in the information on accounts used for bank transfer fraud.

§8. Personally Referable Information (Article 2(7) of the Act)

220. The APPI defines 'personally referable information' as follows:

> Article 2(7) of the APPI provides [that] the term 'personally referable information' as used in this Act means information relating to a living individual which does not fall under personal information, pseudonymously processed information, or anonymously processed information.

221. The PPC Guidelines provide the following specific examples of personally referable information:[31]

> (Case 1) An individual's website browsing history collected via cookies or other terminal identifiers.
> (Case 2) An individual's age, gender, [or] family structure, linked to an e-mail address.
> (Case 3) An individual's product purchase history and service use history.
> (Case 4) An individual's location information.
> (Case 5) Information indicating an individual's interests.

222. If such information falls under personal information, it does not fall under personally referable information. For example, generally, an individual's location information by itself does not constitute personal information, but if location information relating to an individual can be used to identify a specific individual, for example, by continuously accumulating location information, then the information constitutes personal information and does not constitute personally referable information.

223. The APPI also provides a definition of 'personally referable information handling business operator' (Article 16(7) of the Act):

> Article 16(7) provides [that] the term 'Personally Referable Information Handling Business Operator' as used in this chapter [and] Chapters VI and VII means a person who provides for use in business a collective body of information comprising personally referable information which has been systematically organised so as to be able to search using a computer for specific personally referable information or similar others prescribed by Cabinet order as systematically organised so as to be able to search easily for specific personally referable information (referred to as a 'personally referable information database, etc.' in Article 31, paragraph (1)), provided, however, that a person set forth in each item of paragraph (2) is excluded.

224. The PPC General Guidelines provide the following explanation regarding 'personally referable information handling business operator':[32]

> 'Personally Referable Information Handling Business Operator' means a person who uses personally referable information databases for business, excluding national government agencies, local government agencies, incorporated

31. General Guidelines, p. 22.
32. General Guidelines, pp. 22–23.

administrative agencies stipulated in Article 2(9) of the Act (excluding those listed in Annex 2) and local incorporated administrative agencies stipulated in Article 2(10) of the Act.

225. 'A collection of information containing personally referable information which is systematically structured so that specific personally referable information can be retrieved using a computer'. Even if a computer is not used, this also applies to paper-based personally referable information that is organised and classified according to certain rules and placed in a state where it can be easily retrieved by others by attaching table of contents, index, or code, so that specific personally referable information can be easily retrieved.

§9. Pseudonymously Processed Information (Article 16(5) of the Act)

226. Article 2(5) of the APPI provides the following definition of 'pseudonymously processed information':

> The term 'pseudonymously processed information' as used in this Act means information relating to an individual that can be produced from processing personal information so as not to be able to identify a specific individual unless collated with other information by taking action prescribed in each following item in accordance with the divisions of personal information set forth in each said item:
>
> (i) personal information falling under paragraph (1), item (i); Deleting a part of descriptions, etc., contained in the said personal information (including replacing the said part of descriptions, etc., with other descriptions, etc., using a method with no regularity that can restore the said part of descriptions, etc.);
> (ii) personal information falling under paragraph (1), item (ii); Deleting all individual identification codes contained in the said personal information (including replacing the said individual identification codes with other descriptions, etc., using a method with no regularity that can restore the said personal identification codes).

227. The APPI also provides a definition of 'pseudonymously processed information handling business operator' (Article 16(5) of the Act), as follows:

> Article 16(7) provides [that] the term 'Pseudonymously Processed Information Handling Business Operator' as used in this Chapter [and] Chapters VI and VII means a person who provides for use in business a collective body of information comprising pseudonymously processed information which has been systematically organised so as to be able to search using a computer for specific pseudonymously processed information or similar others prescribed by

Cabinet order (referred to as a 'pseudonymously processed information database, etc.' in Article. 41, paragraph (1)), provided, however, that a person set forth in each item of paragraph (2) is excluded.

§10. Anonymously Processed Information (in Relation to Article 16(6) of the Act)

(1) Definition of Anonymously Processed Information

228. Article 2(6) of the APPI provides the following definition of 'anonymously processed information':

> The term 'anonymously processed information' as used in this Act means information relating to an individual that can be produced from processing personal information so as neither to be able to identify a specific individual by taking action prescribed in each following item in accordance with the divisions of personal information set forth in each said item nor to be able to restore the personal information:
>
> (i) personal information falling under paragraph (1), item (i); Deleting a part of descriptions, etc., contained in the said personal information (including replacing the said part of descriptions, etc., with other descriptions, etc., using a method with no regularity that can restore the said part of descriptions, etc.);
>
> (ii) personal information falling under paragraph (1), item (ii); Deleting all individual identification codes contained in the said personal information (including replacing the said individual identification codes with other descriptions, etc., using a method with no regularity that can restore the said personal identification codes).

229. The APPI also provides a definition of 'anonymously processed information handling business operator' (Article 16(6) of the Act), as follows:

> Article 16(6)
>
> The term 'Anonymously Processed Information Handling Business Operator' as used in this chapter [and] Chapters VI and VII means a person who provides for use in business a collective body of information comprising anonymously processed information which has been systematically organised so as to be able to search using a computer for specific anonymously processed information or similar others prescribed by Cabinet order (referred to as an 'anonymously processed information database, etc.' in Article 43, paragraph (1)), provided, however, that a person set forth in each item of paragraph (2) is excluded.

(2) Anonymously Processed Information of an Administrative Organ (Article 60(3) of the Act)

230. Apart from 'anonymously processed information' as defined in the Obligations of a Personal Information Handling Business Operator, a definition of 'anonymously processed information of an administrative organ' is provided. Article 60(3) of the APPI provides the following definition of 'anonymously processed information of an administrative organ':

> The term 'anonymously processed information of an administrative organ, etc.' as used in this chapter means any anonymously processed information that is generated by processing all or part of retained personal information constituting a personal information file that meets all conditions specified in the following items. If a part of these contains non-disclosable information as prescribed in Article 5 of the Administrative Organs Information Disclosure Act (Act No. 42 of 1999), including information prescribed in the proviso of item (ii) of the same Article except information listed in item (i) of the same Article (hereinafter the same applies in this paragraph), non-disclosable information prescribed in Article 5 of the Incorporated Administrative Agencies Information Disclosure Act (Act No. 140 of 2001), including information prescribed in the proviso of item (ii) of the same Article except information listed in item (i) of the same Article, or non-disclosable information prescribed in the information disclosure ordinance of local government (meaning a local government's ordinance which provides for the right of residents, etc. to request the disclosure of information held by a local government agency or local incorporated administrative agency, i.e., information equivalent to non-disclosable information prescribed in Article 5 of the Administrative Organs Information Disclosure Act), the part containing the non-disclosable information is excluded:
>
> (i) the information does not fall under any of the items in Article 75, paragraph (2) or information that is not designated under paragraph (3) of the same Article as an exception to registration in the personal information file register as prescribed in paragraph (1) of the same Article;
>
> (ii) the information for which the head of an administrative organ as prescribed in Article 3 of the Administrative Organs Information Disclosure Act, an incorporated administrative agency, etc., as prescribed in Article 2, paragraph (1) of the Incorporated Administrative Agencies Information Disclosure Act, a local government agency or a local incorporated administrative agency is required to take either of the following actions if that person receives a request to disclose any administrative document in which retained personal information constituting a personal information file is recorded (meaning a request for disclosure which is prescribed in Article 3 of the Administrative Organs Information Disclosure Act or the Information Disclosure Ordinance):

(a) making a decision to disclose all or part of the retained personal information recorded in that administrative document, etc.;
(b) providing an opportunity to submit an opinion under Article 13, paragraph (1) or (2) of the Administrative Organs Information Disclosure Act, Article 14, paragraph (1) or (2) of the Incorporated Administrative Agencies Information Disclosure Act, or the Information Disclosure Ordinance (limited to those with provisions equivalent to Article 13, paragraph (1) or (2)).

(iii) the information is retained personal information that constitutes a personal information file and can be processed into anonymously processed personal information by following the criteria set forth in Article 116, paragraph (1), to the extent that it does not prevent proper and smooth administration of affairs and businesses by administrative organs, etc.

231. The APPI also provides a definition of 'anonymously processed information file of an administrative organ' (Article 60(4) of the Act):

> The term 'anonymously processed information file of an administrative organ, etc.' as used in this chapter means a collection of information containing anonymously processed information of an administrative organ, etc., as set forth below:
>
> (i) a collection of information systematically arranged in such a way that specific anonymously processed information of an administrative organ, etc. can be retrieved by a computer;
> (ii) beyond what is set forth in the preceding item, a collection of information that a Cabinet order designates as being systematically arranged in such a way that specific anonymously processed information of an administrative organ, etc. can be easily retrieved.

Part III. General Principles

Chapter 1. Data Quality Principles

232. Regarding data quality principles, please refer to the following:

> '2. Purpose of Use of Personal Information (related to Articles 17 and 18 and 21(3) of the Act)', '1) Specifying a Utilisation Purpose (Article 17(1) of the Act)', 2) Altering a Purpose of Use (Related to Articles 17(2) and 21(3) of the Act)', '3) Restriction Due to Utilisation Purpose (Related to Article 18(1) of the Act)'.

233. Personal information handling business operators (Article 16(2)) are obliged to specify the purpose of use of personal information and use it within that scope (Article 17(1)):

> The consent of the person concerned is required if the information is to be used beyond the scope of the specified purpose(s) of use (Article 16(1)). The purpose of use may change, but only to the extent that it is reasonably related to the original purpose of use (Articles 17(2) and 21(3)).

Chapter 2. Legal Grounds for Processing Personal Data

234. The Japanese APPI does not have any provisions on the processing of personal data on the basis of lawfulness per Article 6 of the General Data Protection Regulation (GDPR). The lawful processing of personal information is to be determined on the basis applicable under the Obligations of a Personal Information Handling Business Operator.

235. It should be noted that the Draft Bill on the Protection of Personal Information Act as originally submitted set out the 'basic principles' governing the legal grounds for the lawfulness of the processing of personal data.

236. The first Bill on the Protection of Personal Information, which covers the private sector, was presented to the National Diet on 15 March 2002. The Bill provided for the following articles.

Chapter 2: Basic Principles
Article 3
In view of the fact that personal information should be handled with care and under the principle of respect for the individual personality, entities who handle personal information shall endeavour to handle personal information properly in accordance with the basic principles stipulated in the following Article to Article 8.

---

237. The basic principles stipulated based on this article were (i) limitation by purpose of use; (ii) proper acquisition; (iii) ensuring accuracy; (iv) ensuring security; and (v) ensuring transparency.

238. These provisions on the basic principles in Chapter 2 were intended to serve as the basic principles for entities who handle personal information to take voluntary measures for the protection of personal information while referring to the results of the research on legal systems in other countries and in international organisations. The Bill also aimed to clearly define the basic principles for the handling of personal information as a guideline for the development of comprehensive institutional measures for the protection of personal information to be taken by the government and other organisations.

239. Article 3 provides that 'Personal information should be handled with care and under the principle of respect for the individual's personality, and those who handle personal information shall endeavour to handle personal information properly in accordance with the basic principles set out in the following Articles to Article 8.' The content of the 'Basic Principles' encompasses the eight principles of the OECD Privacy Guidelines.

240. However, on 13 December of the same year, the House of Representatives Cabinet Committee decided to discard the original bill submitted in 2002 because the basic principles were the subject of criticism in the mass media. These basic principles, which apply to the lawful handling of 'personal information' in general were deleted from the Bill in response to criticism that it was the so-called Mass Media Regulation Act, and on 7 March 2003, the amended bills on the Protection of Personal Information (Cabinet Bill Nos. 71–75) were submitted to the 156th session of the National Diet, and on 23 May 2003, the five Acts on the Protection of Personal Information were passed and promulgated on 30 May 2003. When the basic principles were deleted, the principle of safety control measures for 'personal information' was also deleted, which resulted in the obligation to take safety control measures limited only to 'personal data' and not encompassing 'personal information'.

Chapter 3. Special Categories of Personal Data

§1. Special Care-Required Personal Information

I. Obligations in Relation to Special Care-Required Personal Information

241. Special care-required personal information must be acquired with the prior consent of the principals concerned. Without the consent of the principals, it is prohibited to acquire special care-required personal information.

242. It is excluded from the application of Article 27(2), which enables the provision of such information to third parties on an opt-out basis. Article 27(2) sets out a procedure to enable provision to a third party without the prior consent of the principals concerned, but by not applying this procedure to personal information requiring special care-required personal information, this prevents personal information from being acquired by a business operator handling personal information by providing it to a third party without the person's knowledge and also prevents the person being subjected to discriminatory treatment on that basis.

II. Personal Information Falling under Special Care-Required Personal Information

243. Article 2(3) provides the definition of the term 'special care-required personal information' as:

> personal information comprising a principal's race, creed, social status, medical history, criminal record, the fact of having suffered damage by a crime, or other descriptions, etc. prescribed by Cabinet order as those of which the handling requires special care so as not to cause unfair discrimination, prejudice, or other disadvantages to the principal.

244. The special care-required personal information specified by Article 2, Item 1 of the Cabinet Order as having other disabilities of physical or mental functions as specified by the Rules of the PPC refers to the information listed in (i)–(iv) below. In addition to this, information which identifies the existence or past existence of such a disability (e.g., that the person is receiving or has in the past received disability welfare services based on the Act for Comprehensive Support of Daily Life and Social Life of Persons with Disabilities (Act No. 123 of 2005)) is also applicable:

> [Cabinet Order to Enforce the Act on the Protection of Personal Information]
>
> Article 2
>
> Those descriptions, etc. prescribed by Cabinet Order under Article 2, paragraph (3) of the Act shall be those descriptions, etc. which contain any of those matters set forth in the following (excluding those falling under a principal's medical record or criminal history):

(i) the fact of having physical, intellectual, or mental disabilities (including developmental disabilities), or other physical and mental functional disabilities prescribed by the Rules of the Personal Information Protection Commission;

(ii) the results of a medical check-up or other examination (hereinafter referred to as a 'medical check-up, etc.' in the succeeding item) for the prevention and early detection of a disease conducted on a principal by a medical doctor or other person engaged in duties related to medicine (hereinafter referred to as a 'doctor, etc.' in the succeeding item);

(iii) the fact that guidance for the improvement of the mental and physical conditions or medical care or prescription has been given to a principal by a doctor, etc., based on the results of a medical check-up, etc., or for reason of disease, injury, or other mental and physical changes;

(iv) the fact that an arrest, search, seizure, detention, institution of prosecution, or another procedure related to a criminal case has been carried out against a principal as a suspect or defendant;

(v) the fact that an investigation, measure for observation and protection, hearing and decision, protective measure, or other procedure related to a juvenile protection case has been carried out against a principal as a juvenile delinquent or a person suspected thereof under Article 3, paragraph (1) of the Juvenile Act.

245. Furthermore, the amended Regulations for Enforcement of the Act on the Protection of Personal Information (Regulation No. 3 of the Personal Information Protection Commission, 5 October 2008) was put into full effect on 30 May 2017. Article 5 of this rule provides 'physical and mental functional disabilities' regarding 'special care-required personal information':

[Article 5 of the Regulations]

Physical and mental functional disabilities prescribed by the Rules of the Personal Information Protection Commission under Article 2, item (i) of the Cabinet Orders[33] shall be those disabilities set forth in the following:

(i) physical disabilities set forth in an appended table of the Act for Welfare of Persons with Physical Disabilities (Act No. 283 of 1949);

(ii) intellectual disabilities referred to under the Act for the Welfare of Persons with Intellectual Disabilities (Act No. 37 of 1960);

(iii) mental disabilities referred to under the Act for the Mental Health and Welfare of the Persons with Mental Disabilities (Act No. 123 of 1950) (including developmental disabilities prescribed in Article 2, paragraph 2 of the Act on Support for Persons with Development

33. Order for Enforcement of the Act on the Protection of Personal Information (Cabinet Order No. 507 of 10 Dec. 2003).

Disabilities, and excluding intellectual disabilities under the Act for the Welfare of Persons with Intellectual Disabilities);

(iv) a disease with no cure methods established thereof or other peculiar diseases of which the severity, according to those prescribed by Cabinet Order under Article 4, paragraph (1) of the Act on Comprehensive Support for Daily and Social Lives of Persons with Disabilities (Act No. 123 of 2005), is equivalent to those prescribed by the Minister of Health, Labour and Welfare under the said paragraph.

246. The PPC General Guidelines provide specific details on the types of personal information that fall into the category of special care-required personal information.[34]

247. 'Special care-required personal information' means personal information that includes the following statements (1)–(11) as requiring special care in its handling so as to avoid unjustified discrimination, prejudice, or other disadvantages. Information that is merely information from which the following information can be inferred (e.g., information relating to the purchase or lending of books on religion) is not included in special care-required personal information:

(1) Race
Race means race, lineage, or ethnic or tribal origin. Note that simple nationality or the information 'foreigner' is just a legal status and is not included in race. Additionally, skin colour is not included in race, as it is merely information from which race can be inferred.

(2) Creed
Creed refers to an individual's basic way of looking at and thinking about things and includes both ideology and religious belief.

(3) Social Status
Social status means a status which is attached to an individual as a condition from which the person cannot easily escape by their own efforts for the rest of their life and does not include mere occupational status or educational background.

(4) Medical History
Medical history means a history of illness and includes the part of the history that indicates a specific medical history (e.g., a specific individual has cancer, suffers from schizophrenia, etc.).

(5) Criminal History
Convictions, i.e., the fact that a conviction has been received and this has been confirmed, are relevant.

(6) Facts of Having Suffered Damage as a Result of the Offence
This refers to the fact that the offender has suffered harm as a result of the offence, whether physical, psychological, or financial harm. Specifically, this

34. General Guidelines, pp. 10–15.

applies to acts that could fall under the constitutive requirements stipulated in the penal laws and regulations and for which proceedings relating to the criminal case have been initiated.

(7) Physical, Intellectual, [or] Mental Disability (including developmental disability) [and] other physical or mental disabilities as defined by the Personal Information Protection Commission rules (Article 2, Item 1 of the Cabinet Order).

(8) The results of medical examinations or other tests for the prevention and early detection of illness (medical examinations), carried out by a doctor or other person engaged in duties related to medical care (Article. 2, Item 2 of the Cabinet Order).

(9) Guidance, medical treatment or dispensing of medicine to improve the physical or mental condition of the person by a doctor based on the results of medical examinations or because of illness, injury or other physical or mental changes (Article. 2, Item 3 of the Cabinet Order).

(10) The results of an arrest, search, seizure, detention, prosecution or other procedures related to a criminal case which have been carried out on the person as a suspect or accused (excluding criminal history). (Article. 2, Item 4 of the Cabinet Order).

(11) The results of an investigation, measures for protective custody, a trial, protective measures or other procedures related to juvenile protection cases have been carried out on the person as a juvenile or a suspected juvenile as defined in Article 3(1) of the Juvenile Act (Act No. 168 of 1948) (related to Article 2(5) of the Cabinet Order).

§2. Anonymously Processed Information (in Relation to Article 2(9) of the Act)

I. Definition of Anonymously Processed Information

248. With the amendment of the APPI in 2015, a new definition of 'anonymously processed information' was provided, and procedures for its literal utilisation have been put in place, such as internal discipline for business operators and the prohibition of re-identification when and after the information is provided to a third party. Since anonymously processed information requires completely anonymised processing, identifying a specific individual is disallowed, as is identifying an individual by cross-checking using other information. Therefore, it has been pointed out that anonymously processed information is insufficient from the point of usefulness.

249. Against the background of technological development, pseudonymously processed information can be analysed in more detail than anonymously processed information via a relatively simple processing method that entails maintaining the same level of usefulness as personal information before processing, while ensuring a certain level of security. Therefore, for the purpose of realising the more active handling of personal information within the business, a new definition of 'pseudonymously processed information', where names and personally identifiable information are deleted from the viewpoint of promoting innovation, such as activating the restriction on the purpose of use, has been provided, and provision to third parties is not permitted; thus, such information can only be used for internal analysis.

250. It is prohibited to provide pseudonymously processed information to third parties. When business operators use pseudonymously processed information, obligations regarding Article 22-2 (security breach notification) and relating to Articles 27–34 (principals' rights) do not apply.

251. The APPI requires the consent of the individual to the use of personal data for purposes other than those for which it was originally intended as well as their consent to the provision of personal data to third parties.

252. Based on the idea of the usefulness of personal information, provisions relating to anonymously processed information have been established as procedures that allow the use of personal information for purposes other than those for which it was originally intended. Furthermore, the provision of personal data to third parties is to be treated as information that does not fall under the category of personal information.

253. Among the obligations relating to the handling of personal information, the procedures for the provision of personal data to third parties require, in principle, the consent of the individual concerned in order to prevent the infringement of individual rights and interests. In light of this and bearing in mind the possibility that a specific individual may be identified and that the handling of such data may infringe the rights and interests of the individual, the provisions on anonymously processed information are concerned with a new type of data that does not require the consent of the individual when the data are provided to a third party. Anonymously processed information is personal data processed in such a way as to reduce the possibility of the identification of a specific individual.

254. For businesses that handle large amounts of personal data, the burden of obtaining the consent of all individuals is significant. In some cases, such businesses may have to hesitate to conduct new business using personal data. To establish a new category of personal data processed to reduce the likelihood of the identification of individuals that can be provided without the consent of the individual while simultaneously setting out the obligations to be assumed by those who handle such data (providers and recipients) including taking necessary measures where needed, provisions relating to anonymously processed information have been established.

II. Overview of Obligations Relating to the Handling of Anonymously Processed Information

255. The procedures for the handling of anonymously processed information stipulate: (i) the creation of anonymously processed information; (ii) the provision of anonymously processed information; (iii) the prohibition of acts of identification; and (iv) security control measures. Each of these will be elaborately sequentially in the following paragraphs:

(i) With regard to the creation of anonymously processed information, the following procedures are stipulated for the creation of anonymously processed information:
  (a) When creating anonymously processed information, the personal information concerned shall be processed in accordance with the standards set out in the PPC Regulations as necessary to make it impossible to identify specific individuals and to restore the personal information used for the creation of the anonymously processed information.
  (b) When anonymously processed information has been created, measures shall be taken for the secure management of this information in accordance with the standards set out in the PPC Regulations as necessary to prevent the leakage of information concerning the method of processing.
  (c) When creating anonymously processed information and handling such anonymously processed information themselves, the anonymously processed information shall not be cross-referenced with other information in order to identify the individuals whose personal information was used to create the anonymously processed information.

(ii) With regard to the provision of anonymously processed information, an anonymously processed information handling business operator (including a personal information handling business operator who has created anonymously processed information) shall not provide anonymously processed information to a third party:
  (a) When providing anonymously processed information to a third party, a business operator handling anonymously processed information (including a business operator handling personal information who has created anonymously processed information) shall, in accordance with the Rules of the Personal Information Protection Commission, make public in advance the items of information concerning individuals contained in the anonymously processed information to be provided to the third party and the method of providing such information and clearly indicate to the third party that the information pertaining to such provision is anonymously processed information.

(iii) With regard to the prohibition of acts of identification, when handling anonymously processed information (excluding information which has been created by processing personal information on its own), the third party shall be informed that the information is anonymously processed information.

(iv) With regard to security control measures, the relevant person shall take necessary and appropriate measures for the security control of anonymously processed information, handle complaints concerning the handling of anonymously processed information, and take other measures necessary to ensure the proper handling of anonymously processed information and shall endeavour to make the details of such measures public.

III. The Concept of Anonymously Processed Information

(i) Protocols for Producers of Anonymously Processed Information

256. Anonymously processed information is data in regard to which the possibility of a specific individual being identified has been reduced. Within any entity that has processed personal data to create anonymously processed data, it is possible to cross-check the resultant data with the data from which it was created. Therefore, if any business operator holds anonymously processed information, it falls under Article 2(1) of the Act as 'personal information'. If it constitutes a personal information database (Article 2, paragraph 2), it falls under Article 2, paragraph 4, as 'personal data'. If the data are personal data that the relevant business entity has the authority to disclose, correct, and delete, such data fall under Article 2, paragraph 5 as 'retained personal data'. As such, the data are subject to Articles 15–31 of the Act. On the other hand, anonymously processed data provided by the relevant business entity to a third party fall under the category of 'personal data', and therefore, when providing such data to a third party, the consent of the individual is required (Article 16(1)(ii) of the Act), unless the provision to a third party is specified as the purpose of use of the relevant personal data or the consent of the individual to the provision of the relevant personal data to a third party is required (Article 16(1)(ii) of the Act); the consent of the individual is required for the provision of the personal data to a third party.

257. However, in the case of the provision of anonymously processed information to a third party, it is not necessary to obtain the consent of the individual to whom the data relates, as the processing makes it difficult to identify a specific individual, and the prohibition of identification has been established with respect to the recipient.

(ii) Risk of Identification of Data Subject Remaining in the Processed Data

258. The APPI provides procedures as to which types of processing may be carried out to allow data to be provided to third parties without the consent of the individual concerned. The purpose of requiring the consent of the individual is to prevent the infringement of rights and interests that may arise from the provision of data to a third party other than the entity handling the personal data. Therefore, it is important to reduce the possibility of third parties identifying the specific individual in order to prevent the infringement of the individual's rights and interests.

259. Additionally, given the wide variety and enormous amount of data, the processing method should be determined on an individual basis in accordance with the actual situation of utilisation. It is difficult to generally define a processing method that completely eliminates the possibility of identifying specific individuals.

(iii) Procedures for Handling Anonymously Processed Information

260. Procedures relating to anonymously processed information are required to take into account the circumstances of the data recipient, which cannot be dealt with without foreseeing and reducing the specific risk to the person creating the anonymously processed information, on the basis of all the circumstances existing in society. However, it is impossible to demand such a response. Therefore, it is important to allocate each risk fairly between the provider and the recipient of the anonymously processed information to ultimately reduce the risk. Thus, anonymised data are personal data that have been processed to delete, in whole or in part, the name, date of birth, or other description contained within the personal data, so that it is impossible to identify a specific individual. Furthermore, the deletion of all of the personally identifiable information contained in the personal data concerned will be applied in the case of anonymously processed information. It is prohibited for the recipient to use this information to identify a specific individual. This clarifies the processing requirements for the providers of anonymously processed information and ensures that recipients receive data that meet the minimum statutory requirements. Additionally, the obligation on the part of the recipient to prohibit the identification of certain individuals reduces the risk, both on the part of the provider and on that of the recipient, thus implying that the identification of certain individuals may lead to the unauthorised handling of personal data.

(iv) Relationship Between Anonymously Processed Information and Personal Information

261. Anonymously processed information are data which, on their own, do not enable a specific individual to be identified, particularly when cross-referenced with information held or available to the recipient.

262. The APPI regulates the handling of personal information by the business operator holding the information and defines ‘personal information’ as an object to be protected by the business operator. On the other hand, anonymously processed information is intended to be circulated by a business operator and handled as non-personal information with a view to providing the data to a third party. Therefore, the business operator who created the anonymously processed information is unable to judge whether a specific individual can be identified based on whether or not the data can be easily cross-checked with other information held by the business operator, but rather based on the risk that a specific individual can be identified by cross-checking with other information which may exist in the world more generally.

263. Additionally, anonymised data are required to reduce the risk of the identification of a specific individual and are unlikely to infringe his/her rights and interests to such an extent that the individual’s consent is not required. To achieve this purpose, it is necessary to ensure that such information itself does not allow for the identification of the specific individual. Additionally, if 'personally identifiable information', as defined in Article 2(1)(ii) of the Act, characteristic or unique information, and IDs used by multiple businesses remain in the processed data, it is possible to use such information to cross-reference particular individual information beyond the 'realm of presumption', and thus, there is a possibility that a specific individual may be identified in the process of analysis through cross-reference with other data. There is a high probability in the process of analysis together with other data that a specific individual may be identified. In this case, it is unreasonable to require the business operator to reduce the risk by deleting or otherwise processing all of the data because the requirement to delete all of the data when processing personal data would impose an undue burden for eliminating the risk of identifying a wide range of specific individuals.

(v) Processing by Deleting All or Part of the Data

264. 'Deletion' means the deletion of an attribution of personal data to be processed that identifies a specific individual and includes not only the deletion of an item but also the replacement of that attribution with other information (including the replacement of detailed information with general or abstract information).

265. Thus, the basic method of processing is deletion. This act is not intended to be any one method, but rather a combination of methods, such as simply deleting items, replacing items, or adding other information, depending on the personal data to be processed, in order to make it impossible to identify a specific individual.

266. The 'objects of deletion' are limitless and will depend on the nature of the items contained within the personal data to be processed. Additionally, for personal data where multiple items can be combined to identify a specific individual, it is required that all or part of the items be deleted, depending on the items contained in the personal data, to make it difficult to identify a specific individual.

(vi) Inability to Identify a Specific Individual

267. The term 'unable to identify a specific individual' means that the anonymously processed information itself cannot identify a specific individual. To make it impossible to identify a specific individual from the data itself, information contained in the data, such as name and date of birth, must be deleted to match the items contained in the personal data. However, for example, where the personal data contain multiple items such as name, address, date of birth, telephone number, purchase history, and web browsing history, in this case, if the name and address are combined, there is usually only one person with that name living at that address, and thus, it is indeed possible to identify a specific person. Accordingly, telephone numbers and e-mail addresses must be deleted or replaced because, when combined with address information, they can identify a person.

(vii) Publicly Distributed Personal Data Items

268. The term 'personal data items which are publicly distributed' refers to information that is publicly used in society and handled by businesses across industries, including information encoded by public institutions, such as passport and driver's license numbers, or information used by multiple companies as ID to provide services (including information numbered in relation to an individual with the same identifying function as an ID).

269. The personally identifiable information and other items of personal data that are publicly used in society referred to in this article are intended to be deleted in their entirety to eliminate as far as possible the risk of identifying a specific individual at the point of distribution of the anonymously processed information to third parties, where such data are intended to be provided to such third parties.

(viii) Public Disclosure Regarding Anonymously Processed Information

(a) Requirements for Processing Anonymously Processed Information

270. Regarding the requirements for processing anonymously processed information, in the case of providing anonymously processed information, the requirement for the consent of the specific individual identified by the personal data is not needed (Article 2(6) of the Act, 'The Data Subject'). However, this still does not eliminate the possibility of identifying a specific individual. Therefore, from the perspective of protecting the rights and interests of individuals, ensuring transparency, and placing the burden on business operators, the items included in the anonymously processed information must be made public in advance when the said data are provided to third parties.

(b) Business Operators Using Anonymously Processed Information for Commercial Purposes

271. 'A business operator using anonymously processed information for business purposes' means an entity that has created anonymously processed information and has received and produced anonymously processed information useful for the purpose of conducting business (Article 2(3) of the Act, 'Use for Business Purposes').

272. The term 'items of such anonymously processed information' means, for example, the type of anonymously processed information provided, including place of residence, age, and names of products purchased.

(c) No-Identification Obligation

273. The 'no-identification' obligation is imposed on any business entity that handles anonymously processed information. The term 'provision of anonymously processed information' is a broad concept that includes not only the transfer of data to a specific person but also includes data that are open to the general public on a website. If the recipient is unaware that the data received constitute anonymously processed information, the business operator cannot hope to fulfil the obligations imposed on him/her in relation to the handling of the data. Therefore, from the perspective of protecting the rights and interests of individuals, when providing anonymously processed information, it must be made clear that the data in question are indeed anonymously processed.

(d) Restriction of Cross-Border Data Transfers

274. Anonymously processed information is data that make it difficult to identify a specific individual, but in the process of distribution, there is a possibility that a specific individual may be identified, and the rules governing the handling of such data rightly ensure that such identification cannot happen. However, if anonymously processed information is transferred to a third party abroad, the obligation to prohibit identification is not required because the third party is not subject to the application and enforcement jurisdiction of the laws of Japan, and the data can be handled in such a way that a specific individual may be, in fact, identified. Additionally, even if the data are personal data that are accessible to the recipient, such data are not subject to the application and enforcement jurisdiction of Japanese law and therefore may not be handled in accordance with the rules on the handling of personal data set out in the APPI. This situation is obviously contrary to the purpose of the Act, which requires, in principle, the consent of the individual with regard to the provision of personal data to third parties and seeks to prevent infringements of the rights and interests of the individual by ensuring that the data are handled as intended by the individual. It must be noted that the provision of anonymously processed information to third parties located in foreign countries is only prohibited; however, in cases where the handling of anonymously processed information is outsourced in whole or in part, or where anonymously processed information is used jointly with a specific person, it is possible for a business operator based in Japan to be monitored and supervised by a third party organisation through this provision, as the said business operator is subject to discipline under the laws of Japan.

(e) Prohibition of the Act of Identification

275. Anonymously processed information are data or datasets that avoid the identification of a specific individual through ‘processing’, such as deleting all or part of the data, in addition to deleting ‘personal identifiers’ and items of personal data that are widely distributed to the public. This reduces the probability of a specific individual being identified, even when the data are combined with other information.

276. However, even if the above processing is carried out, with the development of ICTs, it is possible that any personal information relating to an individual may be accumulated or directly linked to personal data from common items contained in such information by comparing and analysing data held by the business operator handling the anonymously processed information or contained within a large volume and variety of publicly available information. Consequently, it is no longer possible to avoid a state of affairs in which a specific individual can be identified or where there is a high risk of identification.

277. Thus, when a business operator provides anonymously processed information, there is a probability that the data may be restored to 'personal information' by the recipient of the anonymously processed information. Of equal importance is the fact that if a business entity is afraid of reputational risk and withdraws the data from circulation or if the data are processed in such a way that the data lose their usefulness as data through the deletion or replacement of items contained in the data, this may impede innovation and the creation of new business endeavours.

278. To combat this negative effect on business and ensure that significant information can be utilised, Article 45 of the APPI provides for prohibition of the act of identifying as a 'discipline to ensure the significance of anonymously processed information and to prevent infringement of the rights and interests of individuals'.

(f) Handling of Anonymously Processed Information in a Manner not Contrary to the Prohibition of the Act of Identifying

279. The APPI prohibits anonymously processed information identifying a specific individual identified in the personal data from which it was created through 'personal identifiers' included in the personal data and the presence of items of personal data that are widely distributed to the public.

280. Anonymously processed information is expected to be utilised and is effective for the analysis of a large amount and variety of data to create new business endeavours. A business operator who has received anonymously processed information may analyse it together with information held or obtained by the business operator, including personal data and other anonymised data. The law does not prohibit such actions.

281. If anonymously processed information is analysed in the way described above, part or all of it is to be deleted, or the information is to be obtained again through the business operator who has received it or from the identified specific individual. To prevent anonymously processed information from being presented in a format that is prohibited under this article, measures should be taken to systematically limit the handling of information, for example, by stipulating the terms and conditions including provisions such as controlling access rights to the data, so that the information is not handled in a manner that confuses it with personal data held by the business operator.

(g) Security Management Requirements

282. Anonymously processed information reduces the possibility of identifying a specific individual but does not eliminate that possibility entirely. Therefore, in handling such data, necessary and appropriate measures for safety management, such as the prevention of leakage, loss, or damage of data, must be taken. Additionally, the supervision of employees and contractors is also required for security management. Although, anonymised processed data do not fall under Article 2(1) as 'personal information', Article 2(4) as 'personal data', or Article 2(5) as 'retained personal data' per the Law with respect to the recipient, Articles 20–22 of the Law shall apply *mutatis mutandis* and security management measures must be taken.

283. Additionally, persons who process personal data to create anonymously processed information are excluded from the subjects of this article because the provisions of Articles 15–31 of the Act apply only to the handling of such anonymously processed information.

§3. Provisions on the Anonymously Processed Information of an Administrative Organ

284. Apart from the procedures for anonymously processed information handling business operators in the private sector, the procedures for handling anonymously processed information in administrative organs are defined. The handling of anonymously processed information in administrative organs is provided in Chapter 5, section 5 of the Act.

I. Preparation of the Anonymously Processed Information of Administrative Organs

285. When creating anonymously processed information within an administrative organ, the retained personal information shall be processed in accordance with the standards prescribed by the rules, so that specific individuals cannot be identified, and the retained personal information used to create the information cannot be restored (Article 114(1) of the Act). Administrative organs may outsource all or part of the creation of their anonymously processed information (Article 114(1), paragraph 2).

II. Provision of the Anonymously Processed Information of Administrative Organs

286. An administrative organ shall not provide its anonymously processed information unless the information falls under any of the following (Article 107, paragraph 2 of the Act):

(a) Cases based on laws and regulations (including cases in accordance with the provisions of Chapter 5, section 5 of the Act, 'Provision, etc., of Anonymously Processed Information of Administrative Organs' (Item 1 of the same paragraph).

(b) Where the administrative organ may provide retained personal information to a third party for the purpose of use and where the administrative organ anonymously processed information created using the retained personal information is provided to such third party (Item 2 of the same paragraph).
(c) Where the administrative organ, except where required by laws and regulations, provides deleted information (meaning descriptions, etc., and individual identification codes deleted from the retained personal information used to create the administrative organ anonymously processed information) for purposes other than the 'purpose of use' that falls under the category of 'retained personal information' and shall not be used or provided by themselves (Article 107, paragraphs 3 and 4 of the Act).

287. Administrative organs shall confirm that the anonymously processed information they have created has been properly processed before providing it.

§4. Personally Referable Information (Article 2(7) of the Act)

288. The APPI defines 'personally referable information' as follows:

> Article 2(7) of the APPI provides that the term 'personally referable information' as used in this Act means information relating to a living individual which does not fall under personal information, pseudonymously processed information, or anonymously processed information.

Part IV. Data Subjects' Rights

Chapter 1. The Right to Be Informed

289. The APPI provides procedures for receiving information on the handling of personal information by means of procedures relating to notification and publication to the person concerned. Article 21, paragraph 1 of the Act stipulates that personal information handling business operators must, upon acquiring personal information, promptly notify the person concerned of the purpose of its use or make it public, except where the purpose of its use has been made public in advance. In addition to this procedure, the procedures stipulated with regard to 'notifying the person concerned' are as follows:

(i) Regarding the purpose of use
Article 21(3) and (4) of the Act (cases where the purpose of use is changed and notification of the purpose of use is not required)
(ii) Those relating to leakage
Article 26(2) of the Act (notification to the person concerned)
(iii) Those relating to the provision of personal data to third parties
Article 27, paragraphs 2 and 3, and paragraphs 5.3 and 6 of the Act (provision to a third party by opting out, where the third party does not fall under the category of 'third party')
(iv) Those relating to requests for disclosure
Article 32(2) and (3) of the Act and Article 33(3) of the Act (including cases where it is applied *mutatis mutandis* in Article 33(5) of the Act); Article 34(3) of the Act and Article 35(7) of the Act (publication of matters relating to retained personal data, etc., disclosure of retained personal data, disclosure of records of provision to third parties, correction of retained personal data, and suspension of use of retained personal data).

290. Procedures that cannot be notified to the individual are required to be 'disclose[d] to the public'. The procedures stipulated for 'disclos[ure] to the public' as notification or publication are as follows:

(i) Those relating to the purpose of use
Article 21(3) of the Act (change of purpose of use)
(ii) Pseudonymously processed information
Article 41(4) and (6) and Article 42(2) of the Act ('Obligations of the Pseudonymously Processed Information Handling Business Operator').

291. Furthermore, the procedures to disclose to the public matters relating to retained personal data (related to Article 32 of the Act) include making matters relating to retained personal data known to the person concerned (related to Article 32(1) of the Act).

292. In the Basic Policy on the Protection of Personal Information (partially amended on 1 April 2022), '6. Basic Policy on the Protection of Personal Information to be Taken by Personal Information Handling Business Operators, etc.' states that:

> [F]rom the perspective of further protecting the rights and interests of individuals, including their privacy, it is expected that business operators will voluntarily engage in the protection and appropriate and effective use of personal information, including by clarifying their approach and policies (so-called privacy policy, privacy statement, etc.) in promoting personal information protection.

Chapter 2. The Right of Access

293. The APPI provides the right of the individual to disclose, correct, and suspend the use of retained personal data. The principals may request disclosure of 'retained personal data' or 'retained personal information' held by personal information handling business operators and administrative organs in which the individual concerned is identified.

294. Regarding disclosure, the person may request that the personal information handling business operator disclose the retained personal data identifying the person in question. Given that court decisions have been negative as a ground rule for exercising the right to make a specific request based on the 2003 Act, the 2015 amendment to the Act clarifies its position as a judicial 'right to request'. Additionally, when a person intends to file an action pertaining to such a claim, the claimant may not, except in certain cases, file such an action until two weeks have elapsed from the date on which the person made such a request in advance to the person who is to be the defendant in the action and the request reached such person.

295. For details about 'rights of access', please refer to 'Part V: Duties of Controllers and Processors', specifically '9. Publicly Disclose Items Relating to Retained Personal Data – Disclosure, Correction, and Suspension of Use of Retained Personal Data (related to Articles 32–39 of the Act)' and '11. Disclosure (related to Articles 76–89 of the Act)'.

Chapter 3. Rights of Rectification

296. Article 34 of the APPI provides 'rights of correction' as follows:

Article 34(1):

A principal may, when the contents of retained personal data that can identify the principal are not factual, demand of a personal information handling business operator the making of a correction, addition, or deletion (hereinafter referred to as a 'correction, etc.' in this Article) in regard to the contents of the retained personal data.

(2) A personal information handling business operator must, in case of having received a demand pursuant to the provisions of the preceding paragraph, except in cases where a special procedure concerning a correction, etc. of the contents is prescribed in the provisions of other laws or regulations, conduct a necessary investigation without delay to the extent necessary to achieve a utilisation purpose and, based on the result thereof, make a correction, etc. of the contents of the retained personal data.

(3) A personal information handling business operator must, when having made a correction, etc. to the whole or a part of the contents of the retained personal data in connection with a demand pursuant to the provisions of paragraph (1) or when having made a decision not to make a correction, etc., inform the principal without delay to that effect (including when having made a correction, etc. to the contents thereof).

297. For details about the 'rights of access', please refer to 'Part V: Duties of Controllers and Processors', specifically '9. Publicly Disclose Items Relating to Retained Personal Data –Disclosure, Correction, and Suspension of Use of Retained Personal Data (related to Articles 32–39 of the Act)' and '12. Correction' (related to Articles 90–97 of the Act)'.

Chapter 4. The Right to Erasure

298. The individual may request the 'suspension of use or deletion' of retained personal data held by the personal information handling business operator. The suspension of use or erasure includes the suspension of utilisation or the erasure of some part of the personal data. The business operator may choose whether to suspend use or erase.

299. With regard to the relationship between suspension of use and erasure, the ultimate form of suspension of use is erasure, and the right to request erasure is related to and includes the right to request suspension of use. Article 35 of the APPI provides 'rights of suspension of use (cease) or deletion' as follows:

(Utilisation Cease)

Article 35 (1):

A principal may, when retained personal data that can identify the principal is being handled in violation of the provisions of Article 18 or Article 19, or has been acquired in violation of the provisions of Article 20, demand of a personal information handling business operator a utilisation cease or deletion (hereinafter referred to as a 'utilisation cease, etc.' in this Article) of the retained personal data.

(2) A personal information handling business operator must, in case of having received a demand pursuant to the provisions of the preceding paragraph and when it has become clear that there is a reason in the demand, fulfil the utilisation cease, etc. of the said retained personal data to the extent necessary to redress the violation without delay, provided, however, that this does not apply to cases where the utilisation cease, etc. of the said retained personal data requires a large amount of expenses or other cases where it is difficult to fulfil the utilisation cease, etc. and when necessary alternative action is taken to protect a principal's rights and interests.

(3) A principal may, when retained personal data that can identify the principal is being provided to a third party in violation of the provisions of Article 27, paragraph (1) or Article 28, demand that a personal information handling business operator cease the third party provision of the retained personal data.

(4) A personal information handling business operator must, in case of having received a demand pursuant to the provisions of the preceding paragraph and when it has become clear that there is a reason in the demand, cease the third party provision of the retained personal data without delay, provided, however, that this does not apply in cases where ceasing the third party provision of the said retained personal data requires a large amount of expenses or other cases where it is difficult to cease the third party provision and when necessary alternative action is taken to protect a principal's rights and interests.

(5) A principal may demand that the personal information handling business operator fulfil the utilisation cease, etc. of the retained personal data or

cease third party provision if it has become unnecessary for a personal information handling business operator to utilise retained personal data that can identify the principal, if a situation prescribed in the main clause of Article 26, paragraph (1) has occurred in connection with the retained personal data that can identify the principal, or if there is a possibility that handling of the retained personal data that can identify the principal would harm the rights or legitimate interests of the principal.

(6) A personal information handling business operator must, in case of having received a demand pursuant to the provisions of the preceding paragraph and when it has become clear that there is a reason in the demand, fulfil the utilisation cease, etc. or cease the third party provision of the said retained personal data to the extent necessary to prevent an infringement of a principal's rights and interests without delay, provided, however, that this does not apply to cases where the utilisation cease, etc. or ceasing the third-party provision of the said retained personal data requires a large amount of expenses or other cases where it is difficult to fulfil the utilisation cease, etc. or to cease the third-party provision and when necessary alternative action is taken to protect a principal's rights and interests.

(7) A personal information handling business operator must, when having fulfilled a utilisation cease, etc. or decided not to fulfil a utilisation cease, etc. of the whole or part of retained personal data in connection with a demand pursuant to the provisions of paragraph (1) or paragraph (5) inform the principal to that effect without delay.

300. For details about the 'rights of suspension of use (cease) or deletion', please refer to 'Part V: Duties of Controllers and Processors', specifically '9. Publicly Disclose Items Relating to Retained Personal Data – Disclosure, Correction, and Suspension of Use of Retained Personal Data (Related to Articles 32–39 of the Act)' and '13. Suspension of Use and Deletion (Related to Articles 98–103 of the Act)'.

Chapter 5. The Right to Restriction

301. The APPI in Japan has no explicit provision on the right to restriction. The right to restriction under the APPI is a mechanism that is realised by exercising the right to restrict the use of personal information within the scope of the purposes for which it is used in the handling of personal information, as well as to correct, erase, suspend the use of, delete, and cease the provision of personal information to third parties.

Chapter 6. Profiling

302. The APPI has no explicit provisions on the regulation of 'profiling'.

303. In the process of considering the 2015 revision of the APPI, the Outline for the Revision of the System for the Utilisation of Personal Data (24 June 2014) was published, and this document covers the following issues: (i) a new dispute resolution system, (ii) so-called profiling, (iii) Privacy Impact Assessment (PIA), and (iv) data broker regulation. These have been specified as ongoing issues for consideration. However, in the amendment of the APPI, only the countermeasure against (iv) 'data broker regulation' was hastily incorporated into the draft framework in response to a large-scale personal data leakage incident. Therefore, profiling was not specified in the article.

304. The 2020 amendment of the APPI was, in effect, an obligation to specify the purpose of use and specify and publish a notice on profiling.

305. When profiling and analysing information obtained from a person about his or her behaviour and interests, the operator must specify the purpose of use to the extent that the person can predict and assume the type of handling that will occur. This procedure disciplines profiling by imposing an obligation to specify the purpose of use to the extent that the person can reasonably foresee.

306. The PPC General Guidelines provide the following examples[35] of cases where the purpose of use is specified with regard to analysing information about behaviour and interests obtained from the person:

(i) Acquired information on browsing history, purchase history, etc., will be analysed and used for the purpose of advertising new products and services in accordance with hobbies and preferences.
(ii) Acquired information on behavioural history, etc., will be analysed, the results will be scored and said scores will be provided to third parties.

35. General Guidelines, pp. 22.

Chapter 7. The Right to Object

307. The right to object is set out in the procedures for disclosure, correction, suspension of use, and deletion with respect to the exercise of principals' rights.

308. When personal data are provided to third parties including third parties located abroad in violation of the procedures, a request can be made to suspend the provision of the data to third parties (Article 35 of the Act). The difference between the procedure for suspension of the provision of data to third parties under Article 35 and the opt-out procedure under Article 27(2) is that it should be noted that the former permits the suspension of provision to a third party due to a breach of the procedure and requires the suspension of provision only if there is a reason for the request, while the latter, opt-out, differs from the former in that it imposes an obligation to suspend provision to a third party at the request of the individual, regardless of whether there is a reason or not.

Chapter 8. Other Principals' Rights

309. Rights other than those set out in the procedures for disclosure, correction, suspension of use, and deletion are not specified in the APPI.

Part V. Duties of Controllers and Processors

310. The terms 'controller' and 'processor' are not defined in the APPI in Japan. The obligations that apply to controllers and processors are defined as the Obligations of a Personal Information Handling Business Operator and the Obligations, etc., of an Administrative Organ, etc.

Chapter 1. Admin Orgs' Personal Info: Restrictions/Retention

311. One of the differences between private-sector personal information handling business operators and public-sector administrative organs in terms of obligations is that administrative organs are subject to restrictions on the retention of personal information. The private sector does not have this obligation.

312. While administrative organs need to retain personal information to provide administrative services, unnecessary retention of personal information is not only problematic from a security management perspective but may also lead to misuse in some cases. Therefore, the APPI stipulates when administrative organs may retain personal information and requires them to specify the purpose of use when doing so.

313. Administrative organs may retain personal information only when it is necessary for the performance of their legitimate affairs or tasks in accordance with the provisions of the law (Article 61(1) of the Act). The administrative affairs or tasks must have a legal basis and not just be carried out by the administrative organ in fact and must also include the affairs or tasks enumerated in the articles defining 'affairs under jurisdiction' in the laws and regulations on which the establishment is based, as well as the affairs or tasks stipulated in the articles defining 'authority' and those stipulated in the Act on the Law in Action. The office and tasks are included in this category.

314. Additionally, pursuant to the same paragraph, administrative organs must specify, as specifically and individually as possible, for which office or task the personal information is to be used and for which purpose it is to be used. In this case, it is not permissible to weaken the degree of specification of the purpose of use by arbitrary decisions of the administrative organ, and it must be possible to reasonably and clearly determine whether the specific act of use is within the scope of the said purpose of use or not.

315. Furthermore, in accordance with paragraph 2 of this provision, administrative organs must not retain personal information beyond the extent necessary to achieve the specified purpose of use. Therefore, the scope of individuals for whom personal information is held and the content of the personal information must be the minimum necessary in light of the purpose of use.

316. Note that the restrictions on retention are only an obligation for administrative organs and this procedure does not apply to the Obligations of a Personal Information Handling Business Operator.

Chapter 2. Purpose of Use of Personal Information

§1. Specifying a Purpose of Use (Article 17(1) of the Act)

317. Business operators handling personal information must specify the purpose of use as concretely as possible. In specifying this purpose of use, it shall not be merely described in an abstract or general manner but shall be specified to the extent that the individual can generally and reasonably assume the purpose for which the personal information will ultimately be used by the business operator handling the personal information.

318. When it has been decided which personal information will be provided to a third party, the purpose of use must be specified in such a way that the procedures to be followed can be clearly understood.

§2. Altering a Purpose of Use (Related to Articles 17(2) and 21(3) of the Act)

319. Business operators handling personal information are obliged to use personal information within the scope of the purpose of use specified by the purpose of use. However, it is possible to change the purpose of use to the extent that it is reasonably recognised to be related to the original purpose of use and to the extent to which the purpose of use after the change is objectively recognised to be within the limit of what the individual can normally expect in terms of socially accepted norms, in view of the original purpose of use. The changed purpose of use must be notified to the individual or made open to the public.

320. If personal information is to be handled for purposes other than the specified purpose of use, the consent of the individual must be obtained. However, if it is necessary for the protection of the life or body of the individual, and it is difficult to obtain the consent of the individual, or in the cases listed in each item of Article 18, paragraph 3 of the Act, personal information may be handled beyond the scope necessary to achieve the specified purpose of use without obtaining the prior consent of the individual.

§3. Restriction Due to Utilisation Purpose (Related to Article 18(1) of the Act)

321. When a business operator handling personal information handles personal information beyond the scope necessary to achieve the purpose of use specified in accordance with Article 17, paragraph 1 of the Act, they must obtain the consent of the individual in advance.

322. However, it should be noted that the use of personal information for the purpose of obtaining such consent (e.g., sending e-mails or making phone calls) does not fall under the category of use for purposes other than those specified, even if it is not stated as the purpose of use initially specified.

§4. Succession of Business (Related to Article 18(2) of the Act)

323. If a business operator handling personal information acquires personal information as a result of the succession of business from another business operator handling personal information due to a merger, spin-off, or business transfer, and the personal information is handled within the scope necessary to achieve the purpose of use before the succession of the personal information in question, this does not constitute use for other purposes, and consent from the individual need not be obtained.

324. If, after the succession of the business, the business operator will handle personal information beyond the scope necessary to achieve the purpose of use before the succession, the consent of the person concerned must be obtained in advance. However, the use of personal information to obtain such consent (e.g., sending emails or making phone calls), even if not stated as the purpose of use before the succession, does not constitute use for a purpose other than the stated purpose.

§5. Exceptions to Restrictions Regarding Purpose of Use (Related to Article 18(3) of the Act)

325. When a business operator handling personal information handles personal information beyond the scope necessary to achieve the purpose of use specified in accordance with Article 17, paragraph 1 of the Act, they must obtain the consent of the individual in advance. However, Article 18(3) of the APPI provides exceptions to restrictions on purpose of use. The provisions of Article 18(1) and (2) do not apply to those cases set forth in the following:

(i) Cases based on laws and regulations (including local ordinances, hereinafter the same applies in this chapter).
(ii) Cases in which there is a need to protect a human life, body, or fortune, and when it is difficult to obtain a principal's consent.
(iii) Cases in which there is a special need to enhance public hygiene or promote fostering healthy children, and when it is difficult to obtain a principal's consent.
(iv) Cases in which there is a need to cooperate in regard to a national government organ or a local government, or a person entrusted by them performing affairs prescribed by laws and regulations, and when there is a possibility that obtaining a principal's consent would interfere with the performance of the said affairs.
(v) Cases in which the said personal information handling business operator is an academic research institution, etc., and when it is necessary to handle the said

personal information for the purpose of being provided for use in academic research (hereinafter referred to as 'academic research purposes' in this chapter) (including those cases in which part of the purpose of handling the said personal information is for academic research purposes and excluding those cases in which there is a risk of unjustly infringing an individual's rights and interests).

(vi) Cases of providing personal data to an academic research institution, etc., and the said academic research institution, etc., need to handle the said personal data for academic research purposes (including those cases in which part of the purpose of handling the said personal data is for academic research purposes and excluding those cases in which there is a risk of unjustly infringing an individual's rights and interests):

(1) In Cases Based on Laws and Regulations (Related to Article 18(3)(i) of the Act).

In cases based on laws and regulations, Article 18(1) or (2) of the Act does not apply, and personal data may be handled beyond the scope necessary to achieve the specified purpose of use without obtaining the prior consent of the individual.

The PPC Guidelines provide the following specific examples:[36]

> (Case 1) When responding to a police enquiry into matters related to an investigation, (Article 197(2) of the Code of Criminal Procedure, Act No. 131 of 1948).
>
> (Case 2) When responding to an investigation based on a warrant issued by a judge (Article 218 of the Code of Criminal Procedure).
>
> (Case 3) When responding to an investigation by the tax office concerning income tax (Articles 74-2 et seq. of the Act on General Rules for National Taxes, Act No. 66 of 1962).
>
> (Case 4) Where a manufacturer/importer receives an order under Article 39(1) of the Consumer Product Safety Act (Act No. 31 of 1973) (Harm Prevention Order) and takes measures such as recalling the product, and the seller provides information on the purchaser of the product to the manufacturer/importer concerned under Article 38(3) of the same Act.
>
> (Case 5) When responding to an enquiry from a bar association, (Article 23-2 of the Lawyers' Act (Act No. 205 of 1949).
>
> (Case 6) When responding to active epidemiological investigations conducted by health centres (Law on Prevention of Infectious Diseases and Medical Care for Patients with Infectious Diseases, Law (No. 114 of 1998), Article 15, paragraph 1).
>
> (Case 7) Where a general transmission and distribution undertaking provides the necessary information to the relevant administrative authorities or the head of a local authority at the request of the Minister of Economy, Trade and Industry to accelerate power outage restoration in the event of a disaster (Article 34, paragraph 1 of the Electricity Business Act, Act (No. 170 of 1964)).

---

36. General Guidelines, pp. 35–36.

(2) Where it is necessary for the protection of a person's life, body, or property, and it is difficult to obtain the consent of the principals (Article 18(3)(ii) of the Act).
If it is necessary to protect specific rights and interests, such as the life, body, or property of a person (including legal persons), and it is difficult to obtain the consent of the person, personal information may be handled beyond the scope necessary to achieve the specified purpose of use without obtaining the prior consent of the person and without the application of Article 18(1) or (2) of the Act.
The PPC Guidelines provide the following specific examples:[37]

> (Case 1) When, in the event of a sudden illness or other situation, the blood type and contact details of a family member are provided to a doctor or nurse in respect of the person concerned.
> (Case 2) In the event of a major disaster or accident emergency, when information on victims and injured persons is provided to family members, administrative bodies, [or] local authorities.
> (Case 3) When information on anti-social forces such as organised crime groups, information on accounts used for bank transfer fraud, or information on persons who intentionally obstruct business is shared between businesses.
> (Case 4) Where the manufacturer of a product recalls the product because an accident has occurred in relation to the manufactured product or because there is imminent danger of harm to human life or body, although no accident has occurred, and the seller, repair business, or installation business provides the manufacturer with information about the purchaser of the product.
> (Case 5) In addition to Case 4 above, where the manufacturer is requested to provide customer information in an emergency where there is a serious defect in their product, and the protection of human life, body, or property is required, it is necessary to respond to such request.
> (Case 6) Where information relating to the fact of financial crime damage of unauthorised money transfers is provided to other operators for the prevention of related criminal damage.

(3) Where it is particularly necessary for the improvement of public health or the promotion of the sound development of children and it is difficult to obtain the consent of the person concerned (Article 18(3)(iii) of the Act).
If it is particularly necessary for the improvement of public health or the sound upbringing of children undergoing mental and physical development, and if it is difficult to obtain the consent of the person, personal information may be handled beyond the scope necessary to achieve the

37. General Guidelines, p. 36.

specified purpose of use without obtaining the prior consent of the person and without the application of Article 18, paragraph 1 or 2 of the Act.
The PPC Guidelines provide the following specific examples:[38]

(Case 1) When information pertaining to the results of health examinations conducted by health insurance societies and other insurers is used for planning health promotion measures, improving the effectiveness of health services, [or] epidemiological studies.
(Case 2) When exchanging information about a child concerned between relevant organisations, such as child guidance centres, schools, and medical institutions, in order for them to cooperate in responding to a child's non-attendance or delinquent behaviour.
(Case 3) When it is necessary to share information about families with child guidance centres, police, schools, [or] hospitals, where there is a risk of child abuse.

(4) Where it is necessary for the business operator to cooperate with a state body, a local authority, or a person entrusted by them to carry out affairs prescribed by law, and obtaining the consent of the person is likely to impede the carrying out of such affairs (Article 18(3)(iv) of the Act).
In cases where it is necessary for a government organisation (including a local authority or a person entrusted by a local authority) to obtain the cooperation of a private company in the execution of affairs prescribed by law and where obtaining the consent of the person is deemed likely to impede the execution of such affairs, such private company may, without applying Article 18, paragraph 1 or 2 of the Act and without obtaining the prior consent of the person, use personal data for the purposes specified by the government organisation, without obtaining the prior consent of the person. In such a case, the private sector may handle personal information beyond the scope necessary to achieve the specified purpose of use without obtaining the prior consent of the principals and without applying Article 18(1) or (2) of the Act.
The PPC Guidelines provide the following specific examples:[39]

(Case 1) Where a business operator submits personal information in response to a voluntary request by a tax office or customs official.
(Case 2) When a business submits personal information in response to a voluntary request by the law enforcement authority.
(Case 3) Where a business responds to a general statistical survey or a statistical survey conducted by a local authority.

(5) When the business operator handling personal information is an academic research institute, and the personal information concerned needs to be handled for the purpose of academic research, the condition for

38. General Guidelines, pp. 36–37.
39. General Guidelines, pp. 37–38.

receiving the exemption due to academic research is that part of the purpose of handling the personal information concerned is for academic research purposes, and the rights and interests of individuals are not unreasonably infringed. If there is a risk of unjustified infringement of the rights and interests of individuals, the exemption does not apply (Article 18(3)(v) of the Act).

(6) When personal information is provided to an academic research organisation and the academic research organisation needs to handle the personal data for academic research purposes, the condition for receiving the exemption due to academic research is that part of the purpose of handling the personal data is for academic research purposes, and if there is a risk of unjustified infringement of the rights and interests of individuals, the exemption does not apply (Article 18(3)(vi) of the Act).

§6. Administrative Organs' Compliance in Acquiring and Using Personal Information

326. Administrative organs must acquire personal information properly and handle it within the scope of the purpose of its use. On the other hand, it can generally be assumed that the purpose of use may have to be changed due to the need to respond to the development of new administrative services. As Article 1 of the Act stipulates, while the Act aims to protect the rights and interests of individuals, it also stipulates compliance requirements for administrative organs when acquiring and using personal information, taking into account the proper and smooth operation of the administrative organ's affairs and business.

§7. Changes to the Purpose of Use Instigated by Administrative Organs (Article 61(3) of the Act)

327. If an administrative organ changes the purpose of use of personal information, the change must not exceed the extent to which it is reasonably considered to have a reasonable relationship with the purpose of use before the change (Article 61(3) of the Act).

328. If in light of the original purpose of use, it is difficult to envisage the purpose of use after the change, the information cannot be regarded as 'having a reasonable relationship with the purpose of use before the change'.

329. Additionally, the term 'reasonably recognised' is intended to mean that the change is objectively recognised as being socially acceptable. This does not allow for changes based on arbitrary decisions taken by administrative organs.

§8. Clear Statement of the Purpose of Use When an Administrative Organ Acquires Information in Writing from a Data Subject (Article 62 of the Act)

330. Administrative organs shall, when acquiring the personal information of an individual directly from the individual in writing (including electromagnetic records), clearly indicate the purpose of use in advance to the principals in an appropriate manner that the person can recognise (Article 62 of the Law), except in any of the following cases:

(1) when urgently necessary for the protection of a person's life, body, or property (Article 62(1));
(2) when the life, body, property, or other rights and interests of the person or a third party are likely to be harmed by clearly indicating the purpose of use to the person (Item 2 of the same article);
(3) when clarification of the purpose of use to the person concerned is likely to impede the proper execution of the affairs or business conducted by a state organ, independent administrative agency, local incorporated administrative agency, or local incorporated administrative agency (Item 3 of the same article);
(4) when the purpose of use is deemed clear in view of the circumstances of acquisition (Item 4 of the same article).

331. In cases where a document containing personal information has been sent to an administrative organ unilaterally, it is impossible to specify the purpose of use 'in advance' in the first place, and in such cases, the provisions of the said article do not apply.

Chapter 3. Prohibition of Improper Use

§1. Provisions on the Prohibition of Improper Use

332. Business operators handling personal information shall not use personal information in a way that is likely to encourage or induce illegal or unjust acts (Article 19 of the 2020 amended Act). Specific examples of 'unlawful or unjust acts' include (i) discrimination against the individual which is unpredictable to the individual and can be caused by an unspecified number of persons (acts which may be assessed as unlawful under civil law); (ii) infringement of the individual's right to lead a peaceful life due to unsolicited contact by persons engaged in unlawful acts (acts which may be assessed as unlawful under civil law); and (iii) infringement of the individual's right to freedom of expression (acts which may be assessed as unlawful under civil law).

333. The PPC Guidelines provide the following specific examples:[40]

(Case 1) Where the personal information of an individual is provided to an entity suspected of operating illegal activities (e.g., a moneylender who is not registered as a moneylender), even though there is a risk that such an entity's illegal activities may be encouraged, such as the violation of the individual's right to a peaceful life by sudden contact from an entity suspected of operating illegal activities.
(Case 2) Where personal information that has been made public sporadically through public notices issued by courts (e.g., bankruptcy information published in the *Official Gazette*) is aggregated and compiled into a database, even though it is foreseeable that illegal discrimination against the persons pertaining to the personal information may be induced by an unspecified number of persons due to, for example, publication on the Internet.
(Case 3) Personal information on a person identified as falling under the category of an unlawful entity, which is shared among businesses and which is necessary to prevent damage caused by unreasonable demands, despite the foreseeable risk of encouraging or inducing unreasonable demands such as violent demands made by gangsters or by general assemblymen.
(Case 4) When personal information is provided to a third party in violation of Article 27(1) of the Act, even though it is foreseeable that the third party will provide personal information to the party to which the personal information is provided.
(Case 5) Where a business entity that has acquired personal information through recruitment and selection uses the personal information to unlawfully discriminate against a person solely on the basis of specific attributes

40. General Guidelines, p. 39.

such as gender, nationality, etc., without justifiable reason.

(Case 6) Where a business operator engaged in the distribution of advertisements uses personal information obtained by the business operator to distribute advertisements for illegal products, such as illegal drugs, even though it is foreseeable that the products for which the business operator has received a request from a third party to distribute advertisements for such products are illegal products.

§2. Illegal or Unjustified Acts

334. The term 'illegal or unjustified acts' refers to acts that violate the APPI or other laws and regulations or acts that are not immediately illegal but are contrary to the institutional purpose of the APPI or other laws and regulations or public order and morality, or acts that are not deemed appropriate from a socially accepted point of view.

335. The existence of 'a likelihood' is determined by whether or not it is socially accepted as probable that the use of personal data by a business operator handling personal data will encourage or induce illegal or unjustified acts. In making this judgment, in addition to objective circumstances such as the method of use of the personal data, the recognition and foreseeability of the business operator handling personal data at the time of use of the personal data must also be taken into account. For example, even if a business operator handling personal information provides personal information to a third party, and that third party uses the personal information for illegal acts, the business operator handling personal information should be aware of the illegal use of the provided personal information at the time of the provision of the personal information, for example, if the third party has lied about the purpose for which the personal information was obtained. If the business operator handling the personal data could not have foreseen the illegal use of the personal data at the time of provision of the personal data, such as the third party falsifying the purpose for which the personal data were obtained, it is understood that 'a threat' was not recognised.

§3. Prohibition of Improper Use and Acquisition by Administrative Organs (Articles 63 and 64 of the Act)

336. An administrative organ shall not use personal information in a manner that is likely to encourage or induce illegal or unjust acts (Article 63 of the Act) and shall not acquire personal information through deception or other wrongful means (Article 64 of the Act).

337. Specific examples of acquiring personal information through wrongful means include cases where a person is coerced into providing personal information that they did not originally have to provide in return for administrative services.

Chapter 4. Acquisition of Personal Data

§1. Proper Acquisition (Related to Article 20(1) of the Act)

338. The APPI stipulates that a business operator handling personal information must not acquire personal information by deception or other wrongful means.

339. The PPC Guidelines provide the following specific examples of deception or other wrongful means of acquisition:[41]

> (Case 1) Obtaining, without the consent of a family member, personal information relating to any family member, such as income, which is unrelated, considering the circumstances of the specific acquisition, or from a child or disabled person who does not have sufficient capacity to make a decision.
> (Case 2) Obtaining personal information by coercing a person to violate the restriction on providing personal information to a third party as stipulated in Article 27(1) of the Act.
> (Case 3) Obtaining personal information from a person by intentionally presenting false information regarding the entity from which the personal information is obtained.
> (Case 4) Where a business operator instructs another one to obtain personal information by wrongful means.
> (Case 5) Where the personal information is knowingly obtained despite this being a violation of the restriction on provision to third parties as stipulated in Article 27(1) of the Act.
> (Case 6) Where the personal information is acquired in spite of the fact that the person knows or can easily know that the personal information has been acquired by wrongful means.

340. The duty of propriety applies only if the personal information is 'acquired'. Therefore, where information containing personal information is publicly available via the Internet or any social media, and the person merely 'views' the information and does not transcribe it, this is not considered to be acquiring personal information.

§2. Acquiring Special Care-Required Personal Information (Article 20(2) of the Act)

341. Prior consent of the individual must be obtained when acquiring any personal information required. However, in the cases listed in (1)–(9) below, it is not

41. General Guidelines, pp. 40–41.

necessary to obtain the consent of the person. In principle, the consent of the individual is required for the provision of personal information requiring special consideration to a third party, and the provision of such information to a third party by opt-out is not permitted:

(1) When based on laws and regulations (related to Article 20(2)(i) of the Act):

In this situation, personal information may be acquired without obtaining the prior consent of the individual concerned, for example,[42] when a business operator handling personal information conducts medical examinations in accordance with the Occupational Health and Safety Law and thereby obtains information about the physical/medical condition and treatment of an employee from the institution conducting the medical examinations.

(2) When it is necessary for the protection of a person's life, body, or property, and it is difficult to obtain the consent of the person (Article 20(2)(ii) of the Act):

In this situation, the personal information may be obtained without obtaining the consent of the person in advance. The General Guidelines indicate the following cases:[43]

(Case 1) When a doctor or nurse interviews a family member about the person's medical history in the event of a sudden illness or other similar situation.
(Case 2) When the information concerns anti-social forces such as organised crime groups or persons who intentionally interfere negatively with business operations (such persons are those who have been arrested for such interference in the past), this information must be shared between businesses for the purpose of fraud counter-measures.
(Case 3) When information about, for example, illicit money transfers, is obtained from other operators for the prevention of related criminal damage.

(3) Where the information is particularly necessary for improving public health or promoting the sound development of children, and it is difficult to obtain the consent of the person concerned (Article 20(2)(iii) of the Act):

If it is particularly necessary for the improvement of public health or for the sound upbringing of children undergoing mental and physical development, and if it is difficult to obtain the consent of the person, the personal information may be acquired without obtaining the consent of the person in advance:[44]

42. General Guidelines, p. 43.
43. *Ibid.*
44. General Guidelines, p. 44.

(Case 1) Cases in which information about the names of illnesses identified as a result of health check-ups conducted by health insurance societies and other insurers is provided and acquired for epidemiological surveys for the purpose of planning health promotion measures and improving the effectiveness of health services.
(Case 2) Cases in which, in order for child guidance centres, schools, medical institutions, and other relevant institutions to cooperate in responding to a child's truancy or delinquent behaviour, information on the procedures taken by one relevant institution from another, concerning a protection case involving the child concerned, is obtained.
(Case 3) When information pertaining to the fact of victimisation by family members and possible child abuse is obtained by a child guidance centre, police, school, hospital, or other relevant organisation from another relevant organisation.
(Case 4) Cases in which it is necessary for the business operator to cooperate with a governmental organisation, a local public authority, or a person entrusted by such an authority to carry out affairs prescribed by law and in which obtaining the consent of the person is likely to impede the carrying out of such affairs (related to Article 20, paragraph 2, Item 4 of the Act).

When a governmental organisation (including local authorities or persons entrusted by them) is required to obtain the cooperation of private companies in carrying out affairs prescribed by law and obtaining the consent of the person is deemed likely to hinder the carrying out of such affairs, such private companies may acquire special care-required personal information without obtaining the consent of the person in advance, for example, when the business operator acquires the personal information concerned in order to submit personal information falling under the category of special care-required personal information in response to a voluntary request by the police.

(4) In cases where the business operator handling the personal information is an academic research institute, and it is necessary to handle the personal information requiring special consideration for academic research purposes (including cases where a part of the purpose of handling the personal information requiring special consideration is for academic research purposes, except where there is a risk of unreasonable infringement of the rights and interests of individuals) (Article 20(2)(v) of the Act).
(5) When acquiring special care-required personal information from an academic research institute, and when it is necessary to acquire such personal information for academic research purposes (including cases where a part of the purpose of acquiring the relevant special care-required personal information is for academic research purposes and excluding cases where there is a risk of unjustified infringement of the rights and interests of individuals, limited to cases where the business operator handling the personal information concerned and the relevant academic research institute jointly conduct academic research) (Article 20(2)(vi) of the Act).

(6) Where special care-required personal information is disclosed by the individual concerned, a state or local government, an academic research institute, a person listed in any item of Article 57(1) of the Act, or any other person prescribed in the PPC Rules (Article 20(2)(vii) of the Act, related to Article 6 of the Rules):

If the special care-required personal information is made public by any of the following persons, the information may be acquired without obtaining the prior consent of the individual concerned:

(i) the individual concerned;
(ii) any governmental organisation;
(iii) the local authority;
(iv) academic and research institutions, etc.;
(v) broadcasting organisations, newspapers, news agencies, and other media organisations (including individuals who engage in news reporting as a business);
(vi) persons engaged in business writing;
(vii) religious organisations;
(viii) political organisations;
(ix) foreign governments, foreign governmental institutions, foreign local governments, or international organisations;
(x) persons equivalent to those listed in each item of Article 57(1) of the Act in a foreign country.

(7) Cases in which special care-required personal information is obtained by visually observing or photographing the person concerned, which is evident from the external appearance of the person (Article 20(2)(viii) of the Act, Article 9(1) of the Cabinet Order):

If, regardless of the person's intention, the matters included in the special care-required personal information, (e.g., physical disability, etc.) are obvious from the person's external characteristics, this information may be acquired without obtaining the person's prior consent, for example,[45] when a person with a physical disability visits a shop, and in the course of a potential purchase, the owner will have to handle a part of this person's 'records' (e.g., acquisition by visual inspection), or when a person with a physical disability is captured on a security camera installed in the shop (acquisition by filming).

(8) (i)In the cases listed in each item of Article 27(5) of the Act (including the cases where the terms are replaced and applied pursuant to Article 41(6) of the Act and where the terms are replaced and applied *mutatis mutandis* pursuant to Article 42(2) of the Act); (ii) when receiving provision of personal information requiring special consideration that constitutes personal data in the cases listed in Article 20(2)(viii) of the Act and Article 9(2) of the

45. General Guidelines, p. 46.

Cabinet Order (including cases where the provisions of Article 20(2)(viii) of the Act and Article 9(2) of the Cabinet Order apply *mutatis mutandis*):

> When special care-required personal information is provided in accordance with the items of Article 27(5) of the Act (including cases where it is applied *mutatis mutandis* by replacing the terms and phrases pursuant to Article 41(6) of the Act and cases where it is applied *mutatis mutandis* by replacing the terms and phrases pursuant to Article 42(2) of the Act), it is not necessary to obtain the consent of the individual in advance.

§3. Notification or Publication of the Purpose of Use (Related to Article 21(1) of the Act)

342. When acquiring personal data, a business operator handling personal information should publicly disclose the purpose for which the data are to be used in advance. If they have not made it public, they must notify the individual or make public the purpose of use of the information as soon as possible after acquisition.

343. The PPC General Guidelines provide some specific examples[46]regarding cases requiring notification or publication to the individual, as follows:

> (Case 1) When personal information is voluntarily made public by the person in question on the Internet (except in cases where the person merely browses through the information).
> (Case 2) When personal information is obtained from the Internet, official gazettes, or staff records (again, excluding cases where the person has merely browsed).
> (Case 3) If the person has received personal information from a third party.

§4. Direct Acquisition in Writing from the Principals (Related to Article 21(2) of the Act)

344. When a business operator handling personal information obtains personal data directly from a person through a written statement such as a contract or application forms, or through an electromagnetic record such as typing the data into a user input screen, the business operator handling personal data must, in advance, specify to the person the purpose for which the data are to be used. Additionally, in such cases, the purpose of use must be notified to the person (including legal persons) or made public promptly after acquisition, in accordance with Article 21(1) of the Act.

46. General Guidelines, p. 47.

345. The PPC General Guidelines provide some specific examples[47]in which the purpose of use must be clearly indicated to the person in advance, as follows:

> (Case 1) When an application form or contract containing the personal information of a person is obtained directly from the principals.
> (Case 2) Cases where personal information contained in a questionnaire is obtained directly from the principals.
> (Case 3) Cases in which personal information entered on the input screen of a company's website by a person who wishes to participate in a campaign organised by a company is obtained directly from the principals.

346. The PPC General Guidelines also provide some specific examples of cases[48] that fall under the definition of the 'purpose of use', as follows:

> (Case 1) When a contract or other document specifying the purpose of use is hand-delivered or sent to another party.
> (Case 2) When the purpose of use is clearly stated on a company's website accessed by a person or displayed on a person's terminal device on the network.

347. Additionally, the PPC General Guidelines provide that the purpose of use shall be stated in a document (including an electromagnetic record) such as a contractual agreement or terms and conditions of use. The PPC Guidelines provide that it is desirable to pay attention to the fact that the person can actually confirm the purpose of use by, for example, informing the person that the purpose of use is stated in the terms and conditions on the reverse side of the document in a place and font size that the person can recognise from a socially accepted viewpoint, as well as on the front side of the document.

348. Furthermore, when personal information is obtained on a network, this information should be so organised that the purpose of use (including links and buttons that will allow the user to move to a page showing the content of the purpose of use in just one click) catches the attention of the person before he or she clicks on the 'send' button.

§5. Cases in Which Notification of the Purpose of Use Is Not Required (Article 21(4) of the Act)

349. When acquiring personal information, a business operator handling personal information must notify the purpose of use. However, notification of the purpose of use is not required if the following three conditions are met:

---

47. General Guidelines, p. 48.
48. *Ibid.*

(1) Where there is a risk of harm to the life, body, property or other rights or interests of the person concerned or a third party (Article 21(4)(i) of the Act).

Even if there is a risk of harm to the life, body, property, or other rights and interests of the person or a third party by notifying the person of the purpose of use or making it public, Article 21(1) to (3) of the APPI does not apply, and notification of the purpose of use is not required. The PPC General Guidelines provide the following example:[49]

> When a network of relevant organisations such as child guidance centres, schools, and medical institutions is formed to respond to child abuse, and there is a risk that notification or publication of the purpose of use of the personal information of the person who is the perpetrator may aggravate the abuse or cause hindrance to the response to the abuse

(2) Where there is a risk of harm to the rights or legitimate interests of the operator (Article 21(4)(ii) of the Act).

Even if there is a risk of harm to the rights or legitimate interests of the business operator by notifying the person concerned of the purpose of use or making it public, Article 21(1) to (3) of the APPI does not apply, and notification of such purpose of use is not required. The PPC General Guidelines provide the following example:[50]

> When it becomes clear that information about anti-social forces such as organised crime groups, information subject to notification of suspicious financial transactions, or information about malicious persons who sabotage business has been obtained from the person concerned or other business operators, which would cause harm to the company from which the information was obtained

(3) Where it is necessary to cooperate with a governmental organisation or a local authority in affairs prescribed by law (related to Article 21(4)(iii) of the Act).

If it is necessary for a governmental organisation, a local authority, or a person nominated by them to obtain the cooperation of a private company in carrying out affairs prescribed by law, and it is deemed that notification of the purpose of use to the person concerned is likely to impede the performance of these affairs, the private company concerned shall not be subject to Article 21(1) to (3) of the Act.

The PPC General Guidelines provide for cases where there is a risk that the business operator handling the personal information who has received personal information from the police may impede an investigation by notifying the person of the purpose of use or by making it public.[51]

49. General Guidelines, p. 49.
50. *Ibid.*
51. *Ibid.*

(4) Where, in view of the circumstances of the acquisition, the purpose of use is considered to be clear (Article 21(4)(iv) of the Act).

350. If the purpose of use is found to be clear from the circumstances of acquisition, Article 21(1) to (3) of the Act does not apply, and notification of the relevant purpose of use is not required. The PPC General Guidelines provide some specific examples, as follows:[52]

> (Case 1) Where personal information such as addresses and telephone numbers are acquired in the course of selling or providing goods or services, and the purpose of use is to ensure that the goods or services are sold or provided only for the purpose of use.
> (Case 2) Where personal information such as names, affiliations, titles, and contact details are obtained directly from the persons concerned when exchanging business cards as a matter of general practice, and the purpose of use is to send booklets or e-mails for future contact or for advertising and promotion of the company to which the person belongs.

52. General Guidelines, p. 50.

Chapter 5. Management of Personal Data

§1. Ensuring the Accuracy of Data Contents (Article 22 of the Act)

351. To the extent necessary to achieve the purpose of use, business operators handling personal information shall endeavour to keep personal data accurate and up to date by establishing procedures for collation and verification when entering personal data into personal database, by establishing procedures for correction when errors are discovered, updating recorded information and setting retention periods. The important point to make here is that personal data must be kept accurate and up to date. Please note that it is not necessary to uniformly or constantly update all of the personal data held, rather, it is sufficient to ensure that only the important information is accurate and up to date to the extent necessary for the respective purpose of use.

352. Additionally, business operators handling personal data shall not be required to use the personal data they retain when there is no longer a need to use it, i.e., when the purpose of use has been achieved and there is no longer a reasonable reason for retaining the personal data in question in relation to that purpose, or when the purpose of use has not been achieved but the business itself, on which that purpose has been premised, has been discontinued. If the purpose of use has not been achieved, but the business on which the purpose has been premised has been discontinued, efforts must be made to erase the personal data concerned without delay. This does not apply when the given retention period is set by law.

353. The term 'erasure of personal data' means making the personal data no longer usable as personal data and includes, in addition to deleting the data, making it impossible to identify specific individuals from the data.

§2. Ensuring the Accuracy of Retained Personal Information Held by Administrative Organs (Article 65 of the Act)

354. Administrative organs must endeavour to ensure that retained personal information is consistent with past or present facts to the extent necessary to achieve the purpose of use (Article 65 of the Act).

§3. Security Management Measures (Related to Article 23 of the Act)

355. Business operators handling personal data shall take necessary and appropriate measures to prevent leakage, loss, or damage of the personal data that they handle and to otherwise manage personal data securely. Such measures shall take into account the magnitude of the infringement of rights and interests suffered by the individual in the event of a leakage of personal data that are necessary and appropriate in accordance with the risks arising from the size and nature of the business, the circumstances of the handling of the personal data, and the nature of the media on which the personal data are recorded.

§4. SECURITY CONTROL MEASURES IN ADMINISTRATIVE ORGANS (ARTICLE 66(1) OF THE ACT)

356. If personal information is not adequately managed within administrative organs, and the persons handling personal information make its contents known to others without authorisation, the risk of infringement of the rights and interests of individuals increases. To prevent such situations, the Act stipulates that administrative organs are to take certain measures and that these are the obligations of those involved.

357. Administrative organs must take necessary and appropriate measures (security control measures) to prevent the leakage, loss, or damage of retained personal information and to otherwise securely control retained personal information (Article 66(1) of the Act). It is necessary to ensure cyber security to have appropriate security management measures. In taking these cyber security measures, it is also necessary to ensure an appropriate level of cyber security in light of the nature of the retained personal information handled, with reference to the standards for cyber security measures set out in Article 26(1)(ii) of the Basic Act on Cyber Security (Act No. 104 of 2014).

358. If a contractor falls under the category of 'personal information handling business operator' (Article 16, paragraph 2 of the Act), the contractor is also obliged to take security control measures (Article 23 of the Act) concerning personal data. As part of the necessary and appropriate supervision of the contractor, the administrative organ must provide the necessary advice and guidance to the contractor to ensure the proper handling of personal data in accordance with the APPI.

§5. SUPERVISION OF EMPLOYEES (RELATED TO ARTICLE 24 OF THE ACT)

359. When having its employees handle personal data, a business operator handling personal data must provide the necessary and appropriate supervision of such employees to ensure that they comply with the security control measures under Article 23 of the Act. In doing so, it is desirable to take necessary and appropriate measures, such as enhancing the content and frequency of education and training for employees who handle personal data, in accordance with the size and nature of the business and the risks arising from the circumstances in which personal data are handled, taking into consideration the magnitude of the infringement of rights and interests that the individual would suffer if personal data were leaked, etc.

360. The term 'employee' refers to a person who is directly or indirectly engaged in the business of a business operator handling personal data under the direction and supervision of the business operator and includes not only employees in an employment relationship (full-time employees, contract employees, temporary employees, part-time employees, etc.) but also directors, executive officers, board members, auditors, supervisors, temporary employees, etc.

361. The PPC Guidelines provide the following specific examples:[53]

[Cases of failure to provide necessary and appropriate supervision of employees]:

(Case 1) Failure to ensure that employees are performing their duties in accordance with regulations governing personal data security control measures, etc., resulting in the leakage of personal data.
(Case 2) Where a laptop computer or external storage medium containing personal data has been repeatedly taken out of the premises in violation of internal rules, etc., but as a result of neglecting the act, the said computer or storage medium has been lost and personal data has been leaked.

§6. Obligations of Persons Engaged in Administrative Organs (Article 67 of the Act)

362. The APPI provides that the following persons shall not disclose the contents of personal information obtained in connection with their work to others or use it for unjustified purposes (Article 67 of the Law):

(1) Persons who are or were employees of administrative organs engaged in the handling of personal information.
(2) Persons who are or were engaged in the tasks specified in each item of Article 66(2) of the Law.
(3) Dispatched workers (meaning dispatched workers prescribed in item (ii) of Article 2 of the Act on the Securing of Proper Operation of Worker Dispatching Undertakings and Protection of Dispatched Workers (Act No. 88 of 1985) who are engaged in the handling of personal information in administrative organs.

§7. Supervision of Contractors (Related to Article 25 of the Act)

363. The APPI does not provide a definition of 'controller' or 'processor' but imposes an obligation on personal data handlers to supervise contractors. 'Entrustment of the handling of personal data' means that a personal data handling business operator allows another party to handle personal data, regardless of the form or type

53. General Guidelines, p. 52.

of contract. Specifically, this includes outsourcing the input (including acquisition from the person concerned), editing, analysing, output, and other processing of personal data.

364. When a business operator handling personal data outsources all or part of the handling of personal data, the business operator handling personal data must provide necessary and appropriate supervision to the outsourced party to ensure that the outsourced party takes appropriate security control measures for the personal data in question. Specifically, the business operator handling personal data is obliged to supervise the entrusted party to ensure that it takes measures equivalent to the security control measures it should have taken itself in accordance with Article 23 of the Act.

365. It is crucial to ensure that personal data that are not necessary for the content of the business to be outsourced are not provided, and in light of the content of the personal data to be outsourced, the size and nature of the business to be outsourced and the risks arising from the handling of personal data, taking into consideration the magnitude of the violation of the rights and interests to be suffered by the individual if the personal data were leaked, are to be considered. Depending on the risk, the PPC General Guidelines specifically state[54] that the necessary and appropriate measures listed in (I)–(III) below must be taken.

I. Selection of Appropriate Contractors

366. When selecting a contractor, it is desirable to ensure that the security management measures of the contractor are at least equivalent to those required of the contractor under Article 23 of the Act and these Guidelines.

II. Entrustment Contract

367. It is desirable to include in the consignment contract, as a necessary and appropriate security control measure for the handling of the personal data concerned, the details agreed by both the consignor and the consignee, as well as a reasonable understanding by the consignor of the handling status of the consigned personal data at the consignee.

III. Confirming the Status of Personal Data Handling at the Consignee

368. To ascertain the status of the handling of entrusted personal data at the consignee, it is desirable to conduct regular audits to investigate the degree of implementation of the contents incorporated in the consignment contract and then properly evaluate the situation, including considering a review of the contents of the

54. General Guidelines, pp. 52–54.

consignment. Additionally, when a consignee intends to recommission, as in the case of commissioning, the consignor should receive a prior report from the consignee or obtain approval from the consignee regarding the party to whom the consignee recommissions, the content of the business to be recommissioned, the method of handling personal data by the recommissioned party, and through the consignee or by itself as necessary, it is desirable to sufficiently confirm that the sub-consignee properly fulfils the supervision of the consignee under this Article and that the sub-consignee takes security control measures in accordance with Article 23 of the Act, by conducting audits.

369. The PPC General Guidelines provide the following cases[55]of failure to provide necessary and appropriate supervision to the entrusted party:

> (Case 1) When personal data are leaked by a contractor as a result of outsourcing to an external business operator without having the status of security control measures for personal data properly ascertained at the time of signing the contract and thereafter.
> (Case 2) The outsourced party leaks personal data as a result of failing to instruct the outsourced party on the details of the necessary security control measures for the handling of personal data.
> (Case 3) Where the entrustee leaks personal data as a result of the entrustee's re-consignment of the processing of personal data due to the entrustee's failure to give instructions to the secondary entrustee regarding the conditions of re-consignment and to check the status of the handling of personal data by the secondary entrustee.
> (Case 4) Where the consignor fails to take the necessary measures, such as requesting the consignee to report on the re-consignment, despite the fact that the contract includes a requirement for the consignor to monitor the implementation of the re-consignment by the consignee, and the re-consignment is carried out without the consignor's knowledge, resulting in a leak of personal data by the re-consignee in question.

55. General Guidelines, p. 54.

Chapter 6. Reporting of Leaks of Personal Data

§1. Determining a Leakage

370. A personal data 'leakage' means that personal data are leaked to outside parties. It does not constitute a leak if all personal data are collected before being viewed by a third party. Additionally, if a business operator handling personal data provides personal data to a third party based on its own intention, this does not constitute a leak.

371. 'Loss' of personal data means the loss of the content of personal data. If data replicating the content are stored elsewhere, it does not constitute a loss. It also does not constitute a loss if the personal data are deleted by the business operator handling the personal data for reasonable reasons. However, if the forms concerned are not properly disposed of, they may fall under the category of personal data leakage. If personal data are leaked outside the company, such an instance falls under the category of personal data leakage.

372. 'Damage' to personal data means that the content of personal data is unintentionally altered or that the data are rendered unusable while retaining the content. However, it does not constitute damage if identical content is stored elsewhere. If personal data are stolen at the same time, such an instance also falls under the category of personal data leakage.

§2. Measures to Be Taken in the Event of Discovery of a Leakage Incident

373. The PPC General Guidelines stipulate[56] that, in the event of a leakage or other problem that could lead to a leakage risk, the business operator handling personal data must take the necessary measures with regard to the matters listed in (I)–(V) below, depending on the nature of the leakage or other incident. Additionally, the Guidelines stipulate that depending on the nature of the leakage or other incident, it is desirable to promptly disclose the facts and measures to prevent recurrence in order to prevent secondary damage and the occurrence of similar incidents.

I. Reporting Within the Operator and Preventing the Spread of Damage

374. Immediately report the incident to a person in a position of responsibility, and take the necessary measures to prevent the damage caused by the leakage or other incident from spreading beyond the time of discovery.

56. General Guidelines, pp. 56–57.

II. Investigation of Facts and Causes

375. Take the necessary measures to investigate the facts of the leakage incident and determine the cause.

III. Identification of the Scope of Influence

376. Take the necessary measures to identify the scope of the impact based on the facts.

IV. Examination and Implementation of Measures to Prevent Recurrence

377. Take the necessary measures to examine and implement measures to prevent recurrence of incidents such as leaks.

V. Report to the PPC and Notify the Person Concerned

§3. Reporting to the PPC (Related to Section 26(1) of the Act)

378. When a business operator handling personal information becomes aware of a situation listed in the following (1)–(4) (reportable situations), it is mandatory to report the fact and situation to the PPC:

(1) A situation in which leakage of personal data containing special care-required personal information has occurred or is likely to occur (Article 7.1 of the Regulations).
The PPC General Guidelines provide the following special care-required personal information leakage cases requiring reporting to the PPC:[57]

(Case 1) Loss of a USB memory stick containing personal data including patient medical information and dispensing information from a hospital.
(Case 2) Leakage of personal data containing the results of employee medical examinations.

(2) A situation where leakage of personal data that may cause property damage due to unauthorised use has occurred or is likely to occur (Article 7, Item 2 of the Regulations).
The likelihood of property damage being caused shall be judged on the basis of the nature and content of the personal data in question, taking into account the probability of property damage being caused. The PPC General Guidelines provide the following cases[58]requiring reporting:

57. General Guidelines, p. 58.
58. *Ibid.*

(Case 1) Leakage of personal data including credit card numbers from an e-commerce website.
(Case 2) Leakage of personal data including the combination of login IDs and passwords for web services with money transfer or payment functions.

(3) A situation in which leakage of personal data has occurred or is likely to occur, possibly arising from an unauthorised purpose (Article 7(3) of the Regulations).
The entity that may have caused the leakage 'with a wrongful purpose' includes not only third parties but also employees. The PPC General Guidelines provide the following cases[59] requiring reporting:

(Case 1) Leakage of personal data due to unauthorised access.
(Case 2) When personal data are encrypted by ransomware and cannot be restored.
(Case 3) When documents and media containing or recording personal data are stolen.
(Case 4) When an employee illegally removes a customer's personal data and provides it to a third party.

(4) A situation where leakage in which the number of individuals to whom personal data pertains exceeds 1,000 has occurred or is likely to occur (Article 7, Item 4 of the Regulations).

379. The 'number of persons to whom personal data pertains' means the number of persons the personal data handled by the business operator handling personal information concerns with regard to which leakage has occurred or is likely to occur. If this number is less than 1,000 when the situation is first discovered but subsequently exceeds 1,000, then Article 7(4) of the Regulations will apply. In the case of leakage where the number of affected persons cannot be determined, if the maximum number of persons in relation to whose personal data the leakage may have occurred exceeds 1,000, it falls under Article 7(4) of the Regulations.

380. The PPC General Guidelines provide an example[60] where personal data were made available for viewing on the Internet due to a system misconfiguration, and the number of persons pertaining to such personal data exceeded 1,000.

381. These are the reportable situations in which personal data leaks must be reported. On the other hand, even in the case of a leak that does not qualify as a reportable event, a business operator handling personal information may voluntarily report it to the PPC.

382. The 'likelihood' of a reportable event is determined on the basis of the facts known at the time of the event, taking into account the probability of the event for

59. General Guidelines, p. 59.
60. *Ibid.*

each individual case. The 'likelihood' that a leak has occurred applies when there is no proof that a leak has occurred, although leakage is suspected, based on the facts known at the time.

383. Additionally, a report is not required if 'advanced encryption or other measures necessary to protect the rights and interests of individuals' are taken, such as when personal data that have been leaked or are likely to be leaked are kept secret through advanced encryption or other means.

384. Other cases that may fall under situations where a 'leak' may have occurred with regard to cyber-attack cases are as follows, as in the PPC General Guidelines in (a)–(d):[61]

(a) Where there are traces of data theft due to unauthorised access from outside on the server storing the personal data or on a terminal with access rights to the server.
(b) The server storing the personal data or the terminal with access rights to the server is found to be infected with malware that is known to behave in a manner that steals information.
(c) IP addresses and FQDNs (abbreviation of Fully Qualified Domain Name; FQDN is the name of a domain name consisting of sub-domains and domain names) are known to be used by a server (C&C server) that sends and controls malicious commands to computers infected with malware (a string of characters consisting of a sub-domain name and a domain name that identifies a computer (e.g., server) on a network).
(d) If a third party, such as a public authority, security service provider, or expert who detects unauthorised access is contacted on a certain basis about a possible leak.

385. The entity obliged to report a leak is the personal data handling entity handling the personal data with respect to which a leak has occurred or is likely to occur. In cases where the handling of personal data is outsourced, both the outsourcer and the outsourced party are handling the personal data, and therefore, in principle, both the outsourcer and the outsourced party are obliged to make a report if the situation falls under the reporting scope. In this case, the report may be made under the joint names of the consignor and the consignee. If the consignee notifies the consignor, who is obliged to make a report, of the occurrence of such a situation, the consignor is exempted from the obligation to report. Additionally, if the consignor has entrusted the handling of certain personal data (personal data A) to the consignee and has not entrusted the handling of another set of personal data (personal data B) to the same consignee, this consignee is exempted from the reporting

61. *Ibid.*

obligation with regard to personal data B if the consignor has notified the consignee. If a reportable event occurs at the consignor, the consignee is not obliged to report the event; only the consignor is obliged to report the event.[62]

386. When a business operator handling personal information becomes aware of a reportable event, it must promptly report it to the PPC. The PPC General Guidelines define this procedure as a 'preliminary report'. If the PPC has delegated the authority to accept the report to the minister having jurisdiction over the business in accordance with Article 147(1) of the Act, the report shall be made to the competent minister having jurisdiction over the business in question. When reporting to the minister having jurisdiction over the business, the reporting deadline is the same as when reporting to the PPC.

387. The point of 'knowledge' as the starting point for the reporting deadline is determined on a case-by-case basis, but if the business operator handling personal information is a legal entity, it is based on the point at which one of its departments becomes aware of the situation. The standard number of days constituting 'promptly' depends on the individual case but is generally within three to five days from the time when the business operator handling personal information becomes aware of the situation in question.

388. Reports[63] on leaks to the PPC should, in principle, be made by entering the matters listed in (1)–(9) below into the reporting form on the PPC's website. With regard to the contents of the report at the time of the preliminary report, it is sufficient to report the contents that are known at the time when the report is intended:

(1) Summary: An overview of the situation shall be reported, including the date of occurrence, the date of discovery, the incident, the finder, the applicability of each item of Article 7 of the Regulations, the existence or non-existence of a commissioning source and commissioning party, and the factual course of the incident.
(2) Items of Personal Data in Respect of Which a Leak Has Occurred or Is Likely to Occur: Report on the items of personal data that have been or may have been leaked, together with the medium and type (e.g., customer information, employee information, etc.).
(3) Number of Individuals Whose Personal Data Have Been or May Have Been Leaked: The number of persons whose personal data have been or may have been leaked shall be reported.
(4) Causes: Report on the cause of the incident together with the entity (reporter or contractor) from which the incident occurred.
(5) Secondary Damage or Threat of Secondary Damage and Its Description: Report on the existence or non-existence of damage or the threat of damage arising from the incident and the details thereof.

62. General Guidelines, p. 60.
63. General Guidelines, p. 61.

(6) Status of Response to the Person Concerned: Report on the status of implementation of measures (including notification) taken against the person concerned after becoming aware of the situation.
(7) Status of Public Disclosure: Report on the implementation status of public announcements concerning the situation.
(8) Measures to Prevent Recurrence: Report on the measures taken to prevent recurrence of the leakage incident divided into measures already taken and measures to be taken in the future.
(9) Other Matters of Reference.

389. To supplement items (1)–(9) above, the PPC shall be reported to on matters helpful in understanding the situation in question.

390. In addition to the aforementioned preliminary report, a business operator handling personal information shall, when it becomes aware of a reportable event, report the event within thirty days (within sixty days in the case of the event referred to in Article. 7(3) of the Regulation; the same shall apply hereinafter). In addition to the situation referred to in Item 3 of Article 7 of the Regulation, it shall also report the matter within sixty days in the case of the situation referred to in Items 1, 2, and 4 of Article 7 of the Regulation. The report must be submitted to the PPC (or to the competent minister if the PPC has delegated the authority to accept the report to the competent minister pursuant to Article 147(1) of the Act) within thirty days or sixty days, whichever is earlier, as it is advisable to do so as soon as possible.

391. The PPC General Guidelines define this procedure as 'confirmatory reporting'.[64]

§4. Notification to the Person Concerned (Related to Article 26(2) of the Act)

392. The PPC General Guidelines set out the specific details and criteria for notifying the individual concerned when a leak has occurred, and its notification procedure as follows:[65]

I. Situations Subject to Notification and Entities Obliged to Notify

393. When a business operator handling personal information becomes aware of a reportable event, it must notify the principals. The entity obliged to notify is the business operator handling personal information that has handled the personal data in respect of which the leakage has occurred or is likely to occur.

64. *Ibid.*
65. General Guidelines, pp. 64–67.

II. Due Date for Notification

394. When a business operator handling personal information becomes aware of a reportable event, it must, depending on the circumstances of the event, promptly notify the individual concerned.

395. The term 'promptly in accordance with the circumstances of the situation' means that the notification must be made promptly, but the specific point in time for notification must be determined in individual cases, taking into account the details of the situation known at the time, the probability that the rights and interests of the individual will be protected by notification, the harm that will result from notifying the individual, and other factors.

396. Furthermore, the PPC General Guidelines provide the following cases[66] requiring reporting:

> [Cases in which it is not considered necessary to notify the person at that point in time]:
>
> > (Case 1) Where multiple leaked personal data have been uploaded to an Internet noticeboard, and the business operator handling personal information has not completed the necessary initial measures, such as requesting that the administrator of the noticeboard delete the data, and there is a risk that notifying the person in question will instead cause more damage.
> > (Case 2) Where there is a threat of leakage, but the case is still largely unknown, and even if the individual concerned is notified at that time, there is no prospect of measures being taken to protect individual rights and interests, and there is a risk that confusion may result instead.

III. Contents of Notification

397. Matters to be notified to the individual concerned shall include, among the matters to be reported in a report of a leakage, the 'outline' (Article 8, paragraph 1, Item 1 of the Regulations), 'items of personal data in respect of which a leakage has occurred or is likely to' 'occur' (Item 2 of the same paragraph), 'cause' (Item 4 of the same paragraph), 'existence of secondary damage or threat thereof and its details' (Item 5 of the same paragraph), and 'other information which may be of reference' (Item 9 of the same paragraph). It does not mean that the person need not be notified until all these matters are known, but that the person must be notified 'as soon as possible in accordance with the circumstances of the situation'.

398. Notification to the individual is to be made 'to the extent necessary to protect the rights and interests of the individual'. Additionally, if a situation is initially judged to be a reportable situation but is subsequently found not to be a reportable

66. General Guidelines, p. 65.

situation, it is not necessary to notify the person in question, given that notification to the person is 'to the extent necessary to protect the rights and interests of the person'.

399. The PPC General Guidelines provide the following cases[67] requiring reporting:

> [Cases in which notification is made 'to the extent necessary to protect the rights and interests of the person concerned']:
>
> > (Case 1) In cases where personal data have been leaked due to unauthorised access, when notifying the person of the cause of the leak, the necessary details should be selected and notified to the person, instead of reporting the detailed information to the PPC.
> > (Case 2) Where the items of personal data that have been leaked differ from person to person, only the details relevant to the person in question shall be notified to the person in question.

IV. Method of Notification

400. The term 'notification to the individual concerned' means directly informing the individual concerned and, depending on the nature of the business and the circumstances of the handling of personal data, must be made in a reasonable and appropriate manner such that the individual concerned is aware of the contents to be notified. Additionally, unlike a leakage report, the form of notification to the individual is not prescribed by law, but it is advisable to provide notification in a form that is easy for the individual to understand.

V. Exceptions to Notification

401. In cases where notification to the person is required but it is difficult to notify the person, it is permissible to respond by taking alternative measures necessary to protect the rights and interests of the person. The Guidelines state that even if the case is not made public as an alternative measure, it is desirable to make a public announcement from the perspective of preventing secondary damage and the occurrence of similar cases, depending on the nature of the situation in question. The content to be made public is determined on a case-by-case basis, but the basic principle is that the person concerned should be notified.

402. The PPC General Guidelines provide the following cases requiring reporting:[68]

67. General Guidelines, p. 66.
68. General Guidelines, p. 67.

[Cases which fall under cases where it is difficult to notify the person in question]:

(Case 1) Where the personal data held do not include the contact details of the person concerned.
(Case 2) If the contact details are out of date and the person cannot be contacted at the time of notification.

[Cases falling under alternative measures]:

(Case 1) Publication of the case.
(Case 2) Preparing a contact point for enquiries and publicly announcing its contact details so that the individual can check whether these personal data are covered by the case.

§5. Reporting by Administrative Organs to the PPC (Article 68(1) of the Act)

403. If personal information held by an administrative organ is leaked, the rights and interests of individuals may be infringed and public trust in the administrative organ may be lost. Therefore, the APPI requires an administrative organ to report to the PPC and notify the individual(s) concerned in the event of retained personal information leakage with a high possibility to harm the rights and interests of the individual.

404. If any of the following situations stipulated by the Regulations as situations highly likely to cause harm to the rights and interests of individuals occurs with regard to retained personal information, the administrative organ must report to the PPC that such a situation has occurred (Article 68, paragraph 1 of the Act):

(1) Leakage of retained personal information containing special care-required personal information (excluding information for which advanced encryption or other measures necessary to protect the rights and interests of individuals have been taken. The same shall apply hereinafter in (2) to (4)) has occurred or is likely to occur (Article 43(1) of the Regulations).
(2) A situation where there has been or is likely to be a leak of retained personal information that is likely to cause property damage due to unauthorised use (Article 43(1) of the Regulations).
(3) A situation in which a leak of retained personal information has occurred or is likely to occur arising from an unauthorised purpose (Item 3 of the same article).
(4) A situation where a leak has occurred or is likely to occur, where the number of individuals concerned with the retained personal information exceeds 100 (Item 4 of the same article).

§6. NOTIFICATION TO THE PERSON IN THE CASE OF AN ADMINISTRATIVE ORGAN (ARTICLE 68(2) OF THE ACT)

405. In the event of a situation requiring a report to the PPC, the administrative organ shall, in accordance with regulations, notify the person concerned of an outline of the situation, the items of personal information held, the cause, whether or not there is secondary damage or the threat thereof and the details thereof, and any other information that may be helpful to the extent necessary to protect the rights and interests of the person (Article 68(2) of the Act).

406. However, notification is not required if (i) it is difficult to notify the person and alternative measures necessary to protect the rights and interests of the person are taken; or (ii) the retained personal information in question contains any of the 'non-disclosable information' listed in the items of Article 78 of the Act.

407. Additionally, even if the case is not subject to reporting under Article 68(1) of the Act if the information is provided to the PPC as a case that may cause public anxiety, the information shall be provided to the individual to the extent necessary to protect the rights and interests of the individual, including an outline of the situation, the items of retained personal information, the cause, and secondary damage.

Chapter 7. Provision of Personal Data to Third Parties

§1. Principle of Limitation of Provision to Third Parties (Related to Article 27(1) of the Act)

408. Personal information handling business operators shall not provide personal data to third parties without obtaining the prior consent of the individual. In acquiring consent, the business operator must clearly indicate the reasonable and appropriate range of content considered necessary for the individual to decide whether to consent in accordance with the size and nature of the business and the circumstances under which personal data are handled. If it is envisaged in advance that personal information will be provided to third parties, this must be specified in the purpose of use.

409. The mandatory provisions relating to the provision of personal information to third parties set out in the APPI are (1) restrictions on the provision of personal information to third parties, notification and publication of opt-out procedures (Article 27, paragraphs 2–4), and prohibition of the provision of special care-required personal information to third parties by opt-out (Article 27(2)); (2) restrictions on provision to third parties located in foreign countries; (3) preparation of records relating to provision to third parties; and (4) procedures relating to confirmation when receiving provision to third parties. Illegal provision to third parties is also punishable as the crime of providing personal information databases (Article 179).

410. On the other hand, as a procedure not subject to restrictions on third-party provision, there is the provision of anonymously processed information (Articles 2(6) and 43–46) established to enable the provision of personal information to third parties without the consent of the individual for the purpose of promoting the use of personal information.

411. In principle, provision of personal data to a third party requires the consent of the person concerned, with the following exceptions: (a) when based on laws and regulations; (b) to protect the life, body, or property of a person; (c) to improve public health or promote the healthy development of children; and (d) to provide personal data to a third party when the provision of the information is necessary for the following reasons: (1) academic research institutions, (2) opt-out, (3) provision to contractors, (4) business successions such as mergers, and (5) joint use. The provisions on opt-out are set out as a procedure for providing personal data to a third party without the consent of the individual, whereby the provision of personal data to a third party is stopped at the request of the individual.

412. The following (a)–(e) are where personal consent is not required:

(a) Where personal data are provided on the basis of a law or regulation (Article 27(1)(i) of the Act).

(b) Where the provision of personal data is necessary to protect the life, body, or property of a person (including legal persons) whose specific rights and interests are likely to be infringed and where it is difficult to obtain the consent of the person (Article 27(1)(ii) of the Act).
(c) Where the provision of personal data is particularly necessary for the improvement of public health or the sound upbringing of children undergoing mental or physical development and where it is difficult to obtain the consent of the person concerned (Article 27(1)(iii) of the Act).
(d) Where it is necessary to obtain the cooperation of a private company or other entity in carrying out affairs prescribed by law, and where obtaining the consent of the person is likely to impede the carrying out of those affairs if the cooperating private company or other entity provides personal data to governmental organs or another entity (Article 27(1)(iv) of the Act):

(e1) Where an academic research institution provides personal data, and the provision of such personal data is unavoidable for the publication of the results of academic research or for teaching (except where there is a risk of unjustified infringement of the rights and interests of individuals) (Article 27(1)(v) of the Act).
(e2) Where an academic research institution provides personal data and a third party (whether or not it is an academic research institution) conducts academic research in collaboration with the said academic research institution (including where part of the purpose of providing the personal data is for academic research purposes, except where there is a risk of unreasonable infringement of the rights and interests of individuals) (Article 27(1)(vi) of the Act).
(e3) Where an academic research institution receives personal data from a third party and the academic research institution needs to handle the personal data for academic research purposes (including cases where part of the purpose of handling the personal data is for academic research purposes but excluding cases where there is a risk of unjustified infringement of the rights and interests of individuals) (Article 27(1)(vii) of the Act).

§2. Provision of Personal Data to Third Parties by Opting Out (Related to Article 27(2)–(4) of the Act)

413. Notwithstanding the provisions of Article 27(1) of the APPI, a personal information handling business operator may, when providing personal data to a third party, notify the individual in advance of the matters listed in (1)–(9) below or make them readily accessible to the individual, and notify the PPC, without the consent of the individual in advance.

414. It is not possible to provide special care-required personal information to a third party by opting out or to provide personal data that have been provided by opting out again by opting out. When providing personal data falling under these categories to a third party, the consent of the individual must always be obtained in advance, except in cases falling under each of the items of Article 27(1) or Article 27(5) of the Act. Personal data that have been acquired unlawfully may also not be provided to third parties on an opt-out basis.

415. This notification procedure before providing personal data by opting out was established in the revised APPI in 2015. The reason for providing the notification to the PPC is that in order to provide personal data to a third party without the consent of the individual through the opt-out procedure, it is obligatory to notify the individual or make the data readily available to the individual, but because the business generally publishes the method on its website, there are few opportunities for the individual to be aware of this, and the procedures are not formalised. In some situations, it is even difficult for the individual to identify the business operator subject to the opt-out request due to the chain of third-party provisions. Since personal data can be legitimately provided to third parties without the consent of the individual as long as the opt-out requirements are sufficient, the situation where lists of names of dubious origin from the perspective of the obligation to acquire the data properly are sold through the publication of formal opt-out requirements has also been called into question.[69]

416. In light of such problems, it is mandatory to notify the PPC and make a public announcement if personal data are provided with an opt-out requirement, in order to enable the principals to verify this fact.

417. The information that operators are required to notify the PPC with is as follows:

(1) The name and address of the personal information handling business operator and the name of the representative of the legal entity.
(2) The purpose of use of the information to be provided to third parties.
(3) The items of personal data to be provided to third parties.
(4) The method of acquiring the personal data to be provided to third parties.
(5) The method of provision to third parties.
(6) The cessation of provision to third parties at the request of the person in question.
(7) The method of accepting the individual's request.
(8) The method of updating personal data provided to third parties.
(9) The expected date on which the personal data pertaining to the notification will be provided to the third party.

---

69. On 9 Sep. 2014, the Consumer Affairs Commission published 'Opinions on issues to be considered in the future concerning so-called directory agencies' as its opinion on the 'Outline of Institutional Amendments on the Use of Personal Data' (24 Jun. 2014). The following issues have been identified in the General Outline: (1) involvement of third-party organisations in the transfer of personal information whose identifiability has not been reduced; (2) clarification of the responsibility of businesses which obtain and hold lists of personal information such as directories; (3) establishment of traceability which does not allow laundering of information; (4) deletion of personal information that has been leaked by illegal means; (5) regulations on so-called data broker.

418. The matters relating to such notification are published on the PPC's website as 'publication of the opt-out notification', including the name of the business operator and other publication matters specified in the Regulations.

419. Regarding the person concerned with the personal data to be opt-out provided, the scope of the opt-out provision and the method of accepting the cessation of the opt-out provision can be confirmed. Additionally, the person who intends to opt-out can check, among other things, whether the source of the personal data provided has made an opt-out notification. It should be noted that opt-out provision of personal data that have been opt-out provided is prohibited.

420. Specific publication details can be found in 'Opt-out Notification Search and List View of Notifications'.[70]

421. Notification carried out by the operator and publication by the PPC will ensure that the individual has the opportunity to be aware of the fact that opt-out is being implemented, and provision involving third parties in breach of such procedures will be subject to a recommendation or order issued by the PPC.

422. Other special care-required personal information is excluded from the procedure for opt-out provision to third parties.

423. In principle, the consent of the person concerned is required to acquire special care-required personal information, and provision by 'opt-out' as an exceptional procedure for the provision of personal data to third parties is not permitted. The reason for disallowing the provision of special care-required personal information on an opt-out basis is that there is a risk of infringement of rights and interests due to the provision of such information to a third party without the person's knowledge. Note that even special care-required personal information may be provided without the consent of the individual if it falls within the exceptions to the provision to third parties in each of the aforementioned items of Article 27(1).

§3. Cases Where the Person Does Not Fall into the Category of a Third Party (Related to Article 27(5) and (6) of the Act)

424. In principle, the provision of personal data to third parties is subject to the consent of the person concerned. However, in the following cases (1)–(3), although the recipient of personal data falls formally under the category of a third party as an entity separate from the personal data handling entity, it is not a third party because it is reasonable to treat it as one with the personal data handling entity, which is the providing entity in relation to the individual. If such requirements are met, the personal data handling business operator may provide personal data without the prior

70. Opt-out notification form search (revised Act on the Protection of Personal Information) https://www.ppc.go.jp/personalinfo/preparation/optout/publication_2021/.

consent of the individual or opt-out of the provision to a third party, notwithstanding the provisions of Article 27(1) to (3) of the Act.

I. Entrustment (Article 27(5)(i) of the Act)

425. If the personal data concerned are provided in connection with the commissioning of all or part of the work relating to the handling of personal data to the extent necessary for the achievement of the purpose of use, the entity to which the personal data are provided does not fall under the category of a third party. In such a case, the recipient may not handle the personal data concerned other than for the entrusted operations, as it is reasonable for the recipient to be treated as an integral part of the personal data handling business operator, who is the providing entity only within the scope of the entrusted operations and in relation to the person concerned.

426. Additionally, the personal data handling business operator is subject to supervisory responsibility over the entrusted party in accordance with Article 25 of the Act.

II. Succession of Business (Article 27(5)(ii) of the Act)

427. Where personal data relating to a business are provided in connection with the succession of the business due to a merger, spin-off, or business transfer, the party to which the personal data is provided does not fall under the category of a third party.

428. Even after the succession of the business, the personal data must be used within the scope of the purposes for which the personal data were used before they were provided as a result of the succession of the business in question. Additionally, if at the negotiation stage prior to the conclusion of a contract for the succession of a business, the company receives a survey of its own company from the other company and provides its own personal data to the other company, this also falls under this item, and the personal data may be provided without obtaining the prior consent of the person or without performing the opt-out procedure in the provision of personal data to a third party. However, the company must conclude the necessary agreements to ensure that the other company complies with the security control measures, including the purpose of use and handling methods of such data, measures to be taken in the event of leakage, and measures to be taken in the event of unsuccessful negotiations regarding the succession of the business.

III. Joint Use (Article 27(5)(iii) of the Act)

429. Where personal data jointly used with a specific person are provided to that specific person, and the following information (i)–(v) is notified to the person in advance or made readily available to the person upon provision, the recipient of the personal data shall, from the point of view of the person, be treated as an entity that is reasonably considered to be an integral part of the entity that originally provided the personal data in question. The entity is not considered to be a third party because it is considered reasonable that the personal data are treated as an integral part of the entity.

430. Additionally, when personal data that have already been obtained by a specific business operator are used jointly with another business operator, such joint use must be within the scope of those who jointly use the personal data and the purpose of use, which are objectively considered, from a socially accepted perspective, to be within the scope of what is normally expected by the person to whom the personal data pertain. The proprietor must then determine the propriety of joint use in accordance with the content and nature of the personal data concerned and use it jointly within the scope of the purposes of use specified in accordance with Article 17(1) of the Act with respect to the business operator that has already acquired the personal data:

(i) The fact that the data will be jointly used.
(ii) Items of personal data to be jointly used.
(iii) Scope of joint use.

431. The 'purpose of joint use' is to jointly use such personal data to the extent that it is reasonable, from the perspective of the individual concerned, to be treated as an integral part of the entity providing such personal data. Therefore, the scope of the joint users must be sufficiently clear to enable the individual to determine by which entity the personal data will be used in the future. As long as the scope is clear, it is not necessary to list all the names, etc., of the entities individually, but the person concerned must be able to determine by which entities the data will be used.

§4. Purpose of Use by Persons Who Use the Data

432. With regard to personal data used jointly, all purposes of use must be notified to the person concerned or made readily available to the person concerned. If the purpose of use differs depending on the item of personal data, it is desirable to distinguish and describe the purpose of use for each item of such personal data.

§5. The Name and Address of the Person Responsible for the Management of the Personal Data Concerned and, in the Case of a Legal Entity, the Name of Its Representative

433. The term 'person responsible for the management of personal data' refers to a person who accepts requests for disclosure, etc., and complaints and makes efforts to handle them; has the authority to disclose, correct, or suspend the use of the contents of personal data; and is responsible for the management of personal data, including security management. The term 'responsible person' here refers to the person who has the primary authority to receive and process complaints and disclose, correct, etc., among all joint users and does not refer to the person in charge of the internal affairs of one of the joint users. Additionally, the person responsible for the management of personal data must endeavour to keep personal data used among joint users accurate and up to date to the extent necessary to achieve the purpose of use.

§6. Restrictions on Provision to Third Parties Located in Foreign Countries (Related to Article 28 of the Act)

434. Detailed procedures for the restriction of provision to third parties located in foreign countries are set out in the Guidelines on the Act of the Protection of Personal Information ('Provision to Third Parties in Foreign Countries') [updated 17 November 2021].

435. For procedures relating to the provision of information to third parties in foreign countries, *see* 'Part VII: International Transfers'.

§7. Preparation of Records Pertaining to Third Party Provision (Related to Article 29 of the Act)

436. As a procedure to ensure the lawful provision of personal data and the proper acquisition of personal information, the obligations to prepare records pertaining to the provision of personal data to a third party and confirm when personal information is provided to a third party are imposed.

I. Procedures for Provision (to Domestic Third Parties)

437. When personal data are provided to a third party, the obligation to create a record concerning (i) the date on which the personal data were provided; (ii) the name of the third party concerned; and (iii) other matters specified in the PPC Regulations will be imposed, and the record must be preserved for the period as below specified in the PPC Regulations countable from the date it was created:

Methods of Creating Records Retention period	
If the record 'is created by an alternative method, such as a contractual agreement'	Until one year has elapsed from the date of the last provision of the personal data to which the record pertains

If the record 'is created in a batch'	Until three years have elapsed from the date of the last provision of the personal data pertaining to the record in question
In cases other than those mentioned above	Three years

438. The obligation to record is not exempted even with the consent of the person concerned. Therefore, the procedures for provision regarding personal principals with respect to the obligation to record are subject to the following cases: provision of personal data more than once in the same provision case, repeated and continuous provision of personal data between the same entities, provision as a web publication in network-related services, and other cases where it is impractical to record each and every provision at the time of provision. Where it is impractical to record every instance of processing, it is also permitted to comprehensively describe the personal data transferred to and from a particular operator within a certain period of time. In networks, consideration is given to ensuring that compliance with such obligations does not place an undue burden on operators, for example, where analysis and collation of logs can reveal the matters to be recorded. The method of creating the records may be either written or electronic data.

439. The obligation to record is subject to the provision of 'personal data'. There is no obligation to record when providing 'personal information' that is not searchable and does not fall under the category of personal data. Furthermore, the recipient is obliged to confirm how the source acquired the data, but the source is not obliged to confirm the recipient's purpose of use.

440. It should be noted that, initially, at the time of the 2015 APPI amendment, the recording obligation covered 'personal information databases'. However, the scope has changed to 'personal data' during the course of the deliberations on the bill in order to prevent evasion of the Act by carving out personal information databases and providing them to directory agencies.

441. The exceptions to the record-making obligation, where it is not imposed, are (i) when the information is provided to national governmental organs, local government agencies, or incorporated administrative agencies; (ii) when the information falls under the exceptions to the provision to third parties in each item of Article 27(1) of the Act; and (iii) when the information is provided to contractors.

II. Procedures for Provision (to Third Parties Located Abroad)

442. The definition of 'third parties' includes provision to third parties located abroad (i.e., outside Japan). Personally referable information handling companies and subsidiaries whose legal personality differs from that of the personally referable information handling business operator from which the information is provided are also third parties. On the other hand, a foreign branch of that business entity with a Japanese legal personality is not a third party.

443. In the case of provision to a third party in a foreign country, if the provision falls under either (i) provision to a country at the same level as Japan, or (ii) provision to a party that has a security control system equivalent to that of a business operator in Japan, it falls under an exemption from the application of Article 28 of the Act, so the exceptions to the obligation to record are the same as for provision to a domestic third party, and there is no obligation to record when providing information to contractors.

444. On the other hand, provision to parties that do not fall under (i) and (ii) is treated as 'provision to foreign third parties' to which the provisions of Article 28 of the Act apply. In other words, the consent of the individual must be obtained in advance to allow provision to a third party in a foreign country. Hence, the obligation to record the information is imposed even if the information is provided to a contractor.

§8. Confirmation When Receiving Third Party Provision (Related to Article 30 of the Act)

445. Detailed procedures for confirmation when receiving third-party provision are set out in the Guidelines on the Act on the Protection of Personal Information ('Obligation to Verify and Record Regarding Third Party Provision') [updated 17 November 2021].

446. When receiving personal data from a third party, the recipient must confirm (i) the name and address of the third party that is the source of the personal data, and in the case of a legal entity, the name of its representative in addition to such information; and (ii) how the personal data were acquired by the third party that is the source of the data.

447. When confirming (i) and (ii), a record must be made of the date on which the personal data were provided, the matters relating to the confirmation, and other matters stipulated by the PPC Regulations. The exceptions to the obligation to confirm when receiving the provision and the obligation to keep records are the same as the aforementioned procedure when providing the data.

448. In relation to the obligation to make efforts to 'erase' personal data as stipulated in Article 22, it is not necessary to create and preserve records concerning the erasure of personal data relating to the provision.

449. Additionally, third parties who are the source of the provision are prohibited from indicating false confirmations. It is illegal to falsify a name or address, as well as to tell the recipient that the personal information has been acquired properly while providing personal data that have been acquired illegally (violation of Article 20(1)).

§9. Principle of Prohibition of Use and Provision by Administrative Organs for Purposes Other Than the Intended Use (Article 69(1) of the Act)

450. If retained personal information is used or provided for purposes other than the specified purpose of use, it not only causes anxiety and concern to the individual due to the unexpected use and provision of the information but also increases the risk of misuse leading to invasion of privacy and violation of property rights. Therefore, the APPI prohibits administrative organs, in principle, from the use and provision of personal data for purposes other than the intended use and stipulates exceptional cases in which the use and provision of personal data for purposes other than the intended use is permitted.

451. An administrative organ may not use or provide retained personal information for purposes other than the purpose of use, except 'in accordance with laws and regulations' (Article 69(1) of the Act).

452. The same paragraph provides that the information may be used and provided for purposes other than the purpose of use if it is based on other laws and regulations, and the use and provision of the information are not obligatory under the provisions of the same paragraph. The suitability of the actual use and provision of the information must be appropriately determined in accordance with the purpose of the respective laws and regulations.

§10. Where an Administrative Organ Is Permitted to Use and Provide Information for Purposes Other Than the Purpose of Use in Exceptional Cases (Article 69(2) of the Act)

453. Administrative organs may use and provide retained personal information for purposes other than the purposes of use if they find any of the following applicable. However, even in these cases, if it is deemed that there is a risk of unjustified infringement of the rights and interests of the person or a third party, the information may not be used and provided (Article 69(2) of the Act):

(1) When the person concerned has given consent or when the information is provided to the person concerned (Item 1 of the same paragraph).
(2) When an administrative organ uses retained personal information internally to the extent necessary for the performance of a legally prescribed office or task, and when there are reasonable grounds for using the retained personal information (Item 2 of the same paragraph).

(3) Where the retained personal information is provided to another administrative organ, an incorporated administrative agency, or a local incorporated administrative agency, where the person receiving the provision uses the personal information pertaining to the provision within the limit necessary for the performance of the affairs or business prescribed by law, and where there are reasonable grounds for using the said personal information (Item 3).
(4) In addition to the cases described in (1)–(3) above, where the retained personal information is provided exclusively for the purpose of compiling statistics or academic research, where it is clearly in the interest of the individual to provide the information to a person other than the individual, or where there are other special reasons for providing the retained personal information (Item 4 of the same paragraph).

§11. REQUESTS FOR MEASURES BY ADMINISTRATIVE ORGANS TO PERSONS TO WHOM RETAINED PERSONAL INFORMATION IS PROVIDED (ARTICLE 70 OF THE ACT)

454. Where an administrative organ uses retained personal information within the scope of the purposes of use or provides retained personal information to a third party without the consent of the individual pursuant to Article 69, paragraph 2, Items 3 and 4 of the Act, the administrative organ may, when it finds it necessary, request that the person to whom the personal information is provided take measures necessary for the purpose of use, or the Act requires the recipient to take necessary measures for the appropriate management of the personal information, including the prevention of leaks of personal information (Article 70).

455. 'Necessary restrictions' or 'necessary measures' may include, in addition to limiting the purpose or method of use, limiting the scope of handlers of the retained personal information pertaining to the provision, limiting or prohibiting re-provision to third parties, specifying the handling after use such as erasure or return, and requesting required reports on the handling status of the retained personal information pertaining to the provision.

Chapter 8. Third-Party Provision: Personally Referable Information

§1. Regarding the Application of Article 31

456. A personally referable information handling business operator must not provide personally referable information to a third party without verifying that the consent of the person to whom the personally referable information pertains has been obtained in advance.

457. Article 31(1) of the APPI does not apply to the provision of personally referable information by a business operator handling personally referable information to a third party in general, but rather applies to the provision of personally referable information to a third party 'when it is expected that the third party to which the information is provided will acquire the information as personal data'. Therefore, a business operator handling personally referable information who provides personally referable information shall determine whether or not Article 31(1) of the APPI applies, based on the items of personally referable information to be provided and the handling of personally referable information by the third party to whom the information is provided.

458. With regard to examples of cases falling under the presently envisaged cases, the PPC General Guidelines provide the following examples:[71]

> (Case 1) Where the personal information handling business operator at the source explains to the third party at the recipient, who retains personal data such as customer information, that it is possible to acquire personally referable information by linking it to personal data through the use of IDs.
> (Case 2) Where the personally referable information handling business operator from the source is informed by the third party to whom the information is provided that the personally referable information will be acquired by linking it to personal data after it has been received.

459. The term 'acquiring as personal data' used in Article 31(1) of the APPI refers to a situation where the third party to whom the data are provided intends to use the data as personal data, such as by adding personally referable information to the personal data.

460. If the third party to whom the data are provided adds the provided personal data to other personal data held by the third party to whom the data are provided via an ID, the third party to whom the data are provided falls under the category of 'acquiring as personal data'.

461. If the third party to whom the information is provided does not use the provided personally referable information by directly linking it to personal data, such

71. General Guidelines, pp. 91–92.

a case does not immediately fall under the category of 'acquiring as personal data' as used herein, even if readily collated with other information held by the third party to whom the information is provided.

§2. WHERE THE PERSONALLY REFERABLE INFORMATION IS PROVIDED TO A FOREIGN THIRD PARTY

462. Where personal data are provided to a third party located in a foreign country, a business operator handling personally referable information shall, in confirming that the consent of the individual has been obtained in accordance with Article 31(1)(i) of the APPI, confirm not only that consent has been obtained but also that the following information (1)–(3) has been provided to the individual at the time when the consent is to be obtained:

(1) the name of the foreign country concerned (Related to Article 17, paragraph 2, Item 1 of the Regulations);
(2) information on the system for the protection of personal information in the foreign country concerned obtained in an appropriate and reasonable manner (related to Article 17, paragraph 2, Item 2 of the Regulations);
(3) information on measures for the protection of personal information taken by the third party (related to Article 17, paragraph 2, Item 3 of the Regulations).

463. However, in cases falling under either of the following (a) or (b), it is not necessary to confirm that the information described in (1)–(3) above has been provided when obtaining the consent of the individual:

(a) if the third party is located in a country that has a personal information protection legal system that is deemed to be at a level equivalent to that of Japan in protecting the rights and interests of individuals; in other words, a country specified by regulations as a foreign country that has a personal information protection legal system that is deemed to be at a level equivalent to that of Japan in protecting the rights and interests of individuals does not fall under the category of 'foreign country' in Article 31(1)(ii) of the APPI. For this reason, Article 31(1)(ii) of the APPI does not apply where the person to whom the personally referable information is provided is a third party located in that country;
(b) it is given that the said third party has established a legal system necessary to continuously take measures equivalent to those that should be taken by a business operator handling personal information.

§3. The Recording Obligations of Personally Referable Information Handling Business Operators

464. Where a business operator handling personally referable information has conducted a confirmation pursuant to Article 31(1) of the APPI, this business operator shall prepare a record of this confirmation.

465. In the case of continuous or repeated provision of personally referable information to a specific entity within a certain period of time, a batch of records may be prepared instead of preparing records for each individual provision.

§4. Outsourcing, Succession of Business, and Joint Use of Personally Referable Information

466. Article 27(5) provides that the provision of personal data by a business operator handling personal data does not constitute a 'third party' for the purposes of paragraphs 1–4 of Article 27 and that the transfer of personal data between the two parties does not constitute a 'third party' for the purposes of these paragraphs. The cases not restricted by the provisions are listed as those involving outsourcing, business succession, and joint use of personal data.

467. A point of this provision is whether there should be a provision exempting this provision of personally-related information to third parties in connection with outsourcing, business succession, and joint use under the provisions of Article 27(5). No exemption is provided for the provision of personally referable information to third parties.

I. Outsourcing

468. If personal data are provided to a third party as part of an outsourcing arrangement, a restriction is imposed that the entrusted person can only use such personal data to the extent necessary to achieve the purpose of use of the personal data set by the outsourced party.

469. If non-personal data are provided to a third party in the form associated with any specific provision, even if that third party matches it with other information and converts it into personal data, any transfers relating to the provision of personally referable information to third parties would not apply, even if new provisions relating to any transfers of personally referable information to third parties have been established. In this case, the transfer, which has been actioned to avoid the involvement of the individual, is not appropriate, as it can be legitimately implemented by using the outsourcing arrangement. Therefore, even the provision of personally referable information to third parties in connection with outsourcing requires obtaining the consent of the individual in accordance with the transfer relating to the provision of personally referable information to third parties.

II. Succession of Business

470. In the event of business succession, it is common for the legal relationship between the previous business entities and the parties involved, to be passed on to the new business entities, and the new business entity is subject to the restriction that it may only use the personal data it has received to the extent necessary to achieve the purposes for which the personal data were used before the succession took place, based on the premise that the provision of personal data to the new business entity does not fall under the provision of personal data to third parties as stipulated in Article 27.

471. On the other hand, the provision of non-personal data provided to a new business entity in connection with the succession of a business to be converted into personal data by matching it with other information held by the new business entity is considered to be an act beyond the scope of what is normally deemed necessary for the new business operator to continue to carry out the business activities of the business before the succession. Therefore, such acts are considered to fall under this provision, and thus, it is not appropriate to construct the provision mechanism relating to the transfer of personally referable information to third parties, as this would defeat the purpose of establishing the article. Therefore, even in the case of any transfer of personally referable information to a third party in connection with business succession, it is deemed a requirement to obtain the consent of the individual concerned in accordance with the provisions relating to the transfer of personally referable information to a third party.

III. Joint Use

472. If personal data are provided to a third party in conjunction with joint use, the recipient may only use such personal data to the extent necessary to achieve the pre-determined purpose of the joint use and may not exceed the purpose specified in accordance with Article 17(1), subject to the restriction that the recipient may only use such personal data to the extent necessary to achieve the purpose of the joint use imposed.

473. On the other hand, since the personally referable information is generally non-personal information in the first place at the source, and the purpose of use under Article 17(1) itself does not exist, it does not fit the scheme of joint use. Therefore, even if it is necessary to transfer personally referable information to a third party to contribute to the achievement of a common purpose within a specific group, it is required that the consent of the individual concerned be obtained, in accordance with the provisions relating to the transfer of personally referable information to a third party.

Chapter 9. Public Disclosure Items Relating to Retained Personal Data

§1. Public Disclose Items Relating to Retained Personal Data (Article 32 of the Act)

474. With regard to retained personal data, personal information handling business operators must make the following information indicated in (1)–(5) below available to the individual (including responses without delay at the request of the individual):

(1) Name and address of the personal information handling business operator and, in the case of a legal entity, the name of its representative.
(2) The purpose of use of all retained personal data.
(3) Procedures for responding to a request for notification of the purpose of use or a request for disclosure of retained personal data, and the amount of the fee for a request for notification of the purpose of use or a request for disclosure of retained personal data (limited to cases where it has been determined).
(4) Measures taken for the secure management of retained personal data (except those which may hinder the secure management of the retained personal data concerned by making them accessible to the individual).
(5) A contact for complaints about the handling of retained personal data.

475. Additionally, personal information handling business operators shall, except in the following cases (1)–(4), notify the individual concerned without delay when the individual concerned requests to be notified of the purpose of use of retained personal data that identify said individual. If the personal information handling business operator decides not to notify the person, it shall notify the person to that effect without delay:

(1) Where the purpose of use of retained personal data identifying the individual is clear as a result of the measures in (1) above (Article 32(1) of the Act).
(2) Where notifying the person of the purpose of use or making it public is likely to harm the life, body, property, or other rights or interests of the person or a third party (Article 21(4)(i) of the Act).
(3) Where notification or publication of the purposes of use to the individual is likely to infringe the rights or interests of the relevant personal information handling business operator (Article 21, paragraph 4, Item 2 of the Act).
(4) Where it is necessary to obtain the cooperation of a private company in order for a government organ to carry out affairs prescribed by law, and to notify the person of the purpose of use of retained personal data received from the government organ or to make it public is likely to impede the performance of those affairs, render obtaining the consent of the person therefore impossible (Article 21(4), Item 3 of the Act).

§2. Disclosure of Retained Personal Data (Related to Article 33(1)–(4) of the Act)

476. The right to disclose personal information covers data recorded as 'retained personal data'.

477. When a personal information handling business operator receives a request from an individual for the disclosure of retained personal data identifying that individual (including informing the individual to that effect if the data do not exist), it shall disclose the retained personal data to the individual concerned without delay by providing electromagnetic records, by delivering documents, or via any other method requested by the individual concerned from among the methods specified by the business operator.

478. Disclosure may be made via the method requested by the person in question. However, if the person who made the request for disclosure has not specified any particular method of disclosure and has not objected to the method presented by the personal information handling business operator, disclosure may be made via the method presented by the business operator.

479. Disclosure may be carried out by means of providing electronic data as well as by means of paper documents. As for the method of providing electronic data, the personal information handling business operator may specify the specific method, such as file format and recording medium. From the perspective of improving the convenience of the principals in using retained personal data obtained through a disclosure request, it is desirable to respond to the principals' request as far as possible, including by providing the data in a format that is readable and searchable and, where technically feasible, in a format that can be transferred to other operators. Additionally, when it is difficult to disclose using the method requested by the principals, it is preferable to request a change to a method that the personal information handling business operator can handle, rather than immediately disclosing in writing.

480. The PPC General Guidelines provide the following examples of specific disclosure methods,[72] although it is possible to indicate in advance the methods and media that personal information handling business operators can use in the written form to be submitted when requesting disclosure:

[Examples of methods by providing electromagnetic records]:

(Case 1) Storing electromagnetic records on a medium such as a CD-ROM and sending the medium by post.
(Case 2) By attaching the electromagnetic record to an e-mail.
(Case 3) Downloading electromagnetic records on a website such as a members-only website.

72. General Guidelines, pp. 124–125.

[Other methods as stipulated by the personal information handling business operator]:

> (Case 1) Listening to audio data at a location designated by the personal information handling business operator.
> (Case 2) Inspection of documents at a location designated by the personal information handling business operator.

[Examples of cases in which disclosure by such methods is difficult]:

> (Case 1) Where the person requests disclosure by providing electromagnetic records and the personal information handling business operator has to carry out large-scale system modifications in order to respond to the request for disclosure.
> (Case 2) Where the person requests disclosure by providing electromagnetic records, and it is difficult for small and medium enterprises that manage personal information and books and records in writing to respond to the provision of electromagnetic records.

481. However, if disclosure would cause any of the following (I)–(III) to apply, the small and medium enterprises may not disclose all or part of the personal data, but if the decision not to disclose is made as a result of this, or if the retained personal data pertaining to the request do not exist, the small and medium enterprises shall notify the person to that effect without delay. Furthermore, if it is difficult to disclose using the method requested by the principals, the person(s) shall be notified to that effect, and disclosure shall be carried out by way of delivery of a written document.

I. Where There Is a Risk of Harm to the Life, Body, Property, or Other Rights or Interests of the Individual Concerned or a Third Party

482. The PPC Guidelines provide, as a specific example,[73] that 'disclosure of the name of a disease, etc., to a patient at a medical institution may result in the deterioration of the patient's physical or mental condition'.

II. Where There Is a Risk of a Significant Hindrance to the Proper Conduct of the Personal Information Handling Business Operator's Business

483. If the disclosure of retained personal data to the person is likely to cause significant hindrance to the proper conduct of the personal information handling

73. General Guidelines, p. 125.

business operator's business, the retained personal data concerned may not be disclosed in whole or in part. Note that cases falling under the category of 'threat of significant hindrance' are limited to exceptional cases where there is a threat of more serious hindrance, rather than a mere hindrance, to the performance of the personal information handling business operator's business, and this is generally not the case simply because the retained personal data to be disclosed are voluminous.

484. The PPC General Guidelines provide the following specific examples:[74]

> (Case 1) Where disclosure of all scoring information by the examining authority is likely to cause significant hindrance to the maintenance of the examination system.
> (Case 2) Where there is a risk of significant obstacles to business operations, such as when the same person repeatedly requests disclosure of the same details requiring complex responses, effectively occupying the enquiry desk and making it impossible to handle other enquiries.
> (Case 3) Where there is a risk of a significant hindrance to business operations by daring to request in writing data such as audio and video files that are appropriate for the provision of electromagnetic records.

III. Where It Would Violate Other Laws and Regulations

485. Where disclosure of retained personal data to the person concerned would violate other laws and regulations, all or part of the retained personal data concerned may not be disclosed, for example, where disclosure would violate Article 134 of the Criminal Code (Act No. 45 of 1907) (crime of revealing secrets) or Article 4 of the Telecommunications Business Act (Act No. 86 of 1984) (protection of confidentiality of communications).

486. If the provisions of other laws and regulations require the disclosure of retained personal data identifying the person concerned using a method equivalent to the method prescribed in the main clause of Article 33(2) of the Act, the provisions of Article 33(1) and (2) of the Act do not apply, and the provisions of such other laws and regulations shall apply (Article 33(4) of the Act).

487. The PPC General Guidelines provide a specific example:[75]

> When the registration enforcement body stipulated in Article 19 of the Act on Special Measures for the Proper Operation of Taxi Services (Act No. 75 of 1970) responds to a request for the issuance or inspection of a certified copy of the original register pertaining to a registered driver in accordance with Articles 12 and 19 of that Act.

---

74. *Ibid.*
75. *Ibid.*

§3. Disclosure of Records Provided to Third Parties (Article 33(5), Paragraphs 1–3 of the Act)

488. Personal information handling business operators are obliged to record the necessary information when they provide personal data to third parties. Third-party provision records refer to the records referred to in Articles 29(1) and 30(3) of the Act, excluding those listed in (1)–(4) below:

(1) Records which are likely to cause harm to the life, body, or property of the person concerned or a third party if the existence or non-existence of such records is revealed, for example,[76] records created when an organisation aiming to support crime victims or prevent child abuse are provided with personal data in which the perpetrator is the person in question.
(2) Records which may encourage or induce illegal or unjust acts by revealing the existence or non-existence of such records, for example,[77] records created in cases where personal data are provided by a person who falls under the category of anti-social forces, such as organised crime groups, in order to prevent damage from unjustified demands by such forces and groups.
(3) Records which are likely to harm national security, damage relations of trust with other countries or international organisations, or be disadvantageous in negotiations with other countries or international organisations if the existence or non-existence of such records is revealed, for example,[78] records created for VIP security when personal data relating to records of the behaviour of the VIP as the person in question are provided.
(4) Records which may hinder the prevention, suppression, or investigation of crimes or the maintenance of other public safety and order if the existence or non-existence of such records is revealed, for example,[79] records created in cases where personal data on the offender as the person in question have been provided to assist the police in criminal investigations, based on consent acquired in advance.

489. Personal information handling business operators shall disclose (including informing the individual to that effect if it does not exist) the record of the provision of personal data to a third party pertaining to personal data identifying the individual concerned.

490. When a personal information handling business operator discloses a third-party record of provision to the individual, it is sufficient to disclose the matters considered to be matters of record under the APPI in the manner requested by the individual, and it is not necessary to disclose any other matters. For example, if the record is prepared by alternative means to a contract, it is sufficient to extract the

76. General Guidelines, p. 127.
77. General Guidelines, pp. 127–128.
78. General Guidelines, p. 128.
79. *Ibid.*

matters in the contract that are recordable matters and disclose them in the manner requested by the individual, and it is not necessary to disclose the contract itself.

491. If any of the following (1)–(3) applies as a result of disclosing a third-party record, the third-party record may not be disclosed in whole or in part, but when a decision not to disclose is made or when the third-party record pertaining to the request does not exist, the person concerned must be notified to that effect without delay. If it is difficult to disclose the information via the method requested by the person, the person shall be notified to that effect, and the disclosure shall be made by way of delivery of a written document:

(1) Where there is a risk of harm to the life, body, property, or other rights or interests of the individual or a third party.
If disclosure of a third-party record to the person is likely to harm the life, body, property, or other rights and interests of the person or a third party, the business operator may not disclose all or part of the third-party record in question.
The PPC General Guidelines provide the following specific examples:[80]

(Case 1) Where the third-party record contains a personal data item indicating that the individual has an incurable disease, and disclosure of this record will aggravate the mental or physical condition of the patient concerned.
(Case 2) Where the name and related personal information of a representative of a company are provided as part of corporate information used for credit decisions, and a record of provision to a third party is created, and disclosure of the record of provision to a third party may result in confidential information including the fact that the third party receiving the information is making credit decisions, considering an investment, or selecting business partners.

(2) Where there is a risk of a significant hindrance to the proper conduct of the personal information handling business operator's business.
Where there is a risk that disclosure of the third-party provision record to the person concerned may cause significant hindrance to the proper conduct of the personal information handling business operator's business, the third-party provision record concerned may not be disclosed in whole or in part. Even if the fact that the business relationship with another business is contractually confidential information, the disclosure of the record itself does not immediately fall under this category and must be determined on a case-by-case basis:
(3) Where there is a breach of other laws and regulations.

492. If disclosure of the third-party record to the person concerned would violate other laws and regulations, the third-party record may not be disclosed in whole or in part, for example, where disclosure would violate Article 134 (crime of revealing secrets) of the Criminal Code (Act No. 45 of 1907).

80. General Guidelines, p. 130.

§4. Correction of Retained Personal Data (Article 34 of the Act)

493. When a personal information handling business operator receives a request from an individual to correct, add to, or delete the content of retained personal data identifying the individual on the grounds that the data contain an error or are somehow inaccurate, the personal information handling business operator shall comply with the request. If a request for correction, addition, or deletion is received, the business operator shall conduct the necessary investigation without delay to the extent necessary to achieve the purpose of use and, in principle, make the correction based on the results.

494. The provisions of the Act provide separately for 'deletion' and 'erasure'. 'Deletion' refers to the removal of unnecessary information. 'Erasure' is a procedure provided for by Article 35 of the Act that means making retained personal data unusable as retained personal data; 'erasure' includes not only deleting the data concerned but also making it impossible to identify specific individuals from the data concerned.

495. Additionally, when a personal information handling business operator has made a correction to all or part of the contents of the retained personal data pertaining to a request pursuant to Article 34(2) of the Act or has decided not to make a correction, it shall, without delay, notify the person to that effect (including the details of the correction when it has made the correction). The retained personal data holder shall notify the individual of this fact (including the details of the correction) without delay.

496. Additionally, where special procedures are provided in other laws and regulations with regard to the correction of the content of retained personal data, the provisions of Article 34(1) and (2) of the Act shall not apply, and the provisions of such other laws and regulations shall apply.

497. With regard to the relationship between this article and cases where a person requests the correction, etc., of retained personal data identifying that person through judicial action, this shall be handled in accordance with the procedure in 'Advance Request for Judicial Action' of the Guidelines.

§5. Suspension of Use of Retained Personal Data (Related to Article 35 of the Act)

I. Requirements for Suspension of Use

498. In cases falling under any of the following (A)–(C), personal information handling business operators must cease using or erase retained personal data or suspend provision to a third party.

A. Suspension of Use in Case of Violation of the Act

499. A personal information handling business operator shall cease to use retained personal data identifying an individual in the event that the personal information is used for a purpose other than that for which it was originally intended without the consent of the individual in breach of Article 18 of the Act, or is used inappropriately in breach of Article 19 of the Act, or is obtained through deception or other wrongful means in breach of Article 20 of the Act, or is used in a way that does not comply with the provisions of Article 19 of the Act or is used in a manner that is not appropriate for the individual in question.

B. Suspension of Provision to Third Parties in Case of Violation of the Act

500. Where a personal information handling business operator receives a request from a data subject for the cessation of the provision of retained personal data identifying that individual to a third party on the grounds that such retained personal data are being provided to a third party without the consent of the individual in violation of Article 27(1) or 28 of the Act, and the personal information handling business operator finds that there are grounds for the request, the provision of the personal data to a third party must be stopped without delay.

C. Cessation of Use or Cessation of Provision to Third Parties When the Requirements of Article 35(5) of the Act Are Met

501. Personal information handling business operators must, in principle, cease use or cease provision to third parties without delay in cases where any of the following (i)–(iii) applies.

(i) When there is no longer a need to use the information

502. Where a personal information handling business operator receives a request from an individual for the cessation of use or cessation of provision to third parties of retained personal data identifying that individual on the grounds that the personal information handling business operator no longer needs to use that retained personal data, and where it is found that there are grounds for that request, the personal information handling business operator shall, in principle, suspend the use, etc., or cease provision to a third party without delay.

503. The term 'no longer needed by the personal information handling business operator' means, as in Article 22 of the Act, that the retained personal data concerned are no longer needed, i.e., when the purpose of use has been achieved and no reasonable grounds exist for retaining the retained personal data concerned in relation to that purpose, or when the purpose of use has not been achieved but the retained personal data concerned are no longer needed on the premise of the purpose of use. In other words, when the purpose of use has not been achieved, but the business on which the purpose is premised has itself ceased.

504. The PPC General Guidelines provide the following specific examples:[81]

[Cases in which suspension of use or provision to a third party is permitted on the grounds that there is no longer a need to use the information]:

(Case 1) Where a person requests the deletion of information held by a personal information handling business operator for the purpose of sending direct mail after the business operator has ceased sending direct mail.
(Case 2) Where the person requests erasure of information held by a personal information handling business operator for telemarketing purposes after the business operator has ceased telemarketing.
(Case 3) Where the person requests that the personal information handling business operator ceases to use the information of a raffle entrant whose personal information was held for the purpose of sending a raffle prize after the prize has been sent and a reasonable period of time has elapsed to deal with the non-delivery of the prize has passed.
(Case 4) Where the individual requests the suspension of use of the information of an applicant for employment who has not been employed after a reasonable period of time has elapsed to respond to re-application of the person concerned.

(ii) When the situation stipulated in the main clause of Article 26(1) of the Act concerning retained personal data identifying the person in question has arisen

505. Where a personal information handling business operator receives a request from an individual for the suspension of use or the suspension of provision to a third party of retained personal data identifying the individual on the grounds that a situation prescribed in the main clause of Article 26(1) of the Act has occurred, and it is found that the request has grounds, the personal information handling business operator shall, as a rule, notify the individual without delay of such request. In principle, the suspension of use, etc., or the cessation of provision to a third party shall be carried out without delay.

506. The term 'a situation prescribed in the main clause of Article 26(1) of the APPI pertaining to retained personal data identifying the person concerned' means that a leakage incident prescribed in the main clause of Article 26(1) of the APPI has occurred.

81. General Guidelines, p. 134.

(iii) Where the rights or legitimate interests of the person concerned are likely to be harmed

507. Where a personal information handling business operator receives a request from an individual for the cessation of use or cessation of provision to a third party of retained personal data identifying the individual on the grounds that the individual's rights or legitimate interests are likely to be impaired by the handling of such retained personal data, and it is found that there are grounds for such a request, the personal information handling business operator shall, in principle, cease the use or provision of such personal data without delay. The Data Protection Law shall be applied to all personal data held by the Data Protection Agency.

508. The term 'where the rights or legitimate interests of the person are likely to be prejudiced' means where there are legitimate interests deserving protection in light of the purpose of the Act, which are likely to be infringed.

509. With regard to legitimate interests, whether they are 'legitimate' or not is determined by the relationship with the other party and the personal information handling business operator, and unless the personal information handling business operator has special circumstances that outweigh the need to protect the person's rights and interests, the personal information handling business operator must respond to the request. In determining whether there are special circumstances that outweigh the need to protect the rights and interests of the person, the following circumstances are to be taken into account. The PPC General Guidelines give the following examples:[82]

(a) circumstances in which the retained personal data concerned are handled in order to protect the life, body, property, or other rights and interests of the person concerned or a third party;
(b) circumstances in which the retained personal data concerned are handled in order to comply with the law;
(c) circumstances in which the retained personal data concerned are handled in order to fulfil obligations relating to a contract;
(d) circumstances in which the retained personal data concerned are handled in an illegal or unjustifiable manner;
(e) circumstances in which the retained personal data concerned are handled for the purpose of legal assertion, exercise, or defence.

510. The PPC General Guidelines also provide the following examples of cases[83] in which suspension of use, etc., or suspension of provision to a third party is considered to be permitted on the basis that the rights or legitimate interests of the individual may be prejudiced:

82. General Guidelines, p. 136.
83. General Guidelines, p. 135.

> (Case 1) Where a person who has received direct mailings requests the suspension of use, etc., because personal information handling business operators repeatedly send direct mailings despite the fact that the person has indicated his or her intention to request the suspension of sending direct mailings.
> (Case 2) Where a person who has received telemarketing calls requests that the personal information handling business operator stop using principals' personal information because the operator repeatedly engages in telemarketing with respect to the person in question, despite the person having indicated the principals' intention to request that the telemarketing calls be stopped.
> (Case 3) Where the individual requests the suspension of use, etc., because the personal information handling business operator has not taken sufficient security control measures, and there is a risk that the retained personal data identifying the individual may be leaked.
> (Case 4) Where the personal information handling business operator is providing personal information to a third party in violation of Article 27(1) of the Act, and there is a risk that retained personal data identifying the individual concerned may also be provided without the consent of the individual, and the individual requests the suspension of use, etc.
> (Case 5) Where a personal information handling business operator posts information pertaining to a retired employee on its website as if the employee were still an employee of the company, and the person requests the suspension of use as this may cause a disadvantage to the person.

511. Furthermore, the PPC General Guidelines provide the following cases as examples[84] where suspension of use or suspension of provision to a third party is not considered acceptable because there is no risk of harm to the rights or legitimate interests of the person:

> (Case 1) Where a telephone subscriber requests that the telephone company suspend the use of information necessary for billing in order to avoid paying telephone bills.
> (Case 2) Cases where a person who has made an anonymous posting on the Internet requests that the provider stop using the connection authentication logs, etc., held by the provider in order to avoid identification of the sender and subsequent claims for damages through a request for disclosure of sender's information.
> (Case 3) When a person who has been forcibly withdrawn from a service for violating the terms of use in the past requests that the personal information handling business operator providing the service suspend the use of user information, including the fact that the person has been forcibly withdrawn, in order to resume using the service.
> (Case 4) Where a person who has difficulty obtaining a new loan due to loan

84. General Guidelines, p. 136.

screening based on past credit information requests that the personal information handling business operator holding the relevant credit information suspend the use, etc., of the credit information necessary for the current screening or suspend the provision of the credit information to a third party, in order to obtain a new loan.

(iv) To the Extent Necessary to Prevent Infringement of the Person's Rights and Interests

512. In the case of suspension of use or suspension of provision to a third party when the requirements of Article 35(5) of the Act are met, the personal information handling business operator must suspend use, etc., or suspend provision to a third party to the extent necessary to prevent infringement of the rights and interests of the individual.

513. The PPC General Guidelines provide the following examples[85] as possible responses to a request from the individual to the extent necessary to prevent infringement of the rights and interests of the individual:

> (Case 1) Where a person requests the suspension of use of all retained personal data, but only some of the retained personal data are to be used to prevent the possible infringement of the person's rights and interests that may arise from the cessation of use of some retained personal data.
> (Case 2) Where a request is made to erase retained personal data on the grounds that the data have been provided to a third party in violation of Article 27(1) of the Act, and the suspension of use or the suspension of provision to a third party can prevent a possible infringement of the rights and interests of the person in question, the request is dealt with by suspending the use or the provision to a third party.

(v) Alternative Measures Necessary to Protect the Individual's Rights and Interests

514. Even if the requirements for cessation of use are met, if it is 'difficult' to cease use or provision to a third party, a response entailing the implementation of alternative measures necessary to protect the rights and interests of the person is permitted. This 'difficulty' may include cases where the suspension of use or provision to a third party would require significant costs, as well as cases where the personal information handling business operator needs the retained personal data for its legitimate business activities.

85. General Guidelines, p. 137.

515. Alternative measures may vary depending on the case, but they must respond to the threat of infringement of the rights and interests of the person in question and must contribute to the protection of the rights and interests of the person in question.

516. The PPC General Guidelines provide the following examples[86] as possible alternative measures necessary to protect the individual's rights and interests:

> (Case 1) Promising to make corrections when reprinting a list of names already on the market and paying money, if necessary, on the grounds that the reprinting and collection of a list of names already on the market would require a large amount of money.
> (Case 2) Where a serious leakage that is the subject of a report to the PPC has occurred, and it is difficult to stop the use of the personal information because the contract with the person concerned is still in force, and necessary and appropriate preventive measures are taken to ensure that the leakage will not occur again in the future.
> (Case 3) Where, instead of erasing without delay retained personal data required to be retained under other laws and regulations, the business operator promises to erase the data after the end of the retention period stipulated by such laws and regulatio(n.

517. When a personal information handling business operator has suspended the use or made a decision not to suspend the use of personal information in accordance with the above, or when it has suspended the provision of personal information to a third party or made a decision not to suspend the provision of personal information to a third party, it must notify the individual to that effect without delay.

518. Additionally, the relationship between this article and cases where a person requests the cessation of use, etc., or cessation of provision to a third party of retained personal data identifying that person through a judicial action is set out in 3-8-9 ('Advance Request for Judicial Action').

(vi) Explanation of Reasons (Related to Article 36 of the Act), Procedures for Responding to Requests for Disclosure, etc., (Related to Article 37 of the Act), and Fees (Related to Article 38 of the Act)

519. A personal information handling business operator may respond to a request for notification of the purpose of use of retained personal data; a request concerning disclosure, correction, suspension of use or suspension of provision to a third party of retained personal data; or a request concerning disclosure of a record of provision to a third party; in the event that the operator notifies the individual that it will not take a measure or will take a measure different from the requested measure, the operator shall endeavour to explain to the individual the reasons for such a decision.

---

86. General Guidelines, pp. 137–138.

520. The procedures and fees for responding to requests for disclosure are set out in detail in the PPC General Guidelines.[87]

(vii) Advance Requests for Judicial Action (Related to Article 39 of the Act)

521. When a person intends to file a judicial action against a personal information handling business operator for a request for disclosure, correction, suspension of use or suspension of provision to a third party with respect to retained personal data, or for disclosure of a record of provision to a third party pertaining to personal data identifying the person, the person must make said request outside court in advance to the operator. The said action may not be filed until two weeks have elapsed from the date on which the said request reached the personal information handling business operator.

522. However, when the personal information handling business operator refuses said extra-judicial request, a judicial action pertaining to said request may be filed before two weeks have elapsed.

87. General Guidelines, p. 142.

Chapter 10. Admin Orgs': Disclosure/Correction/Utilisation Cease

523. Apart from business operators' disclosure obligation, the APPI establishes a system of requests for disclosure, correction, and utilisation cease as an important mechanism for ensuring the accuracy and proper handling of personal information about oneself held by administrative organs. A request may be made to an administrative organ for the disclosure, etc., of retained personal information about oneself as the principal regarding information held by the administrative organ to which the said organ belongs.

524. Additionally, pursuant to Article 123(2) of the Act, the provisions of Chapter 5, section 4 ('Disclosure, Correction, and Utilisation Cease') of the Act shall apply to the handling by the legal entities listed in Annex 2 of the Act as if they were handled by an incorporated administrative agency.

Chapter 11. Disclosure

§1. Subjects of Disclosure Requests

525. A request for disclosure may be made by all natural persons, including not only Japanese citizens but also foreign nationals. Additionally, requests by a legal representative of a minor or an adult ward or a representative authorised by the principal are permitted (Article 76 (1) and (2) of the Act).

§2. Retained Personal Information Subject to a Disclosure Request

526. The information subject to a disclosure request is considered to be 'retained personal information about the person concerned' (Article 76(1) of the Act).

527. The provisions of Chapter 5, section 4 of the Act are not applicable to retained personal information pertaining to the trial of a criminal case or the execution of a sentence (Article 122(1) of the Act), even if the retained personal information refers to oneself as the principal person. Additionally, among the retained personal information recorded in administrative documents exclusively recording non-disclosable information as prescribed in Article 5 of the Administrative Organ Information Disclosure Act or Article 5 of the Incorporated Administrative Agency Information Disclosure Act, regarding those that have not yet been classified or otherwise arranged and with respect to which it is extremely difficult to search for specific retained personal information because there is a significantly large amount of information pertaining to the same purpose of use, the provisions pertaining to disclosure (excluding those pertaining to requests for examination) are not deemed to hold with respect to administrative organs and are subject to discipline at the stage of being organised (Article 122(2) of the Act).

§3. Obligation to Disclose

528. Administrative organs must disclose the retained personal information pertaining to a disclosure request, except where the retained personal information contains non-disclosable information (Article 78 of the Act).

529. 'Non-disclosable information' is typologically defined in the items of the same article, focusing on the interests to be protected by non-disclosure, in conformity with the composition of non-disclosable information in the national information disclosure legislation, and when disclosing certain retained personal information, it must be confirmed that it does not fall under any of the non-disclosable information in the items of the same article.

530. The types of non-disclosable information specified by the APPI are as follows (Article 78 of the Act):

(1) Information which is likely to harm the life, health, livelihood, or property of the person having made the disclosure request (hereinafter referred to as the 'disclosure requester'; in cases where an agent requests disclosure on behalf of the principal in accordance with Article 76(2) of the Act, it means 'the principal') (Article 78(1) of the Act).

(2) Personal information concerning a party other than the disclosure requester (excluding information concerning the business of an individual who operates a business) and information that contains a personal identification code or an individual identification code, or information that cannot identify a specific individual other than the disclosure requester (including information that can be matched with other information to identify a specific individual other than the disclosure requester), but which, if disclosed, may still be harmful to the rights and interests of an individual other than the disclosure requester.

However, the following information is excluded (Article 78(1) of the Act):

(i) Information that can be or is expected to be known by the disclosure requester pursuant to the provisions of laws and regulations or as a matter of practice (Item (a) of the same article).

(ii) Information that is deemed necessary to be disclosed in order to protect the life, health, livelihood, or property of a person (Item (b) of the same item).

(iii) Where the individual concerned is a public official and the information pertains to the performance of this official's duties, the part of the information pertaining to the position of the public official and the details of the performance of official duties (Item (c) of the same item).

(3) In the case of a juridical person or other organisation (excluding the State, incorporated administrative agencies, local public authorities, and local incorporated administrative agencies), if the information is related to the performance of its duties, the part of the said information related to the public official's position and the content of the performance of the said duties (Item (c) of the same item).

(4) Information concerning the business of a legal person or an individual who operates a business other than the disclosure requester, or the following information concerning the business of an individual who operates a business other than the disclosure requester, which does not constitute information that is deemed necessary to be disclosed in order to protect the life, health, life, or property of a person (Item 3 of the same article):

(i) Information whose disclosure is likely to prejudice the rights, competitive position, or other legitimate interests of the said legal entity or the said individual (Item (a) of the same article).

(ii) Information that has been voluntarily provided at the request of an administrative organ on the condition that it will not be disclosed and that is not normally disclosed to legal persons or individuals, or other information for which the imposition of such conditions is reasonable in light of the nature of the information, the circumstances at the time, and other factors (Item (b) of the same article).

(5) In the case of an administrative organ's decision to disclose or not to disclose ('Disclosure Decision') pursuant to the provisions of Article 82 of the Act, information for which there are reasonable grounds for the administrative organ to consider that disclosure is likely to cause damage to national security, damage to relations of trust with other countries or international organisations, or disadvantage in negotiations with other countries or international organisations (Article 78, Item 4 of the Act).

(6) Information for which there are reasonable grounds for the administrative organ to find that disclosure is likely to hinder the prevention, suppression, or investigation of crimes, the maintenance of prosecution, the execution of punishment, or the maintenance of other public safety and order in cases where the administrative organ makes a disclosure decision (Item 5 of the same article).

(7) Information concerning deliberations, examinations, or consultations within or between state organs, incorporated administrative agencies, local government authorities, and local incorporated administrative agencies, where disclosure is likely to cause unjustified damage to the frank exchange of opinions or the neutrality of decision making, unjustified confusion among the public, or unjustified disadvantage to specific persons (Item 6 of the same article).

(8) Information concerning the affairs or business conducted by a state organ, incorporated administrative agency, local government agency, or local incorporated administrative agency, the disclosure of which is likely to cause the following risks or other risks that may hinder the proper execution of the said affairs or business due to the nature of the said affairs or business (Item 7 of the same article):

  (i) In the case where an incorporated administrative agency makes a disclosure decision and there is a risk that national security will be harmed, that relations of trust with other countries or international organisations will be damaged, or that the incorporated administrative agency will be disadvantaged in negotiations with other countries or international organisations.

  (ii) In the case where an incorporated administrative agency makes a disclosure decision and there is a risk of causing hindrance to the prevention, suppression, or investigation of crimes or the maintenance of other public safety and order.

  (iii) Risk of making it difficult to ascertain accurate facts or risk of facilitating illegal or unjust acts or of making it difficult to discover such acts in connection with affairs pertaining to audits, inspections, controls, examinations, or the imposition or collection of taxes.

  (iv) Risk of causing unjust harm to the property interests of the State, local incorporated administrative agencies, local public bodies, or local incorporated administrative agencies or their status as a party in connection with affairs pertaining to contracts, negotiations, or disputes.

(v) Risk of unreasonably impeding the fair and efficient execution of affairs pertaining to research and study.
(vi) With regard to affairs pertaining to personnel management, the risk of hindering fair and smooth personnel management.
(vii) Risk of harm to the legitimate interests of an incorporated administrative agency, a company managed by a local public entity, or a local incorporated administrative agency in the management of the business.

(i) Partial Disclosure

531. Administrative organs shall disclose partial information excluding specific information in each of the following cases (Article 79 of the Act):

(1) Where the retained personal information pertaining to the disclosure request contains non-disclosable information, and the part of the retained personal information which corresponds to the non-disclosable information can be easily classified and excluded (Article 79(1) of the Act).
(2) Where the retained personal information pertaining to the disclosure request contains information referred to in Article 78(2) of the Act (limited to information that can identify a specific individual other than the disclosure requester), if it is found that there is no risk of infringement of the rights and interests of an individual other than the disclosure requester by excluding descriptions and individual identification codes that can identify a specific individual other than the disclosure requester from the said information (Article 79(1) of the Act).

(ii) Discretionary Disclosure

532. Even if the retained personal information pertaining to a disclosure request contains non-disclosable information, if the administrative organ finds it particularly necessary in order to protect the rights and interests of the person, the administrative organ may disclose the information based on its administrative decision (Article 80 of the Act).

(iii) Information on the Existence or Non-Existence of Retained Personal Information

533. If simply clarifying the existence or non-existence of the retained personal information pertaining to a disclosure request would result in the disclosure of non-disclosable information as stipulated by the Act, it is possible to reject the disclosure request without clarifying the existence or non-existence of the retained personal information (Article 81 of the Act).

(iv) Procedures in Response to Disclosure Requests

534. In principle, the period is within thirty days from the date of a disclosure request (in cases where an amendment is requested pursuant to Article 77, paragraph 3 of the Act, the number of days required for the amendment is not included) (Articles 82(1) and (2) and 83(1) of the Act).

535. The due date for making a disclosure decision may be extended for up to thirty days in cases of administrative difficulties or other justifiable reasons (paragraph 2 of the same article). If, due to an extremely large volume of retained personal information pertaining to the disclosure request, there is a risk of a significant hindrance to the performance of the affairs by making a disclosure decision regarding all of the retained personal information within sixty days of the date of the disclosure request, a disclosure decision for a reasonable portion of the retained personal information pertaining to the disclosure request shall be made within that period, and it is sufficient to make a disclosure decision for the remaining retained personal information within a reasonable period of time (Article 84 of the Act).

536. Since the disclosure decision, etc., constitutes a disposition on an application as stipulated in the Administrative Procedure Act, each administrative organ is required to indicate the reasons for the disposition in accordance with Article 8 of the Administrative Procedure Act.

537. Additionally, in the disclosure decision, each administrative organ must provide an instruction based on the provisions of Article 82 of the Administrative Appeal Act (Act No. 68 of 2014) (instruction to the effect that a request for review may be filed) and an instruction based on the provisions of Article 46 of the Administrative Case Litigation Act (Act No. 139 of 1962) (instruction on matters concerning the filing of revocation proceedings).

(v) Transfer of Disclosure Request Cases

538. When the retained personal information pertaining to a disclosure request has been provided by an administrative organ other than that to which the administrative organ of note belongs, or when there are other justifiable grounds for making a disclosure decision in another administrative organ, the administrative organ may, upon consultation with that other administrative organ, transfer the case to that other administrative organ. The administrative organ that has transferred the case must notify the disclosure requester to that effect in writing (Article 85(1) of the Act).

539. The administrative organ that has received the transfer must make disclosure decisions on the transferred case, and any action taken by the administrative organ that has transferred the case before the transfer is deemed to have been taken by the administrative organ that has received the transfer (paragraph 2 of the same article).

540. Additionally, if the administrative organ that has received the transfer makes a disclosure decision (referring to the decision under Article 82(1) of the Act), the administrative organ that has transferred the case shall cooperate as necessary for the implementation of such disclosure (Article 85(3) of the Act).

541. The transfer of a case can be carried out between administrative organs, such as between national administrative organs and incorporated administrative agencies.

(vi) Implementation of Disclosure

542. Disclosure of retained personal information shall be carried out by inspection or delivery of a copy when the information is recorded in documents or drawings, or via a method determined by an administrative organ when the information is recorded in electromagnetic records (Article 87(1) of the Act), depending on the administrative organs where the retained personal information is recorded.

543. Administrative organs may also disclose by means of electromagnetic records, but they must make their provisions on the method of disclosure for electromagnetic records available for public inspection (paragraph 2 of the same article).

544. Additionally, the person who receives disclosure of retained personal information based on a disclosure decision must, as a general rule, within thirty days from the date of notification of the disclosure decision, offer the administrative organ that made the disclosure decision the method of implementation of the disclosure sought and other matters specified by the relevant Cabinet order (paragraphs 3 and 4 of the same article).

(vii) Coordination with the Implementation of Disclosure under Other Laws and Regulations

545. Where other laws and regulations provide for the disclosure of specific retained personal information to the disclosure requester, and the method of disclosure is identical to the method of disclosure prescribed in the main clause of Article 87(1) of the Act (when recorded in documents or drawings, by inspection or delivery of copies; when recorded in electromagnetic records, by a method prescribed by an administrative organ), the disclosure requester may request that the administrative organ disclose the information in accordance with the provisions of the other laws and regulations.

(viii) Fees Associated with Disclosure Request

546. A person making a request for disclosure must pay a fee within the scope of the actual cost, in accordance with the provisions of the relevant Cabinet order when making a request to an administrative organ, or in accordance with the provisions of the incorporated administrative agency when making a request to an incorporated administrative agency (Article 89 of the Act).

Chapter 12. Correction

§1. Subject of Correction Request

547. If a person believes that the content of certain retained personal information about principals is incorrect, the principals may make a request for the correction of said retained personal information. A request by a representative is also permitted (Article 90(1) and (2) of the Act).

§2. Retained Personal Information Subject to Correction Request

548. The information subject to a request for correction is limited to the following information among the 'retained personal information about the person concerned' (Article 90(1) of the Act):

(1) Retained personal information that has been disclosed based on a disclosure decision (Item 1 of the same paragraph).
(2) Retained personal information pertaining to a disclosure decision, which has been disclosed in accordance with the provisions of other laws and regulations under Article 88(1) of the Act (Article 90(1)(ii) of the Act).

§3. Due Date for Correction Requests

549. A request for correction must be made within ninety days from the date of disclosure of the retained personal information (Article 90(3) of the Act).

§4. Correction Obligations

550. When an administrative organ finds grounds for a correction request, it shall correct the retained personal information pertaining to the correction request to the extent necessary to achieve the purpose of use of the retained personal information (Article 92 of the Act).

551. Since a decision to make a correction or a decision not to make a correction constitutes a disposition on an application as prescribed in the Administrative Procedure Act, each administrative organ is required to take appropriate public measures, such as formulating examination criteria and publishing them on its website, in accordance with the provisions of Article 5 of the Administrative Procedure Act.

§5. Procedures for Responding to Correction Requests

552. Administrative organs shall, as a general rule, notify the effect of correction or the fact of correction within thirty days from the date of the request for correction (in cases where an amendment is requested pursuant to Article 91(3) of the Act, the number of days required for the amendment shall not be included). The administrative body shall, as a general rule, decide to make a correction or not to make a correction within thirty days from the date of the request for correction (where an amendment is requested under Article 91(3) of the Act, not including the time required for the amendment) and notify the correction requestor to that effect in writing (Articles 93(1) and (2) and 94(1) of the Act).

553. The due date for making correction decisions, etc., may be extended for up to thirty days in cases of administrative difficulties or other justifiable reasons (paragraph 2 of the same article). If a correction decision, etc., are deemed to require a long period of time, notwithstanding the provisions of Article 94 of the Act, it is sufficient to make the correction decision within a reasonable period of time, in which case the correction applicant shall be notified in writing within thirty days (Article 95 of the Act).

§6. Transfer of Correction Request Cases

554. When the retained personal information pertaining to a correction request relates to a disclosure with respect to which a disclosure decision has been made by another administrative organ to which a disclosure request has been transferred pursuant to the provision of Article 85, paragraph 3 of the Act ('Transfer of Case of Disclosure Request'), or when there are other justifiable grounds for making a correction decision, etc., at the other administrative organ, the administrative organ shall, after consultation with the other administrative organ, transfer the case to that other administrative organ (Article 96, paragraph 1 of the Act).

555. The administrative organ that has received the transfer must make the correction decision for the case which has been transferred, and any actions taken by the administrative organ that has transferred the case before the transfer are deemed to have been taken by the administrative organ that has received the transfer (paragraph 2 of the same article).

§7. Notification to the Recipient of Retained Personal Information

556. Where an administrative organ has implemented the correction of retained personal information based on a correction decision, if it finds it necessary after making an individual decision in consideration of the content of the retained personal information pertaining to the provision and the purpose of use at the recipient, it must notify the recipient of the retained personal information in writing to that effect without delay (Article 97 of the Act).

Chapter 13. Suspension of Use and Deletion

§1. Subject of Request for Suspension of Use

557. Where certain retained personal information about the person concerned is held beyond the scope necessary to achieve the purpose of use, where it is used in a way that encourages or may encourage illegal or unjust acts, where it is acquired through deception or other wrongful means, or where it is used for purposes other than the purpose of use even though the prescribed grounds do not apply, the person concerned shall be informed in writing without delay (Articles 98–103 of the Law). If the principals consider that the personal information is being used or provided for a purpose other than the purpose for which it is being used, the principals may request the cessation of use, erasure, or cessation of provision of the retained personal information in question. A request by a representative is also permitted (Article 98(1) and (2) of the Act).

§2. Retained Personal Information Subject to a Request for Suspension of Use

558. The information subject to a request for cessation of use is limited to 'retained personal information about the person in question' that has been disclosed pursuant to a disclosure decision or other legal provisions (Articles 90(1) and 98(1) of the Act).

§3. Due Date for Requests for Suspension of Use

559. A request for suspension of use must be made within ninety days from the date of disclosure of the retained personal information (Article 98(3) of the Act).

§4. Obligation to Suspend Use

560. If the administrative organ finds grounds for the suspension of use request, it must suspend the use of the retained personal information pertaining to the suspension of use request to the extent necessary to ensure the proper handling of personal information in the administrative organ to which the said administrative organ belongs (Article 100 of the Act).

561. The decision as to whether there are grounds for the request for suspension of use must be made objectively on the basis of facts, taking into consideration the affairs under the jurisdiction of the administrative organ pertaining to the request, the purpose of use of the retained personal information, and the purpose of the Act.

562. Even if it is found that there are grounds for the request for cessation of use if the cessation of use of the retained personal information concerned is likely to cause significant hindrance to the proper performance of affairs or business pertaining to the purpose of use of the retained personal information concerned due to the nature of the affairs or business, the administrative organ is not obliged to suspend the use of the personal information (Article 100 of the Act).

563. Since a decision to suspend use or a decision not to suspend use constitutes a disposition on an application as stipulated in the Administrative Procedure Act, each administrative organ is required to take appropriate public measures such as formulating examination criteria and publishing them on its website in accordance with the provisions of Article 5 of the Administrative Procedure Act.

§5. Procedures for Responding to Requests for Suspension of Use

564. Administrative organs shall, in principle, notify the suspension of use or the fact that the use will be suspended within thirty days from the date of the request (in cases where an amendment is requested pursuant to Article 99, paragraph 3 of the Act, the number of days required for the amendment shall not be included). The administrative organs shall, in principle, decide to suspend use or not to suspend use within thirty days from the date of the suspension of use request (if an amendment is requested pursuant to Article 99(3) of the Act, the number of days required for such amendment shall not be included) and notify the suspension of use requester in writing (Articles 101 and 102(1) of the Act).

565. The due date for a decision to suspend use may be extended for up to thirty days in cases of administrative difficulties or other justifiable reasons (paragraph 2 of the same article).

566. If a suspension of use decision is deemed to require a long period of time, notwithstanding the provisions of Article 102 of the Act, it is sufficient to make a suspension decision, etc., within a reasonable period of time, in which case, the suspension requester must be notified in writing within thirty days (Article 103 of the Act).

Chapter 14. Request for Review

§1. Exemptions to the Provisions on Hearing Procedures Presided over by a Hearing Examiner

567. With regard to a request for review of a disclosure decision, a correction decision, a decision to suspend use, or inaction pertaining to a disclosure request, correction request, or discontinuation of use request with respect to an administrative organ, the provisions of the Administrative Appeal Act concerning hearing procedures presided over by a hearing examiner (Articles 9, 'Hearing Examiner', 17, 'List of Persons to Serve as Hearing Examiner', and 24 of the same Act) apply ('Dismissal Decision Without Proceedings', Chapter II, section 3 'Proceedings', and section 4 'Consultation with the Administrative Appeal Board'), and the provision of Article 50, paragraph 2 ('Attachment of the Hearing Officer's Opinion When Consultation With the Administrative Appeal Board is Not Required') shall not apply (Article 104, paragraph 1 of the Act).

568. Additionally, the provisions in the Administrative Appeal Act that are to be conducted by a hearing examiner and which are necessary for the request for review of a disclosure decision, a correction decision, a decision to suspend use, or inaction related to a request for disclosure, correction, or suspension of use shall be read in accordance with the above exclusion provision (paragraph 2 of the same article).

§2. Consultation with the Information Disclosure and Personal Information Protection Board

569. The administrative organ that received the request for review shall consult the Information Disclosure and Personal Information Protection Review Board (in the case of the Board of Audit, the review board separately prescribed by law) on the request for review pertaining to a disclosure decision, correction decision, suspension of use decision, or inaction pertaining to a disclosure request, correction request, or suspension request, except when any of the following applies (section 105(1) of the Act):

(1) Where the request for review is unlawful and is to be dismissed (paragraph 1 of the same section).
(2) Where the Board, in its decision, grants the request for review in its entirety and decides to disclose all of the retained personal information pertaining to the request for review (except where a written objection to the disclosure of the retained personal information in question has been submitted) (Item 2 of said paragraph).
(3) Where the decision is to approve the request for review in its entirety and correct the retained personal information pertaining to the request for review (Item 3 of the said paragraph).

(4) Where the decision approves the request for review in its entirety and decides to suspend the use of the retained personal information pertaining to the request for review (Item 4 of the said paragraph).

570. Additionally, the administrative organ that has made the above-mentioned consultation must notify the following persons to the effect that it has made the consultation (paragraph 2 of the same article):

(1) The person requesting the review and the intervenors.
(2) The disclosure requestor, the correction requestor, or the suspension requestor.
(3) The third party who submitted a written objection to the disclosure of the retained personal information pertaining to the review request.

§3. Procedures in the Case of Dismissing a Request for Review from a Third Party

571. In any of the following cases, the administrative organ must, by applying the provisions of Article 86(3) of the Act *mutatis mutandis*, allow at least two weeks between the date of the decision on disclosure and the date of implementation of disclosure and must, immediately after the decision, notify the third party in writing of the decision made, the reasons thereof, and the date of implementation of disclosure (Article 106(1) of the Act):

(1) A decision to reject or dismiss the third party's request for review of the disclosure decision (Item 1 of the same paragraph).
(2) A decision to disclose (excluding a decision to disclose all of the retained personal information pertaining to the disclosure request) pertaining to the request for review or a determination to the effect that the request for review (excluding a determination to disclose all of the retained personal information pertaining to the request for review) shall be changed and the retained personal information pertaining to the request for review shall be disclosed (limited to cases where a third party intervenor has expressed opposition to the disclosure of information concerning that third party) (Item 2 of the same paragraph).

Chapter 15. Complaint Consultation

572. Personal information handling business operators must endeavour to handle complaints about the handling of personal information appropriately and promptly. Additionally, to handle complaints appropriately and promptly, they must endeavour to establish the necessary systems, such as setting up a complaint-consultation contact point and concomitant procedures. However, they are not obliged to comply with unreasonable demands.

573. Additionally, the personal information handling business operator must provide concerned individuals with a contact point for complaints about the handling of retained personal data, including the name of the organisation and the contact person for the resolution of complaints if the business operator handling personal data is an entity subject to an authorised personal data protection organisation.

574. To accept the offer of complaint resolution, the company shall formulate a 'policy on the promotion of personal information protection (privacy policy, privacy statement)' to build a relationship of trust with concerned individuals and ensure public confidence in its business activities, and the company shall make it public by posting it on its website or in an easily visible location in its shops, etc., It is also necessary to promote transparency in outsourced processing by, for example, clarifying whether or not outsourcing is carried out and the nature of the outsourced work.

Chapter 16. Obligations of PPI Handling Business Operators

575. The obligations of PPI, (pseudonymously processed information) handling business operators are set out in the following guidelines. For details about the guidelines and regarding the explanation of specific handling of the aforementioned information, refer to the Secretariat's Report:

Guidelines

Guidelines on the Act on the Protection of Personal Information (Pseudonymously Processed Information and Anonymously Processed Information) [Updated 17 November 2021]

Secretariat's Report

Pseudonymously Processed Information/Anonymously Processed Information: Towards the Trustworthy Utilisation of Personal Information – System (11 May 2022)

Pseudonymously Processed Information/Anonymously Processed Information: Towards the Trustworthy Utilisation of Personal Information – Case Studies (11 May 2022)

Chapter 17. Handling of PRI, PPI, and API by Administrative Organs

576. Based on the provisions on the handling of PRI, (personally referable information) and PPI, (pseudonymously processed information) in the private sector established in the 2021 Amendment Act, and taking into account the characteristics of administrative organs, the provisions on the handling of personally referable information and pseudonymously processed information by administrative organs have been developed in this Amendment Act. Additionally, as a result of the revision of the definition of 'personal information', API, (anonymously processed information) acquired by administrative organs from private entities will no longer fall under the category of personal information. Provisions on the handling of anonymously processed information in administrative organs have also been developed.

Chapter 18. Handling of PRI in Administrative Organs

577. Where an administrative organ provides PRI, (personally referable information) to a third party who is expected to acquire such information as personal information, the administrative organ may, if it deems it necessary, impose on the third party restrictions on the purpose or method of use of the personally referable information or other necessary restrictions, or impose on the third party the necessary measures to prevent the leakage of the personally referable information. The third party shall be required to take necessary measures for the prevention of leakage or other appropriate management of the personally-related information (Article 72 of the Act).

Chapter 19. Handling of PPI Within Administrative Organs

578. Administrative organs shall handle PPI, (pseudonymously processed information) that does not constitute 'personal information' as follows (Article 73 of the Act):

(1) Except where required by law, pseudonymously processed information shall not be provided to third parties (except those who have been entrusted with the handling of such pseudonymously processed information) (Article 73(1) of the Act).
(2) Necessary and appropriate measures must be taken with regard to such pseudonymously processed information to prevent leakage and otherwise to ensure the secure management of the pseudonymously processed information (Article 73(2)).
(3) Except where required by law, information relating to descriptions, etc., deleted from personal information, individual identification codes, and processing methods (e.g., deleted information) must not be acquired or the pseudonymously processed information must not be cross-checked with other information in order to identify the person whose personal information was used to create the pseudonymously processed information in question (paragraph 3 of the same article).
(4) Except where required by law, pseudonymously processed information shall not be used to send communications via telephone, post, or the general letter service operator, as prescribed in Article 2(6) of the Act on the Service of Letters by Private Business Operators (Act No. 99 of 2002), or, per the specified letter service operator prescribed in Article 2(9) of the same Act, via telegram, and the contact details and other information contained in pseudonymously processed information shall not be used for communications via facsimile or electromagnetic means (methods using electronic data processing systems or other methods using ICT, as prescribed by regulations) or to visit the residence of concerned individuals (Article 73(4) of the Act).

579. Additionally, a person whom an administrative organ has entrusted with the handling of pseudonymously processed information that does not constitute personal information (including entrustment over two or more stages) shall, when performing the entrusted operations, handle it in the same way as indicated in (1)–(4) above (Article 73(5) of the Act).

Chapter 20. Handling of API Within Administrative Organs

580. On handling API, (anonymously processed information) with respect to an administrative organ, *see* Chapter 3, 'Special Categories of Personal Data', specifically '4. Provisions on Anonymously Processed Information of an Administrative Organ'.

Part VI. Codes of Conduct and Certification

Chapter 1. The Personal Information Protection Certification System

581. As a certification system for personal information protection, the Personal Information Protection Management System – Requirements (JIS Q 15001:2017) have been established. This standard is one of the JISs notified by the Ministry of Economy, Trade and Industry (METI) after deliberation by the Japanese Industrial Standards Committee in accordance with the Industrial Standardisation Act.

582. Based on this JIS standard, a third-party certification system called the Privacy Mark is in operation.

583. In the private sector, the Guidelines for the Protection of Personal Information Pertaining to Computer Processing in the Private Sector (Ministry of International Trade and Industry Bulletin No. 98 of 4 March 1997) were established by the then MITI. As the need for the protection of personal information increased with the development of the networked society, as of 1 April 1998, the Privacy Mark System was launched as a system whereby JIPDEC certifies businesses that properly handle personal information and grants them the 'privacy mark'. The Privacy Mark System was subsequently changed from governance by the MITI guidelines, which were the standards for certification at the time the Privacy Mark System was launched, to the National Privacy Mark System (JIS) on 20 March 1999, and on 2 March 1999, the JIS Q 15001 was adopted as a national JIS standard. On 20 March 1999, JIS Q 15001 'Requirements for Compliance Programmes for the Protection of Personal Information' was established as a national standard, and this standard was used as the accreditation criteria for granting the privacy mark.

584. As of July 2022, approximately 17,000 Japanese companies have been certified. The advantage of using a third-party certification (Privacy Mark System) is that it can certify and externally state that voluntary initiatives are at an appropriate level through confirmation by a third party, so that when a principal provides personal data, the company can, by displaying the mark, confirm that it appropriately handles and protects personal information. The company can then recognise that the response it is implementing as a voluntary initiative to protect personal information is an appropriate response based on clear standards, and the company can actively promote internal initiatives aimed at maintaining and further improving this situation.

Chapter 2. Nature of JIS Q 15001

585. The Personal Information Protection Management System – Requirements (JIS Q 15001:2017) is an industrial standardisation among the JISs published by the Minister of Economy, Trade and Industry on 20 December 2017, based on the Industrial Standardisation Act and after deliberations by the Japanese Industrial Standards Committee.

586. This standard was established on 20 March 1999 as the Requirements for Compliance Programme on Personal Information Protection (JIS Q 15001:1999) and was revised for the first time in 2006.

587. As the APPI was amended in September 2015 and came into full force on 30 May 2017, the JIS standard was amended to comply with the amendment of the APPI, and the JIS standard will also be amended to comply with the 2020 amendment of the Act.

Chapter 3. Meaning of 'JIS' and 'Q'

588. 'JIS' is an abbreviation for JISs, which are national standards established in accordance with the Industrial Standardisation Law.

589. The letter of the alphabet following 'JIS' is a classification symbol indicating the content of the standard, which can refer to one of the nineteen fields indicating the classification of the given standard, such as 'C' (electronic equipment and electrical machinery) and 'S' (daily necessities). 'Q' is a symbol for 'standard substances and management systems' and indicates that this standard is classified as a management system, as indicated by the title.

590. The Industrial Standardisation Law, the law on which JIS is based, defines industrial standardisation in Article 2 as 'nationwide unification or simplification'; Article 2(2) accordingly stipulates 'production methods, design methods, drawing methods, usage methods or basic units of mineral or industrial products, or work methods or safety conditions'.

591. The personal information management system referenced in this Standard was developed on the premise of an information network society. It standardises management methods for the handling of personal information in general, with a focus on the use of computers. This Standard corresponds to the 'methods of use' of 'mineral industrial products' (computers) as defined in Article 2(2) of the Act.

Part VII. International Transfers

Chapter 1. General Principles

§1. Response to Globalisation

592. The Japanese APPI recognises that personal information has been distributed across national borders, as large amounts of information are acquired and used on a daily basis in networks. It is therefore an urgent issue pertaining to the development of the network and information society to ensure a fair and just law enforcement environment for the proper handling and protection of personal information and to maintain safe and secure handling of personal information for both business operators and consumers. Procedures in response to globalisation have thus been established. To achieve this objective, the APPI is based on the idea that uniform and effective domestic enforcement of the law as well as an enforcement system corresponding to international standards and cross-border enforcement networks are necessary. Hence, the 2015 Amendment Act established (i) the extraterritorial application of the APPI; and (ii) the procedures for the provision of information to foreign enforcement authorities and the aforementioned foreign third parties.

593. Due to the globalisation of business activities and logistics and the spread of cloud services, there are many businesses that have their bases of operation in foreign countries but provide sales and services via the Internet to the Japanese market and obtain personal information from Japanese residents. If such businesses are not covered by Japanese law, the Japanese Government will be unable to take any effective measures to protect the personal data of Japanese residents from being improperly handled, and this will mean insufficient protection for Japanese residents.

594. In some cases, it may be necessary for Japan to take measures to ensure the appropriate handling of personal information held by business operators based outside Japan. Additionally, as far as the general public who use services in Japan via Japanese telecommunications lines is concerned, it is normal to expect that, as long as these services are provided to the citizens of Japan, concomitant operations are subject to Japanese law, regardless of where the business operator is based.

595. It is important to re-emphasise, that in the light of such globalisation of business activities and the general belief that foreign laws and regulations focus the application of the law on the basis of the provision of services rather than on the basis of physical location, the scope of application of the Law has been defined to meet the normal expectations of persons residing in Japan.

§2. Extraterritorial Application (Article 171 of the Act)

I. Overview of Extraterritorial Application

596. Article 171 of the APPI provides that:

> This Act also applies in those cases where a personal information handling business operator, a pseudonymously processed information handling business operator, an anonymously processed information handling business operator, or a personally referable information handling business operator, in relation to supplying a good or service to a person in Japan, handles the personal information that has a person in Japan as the principal, personally referable information that is to be acquired as that personal information, pseudonymously processed information, or anonymously processed information produced by using that personal information, in a foreign country.

597. This article provides that the provisions of this Act shall apply, in certain cases, to foreign business operators who provide services for the Japanese market and handle personal information in a foreign country. Even if the foreign business operator acts in a foreign country, if the foreign business operator provides services for the Japanese domestic market and handles personal information that originates in Japan and is obtained through domestic systems, this personal information can be protected under Japanese law.

598. The PPC General Guidelines stipulate that a personal information handling business operator in a foreign country may, in relation to the provision of goods or services to a person in Japan, such as a resident of Japan, should handle personal information of which the person in Japan is the principal, personally referable information which is to be acquired as such personal information, or pseudonymously processed information or anonymously processed information created by using such personal information, in a foreign country. Extraterritorial application is not limited to cases where a personal information handling business operator in a foreign country acquires such information directly from the individual concerned and handles it, but also includes cases where it is provided by a third party other than the individual concerned.

II. Details of the Provisions

599. This article provides that the provisions of this Act shall apply to a business operator who provides goods or services from a foreign country to a person in Japan and when the business operator handles the personal information of a person in Japan in connection with the provision of goods or services.

600. The entity to which the Act applies under this article is defined as 'a person (limited to a business operator handling personal information) who provides goods or services from a foreign country to a person in Japan (limited to a business operator handling personal information)'.

601. 'Personal information' subject to the APPI is not limited to Japanese citizens but also includes foreign nationals (Guidelines – General Rules, Part 2, Definitions, 2-1 'Personal Information'; related to Article 2.1 of the Act).

602. A person in Japan, such as a resident of Japan, does not necessarily have to be the same as a 'person in Japan 'who is the subject of the provision of goods or services' or a 'person in Japan' whose identity is contained in the 'personal information'. For example, if a personal information handling business operator in a foreign country handles personally referable information in relation to selling a list of names containing the personal information of a person A in Japan to a person B in Japan, the personal information is subject to extraterritorial application (Guidelines, p. 166 *2).

603. 'Personal information handling business operators located in foreign countries' are not limited to business operators that only have a base of activity in a foreign country (including personal information handling business operators that have moved their base of activity from Japan to a foreign country). For example, the head office in a foreign country of a personal information handling business operator that has a branch or sales office in Japan, or a branch or sales office in a foreign country of a personal information handling business operator that has a head office in Japan are also included (Guidelines, p. 166 '1).

604. The term 'from abroad' means that the entity is providing goods or services in the territory of a foreign country. Even if a business operator has some activities in Japan, as long as these activities are located within the territory of a foreign country, it is considered that such activities are not naturally regulated by Japanese law (the so-called territotiality principle), and therefore, it is assumed that the activities in question will be regulated by Japanese law for the first time by applying this provision.

605. Second, the term 'a person who provides goods or services to a person in Japan' is used because the need to apply Japanese law to business operators in foreign countries is considered limited to cases where Japan needs to protect information, regardless of whether or not the person has paid compensation 'for the provision of goods or services',[88] i.e., where the information-holder to be protected is located in the territory of Japan, and their personal information is acquired and handled in connection with the provision of goods or services to such a person. The term 'provision of goods' means the sale or rental of tangible goods, and 'provision of services' means the sale of music or video, or information, or the provision of other services.

---

88. General Guidelines, p. 166 *3.

606. Specific examples of cases where this requirement applies are when a company has set up a website in Japanese with a person in Japan as the counterparty to the business or where a company is engaged in a business involving the sending of goods to Japan. Additionally, in cases where the service is provided via the Internet, in view of the current Internet environment where the distribution area (country) can be easily restricted, there must be a recognition of providing services to foreign countries including Japan, not only in the case where Japan is set as the distribution area but also in cases where the distribution is not restricted to the home country. In this regard, it is normal that there should be a clearly identifiable objective as well as recognition to provide services to foreign countries including Japan, and it can be said that this objective and recognition to provide fall under the category of a person who provides goods or services to a person in Japan.

III. Rules and Enforcement to Be Applied

607. If a foreign operator to which the Act applies according to Article 171 of the Act violates the APPI, the PPC may issue guidance, advice, recommendations, or orders (Guidelines, p. 166 *4).

608. Where, pursuant to this article, the provisions of this Act apply to the conduct of an undertaking in a foreign country, all of the provisions of this Act will apply. Consequently, there exist obligations to properly acquire personal data (Article 20), implement security management measures in relation to the personal data acquired (Article 23), provide personal data to third parties subject to certain conditions such as obtaining the consent of the principals (Article 27 of the Act), and respond to requests from the principals for disclosure (Articles 32–37 of the Act).

609. With regard to law enforcement by the PPC, the collection of reports, recommendations, and orders shall not be denied, but the on-site inspection of any possible infringement of the law within the territory of a foreign country is considered to be inadequate per the point of the sovereignty of the foreign country.

IV. Exemptions from Extraterritorial Application

610. Exemptions from extraterritorial application are provided for the acquisition of special care-required personal information.

611. Article 20(2) of the Act provides that a personal information handling business operator must not acquire special care-required personal information without obtaining the principals' consent in advance. However, Item 7 of the same article provides that it is not necessary to acquire the principals' consent in 'cases in which the said special care-required personal information is being opened to the public by principals, a governmental organ, a local authority, an academic research institution, a person set forth in each item of Article 57, paragraph (1) or other persons prescribed by the rules of the PPC'. Based on this provision, Article 6 of the Regulations stipulates that the persons specified by the Regulations of the Personal Information Protection Commission under Article 20(2)(vii) of the Act shall be those falling under any of the following items:

(1) Foreign governments, foreign government agencies, foreign local government agencies, or international organisations.
(2) A person who is equivalent to an academic research institution, etc., provided for in Article 16(8) of the Act in a foreign country.
(3) Persons equivalent to those listed in each item of Article 57(1) of the Act in a foreign country.

V. Other Laws with Extraterritorial Application

612. There are many examples of Japanese laws and regulations that permit extraterritorial application in the fields of (i) competition law (e.g., the Anti-Monopoly Act), (ii) securities law (e.g., the Financial Instruments and Exchange Act), (iii) criminal law (e.g., the Penal Code and the Act on Prevention of Unauthorised Computer Access), (iv) tax law, and (v) in other fields, the Act on the Proper Transmission of Specified Electronic Mail. Each of these will be elaborated on in the following paragraphs.

613. In the competition law sector, the Act on Prohibition of Private Monopolisation and Maintenance of Fair Trade (Anti-Monopoly Act) has been enacted. This law prohibits private monopolisation and unfair trade with respect to 'business operators' without any limitation in the regulations (Articles 2 and 3) and restricts companies, including foreign companies (corporations and other foreign organisations established in accordance with foreign laws and regulations, which are the same as or similar to a company), from excessive concentration of business control through shareholding (Article 9). Additionally, there is a provision on enforcement cooperation with foreign enforcement authorities (Article 43).

614. In the securities law sector, the Financial Instruments and Exchange Law prohibits foreign securities dealers operating in accordance with the laws and regulations of a foreign country from engaging in certain acts with persons located in Japan (Article 58-2) and applies a licence system to corporations incorporated under the laws and regulations of a foreign country that conduct business in a foreign country in order to engage in financial instruments debt underwriting business (Article 156-20-2). The licensee shall be obliged to maintain confidentiality (Article 156-20-7) and shall be subject to report collection and inspection by the prime minister (Article 156-20-12). Additionally, there is a provision for cooperation with foreign financial instruments regulatory authorities regarding investigations (Article 189).

615. The Japanese Penal Code provides for the application of the law to crimes committed outside Japan, including crimes of internal disturbance and counterfeiting and use of currency (Article 2). The Law on the Use of Numbers to Identify Specific Individuals in Administrative Procedures (the 'My Number Law'), which is a law related to the APPI, provides that the law shall apply even if the crime is committed outside Japan (Article 2). This law also provides for foreign criminal penalties for certain acts, such as the unlawful provision of number information (Articles 67 and 68), leakage of secrets (Article 69), and unlawful acquisition by fraud (Article 70).

616. In the taxation law sector, the Income Tax Act provides that non-residents and foreign corporations shall be subject to taxation on certain domestic source income (Article 7). Additionally, the Consumption Tax Act imposes consumption tax on any transfer of taxable assets that takes place in Japan, irrespective of whether the business is located in or outside Japan (Article 5) and determines whether or not the transfer of assets takes place in Japan based on whether or not the place of service provision is in Japan.

617. In other areas, the Act on the Legality of Transmission of Specified Electronic Mail (the Unsolicited E-mail Act) prohibits the transmission of specified electronic mail (Article 3) and has provisions on enforcement cooperation with foreign enforcement authorities (Article 30) in relation to 'senders', without any limitation in the regulations.

§3. Restrictions on Transfers to Foreign Countries (Related to Article 28 of the Act)

I. Onward Transfer to a Foreign Country

618. To be consistent with the international framework on the protection of personal information, Article 28 stipulates the procedure regarding the provision of personal data to third parties located in foreign countries. This procedure was established by the 2015 Amendment. Among the obligations of a personal information handling business operator set out by the APPI, the obligations and details of procedures to provide personal data to a third party located in a foreign country are set out in the Guidelines on the Act of the Protection of Personal Information ('Provision to Third Parties in Foreign Countries') [updated 17 November 2021]. These Guidelines are separate from the General Guidelines.

619. When a personal information handling business operator provides personal data to a third party in a foreign country, it is necessary to obtain 'the consent of the individual to the effect that the provision of personal data to a third party in a foreign country is permitted' in advance, except in cases falling under any of the following (1)–(3), in accordance with Article 28(1) of the Act:

(1) Where the third party concerned is in a country defined in the Enforcement Regulations of the Act on the Protection of Personal Information (Regulation No. 3 of the Personal Information Protection Commission, 2016) as a country with a personal information protection system recognised as being at the equivalent level as that in Japan;
(2) Where the third party concerned has established a system which conforms to the standards set out in the Regulations as a system necessary to continuously take measures equivalent to those to be taken by personal information handling business operators;
(3) Where the data transfer falls under any of the items of Article 27(1) of the Act.

620. The APPI envisages that an 'onward transfer' to a foreign country may take place in the following situations:

(1) Cross-border transfers within a business entity: the transfer of personal data obtained in Japan to a branch or base of the same business entity in a foreign country;
(2) Transfer of personal data to a third party outside Japan: where personal data obtained in Japan are transferred to a foreign country in connection with the provision of such data to a foreign third party;
(3) Transfer of personal data to a third party outside Japan: when personal data are transferred to a foreign country in conjunction with the outsourcing of all or part of the handling of personal data obtained in Japan to a foreign business entity (where the provisions of Article 27(5)(i) apply);
(4) When personal data are transferred to a foreign entity for the purpose of business succession: when personal data acquired in Japan are transferred to a foreign country in conjunction with the succession of business to a foreign business entity (where Article 27(5)(ii) applies);
(5) When personal data are transferred to a foreign country in order to be used jointly with a foreign business entity: in the event that personal data are transferred to a foreign country in conjunction with the joint use of personal data obtained within the scope of the APPI with a specific business entity, such as a group company (where Article 27(5)(iii) applies).

621. In the case of a business entity, whether it has a separate legal personality from the personal information handling business operator to which it provides personal data determines whether it constitutes a 'third party'. For example, if a Japanese company provides personal data to a local subsidiary of the said company that has acquired a business entity in a foreign country, it falls under the provision of personal data to a 'third party in a foreign country' for the said Japanese company, but if the personal data are transferred within the same legal entity, such as a local business office or branch, it does not constitute a third party provision of personal data.

622. The exchange of data between the head and branch offices within the same business or the transfer of data to a server located in a foreign country is necessary for facilitation purposes in the course of business activities. Moreover, while the transfer of personal data to a third party is permitted by the conclusion of a contract that meets certain criteria, there is no reason the exceptions that allow the transfer within the same business entity should be limited. Therefore, in cases where the cross-border transfer of personal data takes place within the same undertaking, the transfer is permitted on the basis of a guarantee that the personal data will be treated in the overseas office in the same way as the data would be treated in Japan.

II. Foreign States or Territories Specified by the Rules of the Personal Information Protection Commission as Having a System of Personal Information Protection Considered to Be of a Level Equivalent to That of Japan

623. Article 28(1) permits the transfer of personal data without the consent of the individual concerned to a country or territory that has a system of personal information protection that is sufficient to meet a level equivalent to that of Japan.

624. The EU and the United Kingdom fall under foreign countries that have a system for the protection of personal information that is recognised as being at the same level as that of Japan in protecting the rights and interests of individuals based on Article 15 of the Regulations of the APPI. The EU refers to countries defined as 'foreign countries which have a legal system for the protection of personal information that is recognised as being at the same level as that of Japan in protecting the rights and interests of individuals'. The EU does not include the United Kingdom. Therefore, to ensure smooth mutual transfer of personal data between the EU and Japan, the United Kingdom is also designated, since the European Commission's decision to recognise a country or region as having an adequate level of protection for personal data, in accordance with GDPR Article 45 of the European Commission's Mutual Adequacy Findings for Japan.

625. Clearly, the reason this article restricts the transfer of personal data to foreign countries is that the transfer may involve a recipient country or territory with a lower level of protection for personal data than Japan, which may lead to a greater risk of infringement of the rights and interests of the individual. Therefore, if the transfer is to a country or region known to have a system of personal data protection at a level comparable to that of Japan, then there is no significant risk of unforeseen infringement of the rights and interests of the individual, and allowing the transfer of personal data to such a country or region would not be contrary to the purpose of establishing this article.

626. It is possible for personal data to be transferred outside Japan without the consent of the individual concerned, in accordance with a contract with the person to whom the personal data are to be transferred, provided that this transfer meets certain criteria. The Guidelines indicate the procedure that permits the transfer of personal data to a foreign country when a contract that conforms to the standards set out in the PPC Regulations has been concluded in advance with the party to whom the personal data are to be transferred, specifically when necessary and appropriate supervision of the party to whom the personal data are to be provided is carried out, even after the transfer of the personal data.

627. In light of the fact that the previous item allows for the transfer of personal data without the consent of the individual to countries or regions that have personal data protection legal systems that are of an equivalent standard to those in Japan, it is possible that any given legal system will not allow for exceptions to be made for the conclusion of contracts, and instead, consolidate procedures for the transfer of personal data outside Japan in accordance with Item 1. However, if the period of time required to certify the system as a system of personal data protection that is equivalent to that of Japan lengthens, the transfer of personal data to that country or region will be prohibited during that period; this may impede the business activities of business operators handling personal data. It has been considered the standard legal system in the international community to ensure the proper handling of personal information and thereby the protection of the rights and interests of individuals by requiring certain contracts to be entered into and by requiring the provider to take the necessary and appropriate measures for the safe management of personal data at the recipient's end. Therefore, to ensure the same level of security management at the recipient's end as in Japan, this contract-based procedure allows for the transfer of personal data to a third party located in a foreign country, provided that the third party enters into a contract in advance that conforms to the standards set out in the PPC Regulations and that the third party is subject to necessary and appropriate supervision even after the transfer of the personal data.

III. Administrative Organs' Provision to Third Parties in Foreign Countries for Purposes Other Than the Purpose of Use (Article 71(1) of the Act)

628. When providing retained personal information to a third party in a foreign country for a purpose other than the purpose of use, an administrative organ shall, except in any of the following cases, obtain the consent of the individual concerned to the effect that the provision to the third party in the foreign country is permitted in advance:

(1) Where the third party is located in a country that is stipulated by regulation as having a personal information protection legal system recognised as being of an equivalent standard to that of Japan.
(2) Where the third party concerned has established a system that conforms to the standards stipulated by the regulations as necessary to continuously take measures equivalent to those required to be taken by personal information handling business operators.
(3) Exemption based on laws and regulations.
(4) In cases listed in Article 69(2)(iv) of the Act.

629. Additionally, where an administrative organ intends to obtain consent to allow the provision of information to a third party located in a foreign country, the following information must be provided to the individual in advance, as required by the Regulations (Article 71(2) of the Act):

(1) Name of the foreign state concerned (Article 47(2)(i) of the Regulation).
(2) Information on the system for the protection of personal information in the foreign country concerned obtained by appropriate and reasonable means (Item 2 of the said paragraph).
(3) Information on measures taken by the third party for the protection of personal information (Item 3 of the said paragraph).
(4) Other information which should be of reference to the person concerned (Article 71(2) of the Act).

630. Furthermore, where an administrative organ has provided retained personal information to a third party in a foreign country that has established a standards compliance system for a purpose other than the purpose of use, the administrative organ shall, in addition to cases based on laws and regulations and cases listed in Article 69, paragraph 2, Item 4 of the Act, ensure the continuous implementation of the corresponding measures by the third party as prescribed by regulations. In addition to taking the necessary measures to ensure the continuous implementation of the corresponding measures by the third party concerned, the following information shall, in principle, be provided to the individual concerned at the request of the individual (Article 71(3) of the Law), as specified in the Regulations:

(1) The method by which the third party concerned established the system stipulated in paragraph 1 of the same article (Article 48(3)(i) of the Regulations).
(2) An outline of the corresponding measures to be implemented by the third party concerned (Item 2 of the same paragraph).
(3) The state of implementation of the corresponding measures by the third party and the frequency and method of checking the existence or non-existence of the foreign system and its contents that may affect the implementation of the corresponding measures (Item (iii) of the said paragraph).
(4) The name of the foreign state concerned (Item 4 of the same paragraph).
(5) Existence or non-existence of a system in the foreign country that may affect the implementation of the corresponding measures by the third party and an outline of the system (Item 5 of the said paragraph).
(6) Existence or non-existence of obstacles to the implementation of the corresponding measures by the third party concerned and an outline of such obstacles (Item (vi) of the said paragraph).
(7) An outline of the measures to be taken by the relevant administrative organ in relation to the impediment referred to in (6) above (Item 7 of the same paragraph).

Chapter 2. Transfers in the Context of International Agreements

§1. Consultation on the Establishment of a Framework for the Smooth Mutual Transfer of Personal Data Between Japan and the EU

631. The PPC and the European Commission have been discussing the establishment of a framework for the smooth mutual transfer of personal data between Japan and the EU since April 2016. The final agreement was confirmed on 17 July 2018, with the EU designating Japan as adequate under Article 28 of the APPI as of 23 January 2019 and the European Commission deciding on the same day on the mutual adequacy decision for Japan under Article 45 of the GDPR thus bringing the new data transfer framework between Japan and the EU into force.

632. The EU's designation under Article 28 of the APPI is based on the following criteria per 'foreign states that have systems for the protection of personal data which are recognised as being at a level comparable to that of Japan in protecting the rights and interests of individuals' (PPC Notice No. 1 of 1991):

(1) There are laws and other norms corresponding to the provisions concerning the obligations of business operators handling personal information as set out in the Personal Information Protection Law, and a system for complying with these norms is recognised;
(2) There is an independent personal information protection agency, and the agency has secured an enforcement system to conduct the necessary supervision;
(3) Mutual understanding, coordination, and cooperation regarding the proper use of personal information and the protection of the rights and interests of individuals are possible;
(4) It is possible to establish a framework for the smooth mutual transfer of personal information while ensuring its protection;
(5) The necessity for Japan to designate the foreign state as recognised.

633. Consequently, the Supplementary Rules Under the Act on the Protection of Personal Information for the Handling of Personal Data Transferred from the EU Based on an Adequacy Decision[89] have been applied to personal data transferred from within the EU under the mutual adequacy findings since the same date.

§2. Significance of EU–Japan Mutual Adequacy Findings

634. Due to the current procedures relating to the provision of personal data from Japan to a foreign third party within the EU, it is now possible to provide

89. Supplementary Rules under the Act on the Protection of Personal Information for the Handling of Personal Data Transferred from the EU based on an Adequacy Decision.

personal data to a third party in accordance with Article 27 of the APPI (the same procedures as for the provision of personal data to a domestic third party), rather than the procedures relating to the provision of personal data to a foreign third party as set out in Article 28 of this Act, and it is now possible to transfer personal data from within the EU to Japan based on an adequacy determination in accordance with Article 45 of the GDPR in relation to restrictions on the transfer of personal data to a third country.

635. Additionally, following a request by the European Commission, it has issued a consultative document explaining the Japanese legal system for the handling of personal data transferred from the EU to a Japanese private sector entity, where such data are collected and used by a Japanese administrative body. This agreement is expected to increase the number of options for the means of transferring personal data and reduce the burden on companies. This consultation covers procedures for Japanese companies transferring personal data from the EU, as well as procedures for EU entities transferring personal data handled in Japan. The aim of the consultation is to mutually recognise the homogeneity of the two systems, rather than unilaterally recognise the EU system as meeting the EU's adequate level of protection. This would also provide an opportunity for Japanese companies to understand the purpose of the consultation and reaffirm that compliance with the obligations set out in the APPI is a prerequisite for complying with the EU's system, which is described as strict.

Part VIII. Enforcement

Chapter 1. Supervisory Authorities

§1. The Japanese Personal Information Protection Commission

636. It should be noted here that the duties of the Japanese PPC encompass the protection of the rights and interests of individuals while taking into consideration the proper and effective use of personal information, including My Number.

637. Founded in accordance with the recommendations of the APPI, the PPC is one of the most independent organs in the Japanese legal framework, with the chairperson and Commission members exercising their authority independently.

§2. Organisation of the Personal Information Protection Commission (PPC)

638. As stated above, the PPC is a highly independent body established to ensure the proper handling of personal information (including specific personal information relating to My Number). Specifically, the PPC executes the following tasks in accordance with the APPI and the Act on the Use of Numbers to Identify a Specific Individual in Administrative Procedures (Act No. 27 of 31 May 2013):

(1) Formulation and promotion of a basic policy on the protection of personal information;
(2) Supervision of the handling of personal information; the PPC provides necessary guidance and advice, collects reports, and conducts on-site inspections of businesses that handle personal information and may issue recommendations and orders for enforcement;
(3) Administrative procedures concerning authorised personal information protection organisations, which are corporations that the PPC has authorised to make voluntary efforts to promote the protection of personal information in the private sector within each industry and business field. When the PPC receives an application for accreditation from a corporation that intends to handle complaints or provide information, it accredits the corporation as an

'authorised personal information protection organisation' based on the relevant laws and regulations. It should be noted that the authorised personal information protection organisation may be subject to measures such as collection of reports and orders;

(4) Monitoring and supervision of the handling of specified personal information: The PPC provides necessary guidance and advice, collects reports, and conducts on-site inspections of administrative agencies, businesses, and any persons handling specified personal information and may issue recommendations, orders, and other measures for enforcement;

(5) Issues concerning the evaluation of the protection of specific personal information including the evaluation of the protection of specified personal information of national administrative organs, local public entities, etc., and the evaluation of the risk of information leaks, etc., prior to the possession of specified personal information files, as well as the description of countermeasures in writing in advance of publication to the general public. The Committee also prepares guidelines stipulating the contents and procedures for such evaluation and approves the evaluation reports prepared by national administrative organs on the protection of specified personal information;

(6) Administrative procedures related to complaint mediation including the answering of general questions regarding the interpretation of the APPI and its associated legal system and the provision of necessary advice and mediation regarding complaints about the handling of personal information. It should be noted also that a Personal Information Protection Law Consultation Call Centre has been established, and consultation is available there. Additionally, a My Number Complaint Mediation Desk has been set up to answer general questions about the guidelines for the handling of specific personal information relating to My Number and to provide necessary advice and mediation for complaints against any other parties;

(7) International cooperation including participation in international conferences concerning the protection of personal information: The PPC exchanges information with relevant overseas organisations and strives to build cooperative relationships;

(8) Publicity and promotional awareness: The PPC promotes the protection of personal information and its required appropriate and effective use by means of pamphlets, websites, and public information sessions;

(9) Other duties: In addition to the abovementioned, the PPC provides reports for the Japanese Diet to indicate the status of the processing of its duties under its jurisdiction and conducts necessary surveys and research.

Chapter 2. Composition

639. The PPC is composed of the chairperson and eight Commission members appointed by the prime minister with the consent of both Houses of the Japanese Diet. The term of office of the chairperson and the Commission members is five years. The chairperson and commission members exercise their authority independently and should meet the following personal criteria:

640. A person who has knowledge of and experience in the protection of and shows appropriate and effective use of personal information and/or has knowledge of/experience in the protection of consumers and/or has knowledge of/experience in information processing technology and/or has knowledge of/experience in the administrative fields used in specific personal information and/or has extensive knowledge of/wide experience in matters relating to the practices of private enterprises and/or is a person recommended by federations composed of governors, mayors, and presidents of the local councils.

Chapter 3. Competence, Tasks, and Powers

§1. Law Enforcement Mechanism Provided by the APPI

I. Step-by-Step Law Enforcement Mechanism

641. The APPI stipulates a step-by-step law enforcement mechanism via the PPC in response to violations of obligations by business operators handling personal information and administrative organs that entails (1) calling for a report and on-site inspection and issuing (2) guidance and advice, (3) recommendations, and (4) orders (emergency orders). Each of these will be elaborated on in the following paragraphs:

(1) With regard to calling for a report and on-site inspections, the PPC may, to the extent necessary for the enforcement of the provisions of Chapter 4, sections 1–4 and 6 and Chapter 5 of the APPI, request the submission of necessary reports and materials from business operators handling personal information, enter the offices and other related locations of the said business operators handling personal information, ask questions concerning the handling of personal information, and inspect books and documents and other objects (Article 146, paragraph 1 and Article 156 of the Act).
(2) With regard to guidance and advice, the PPC may provide necessary guidance and advice to business operators handling personal information with regard to the handling of personal information (Articles 147 and 157).
(3) With regard to recommendations and (4) orders (emergency orders), the PPC may make recommendations (Article 148, paragraph 1 and Article 158) when it finds it necessary to do so in order to protect the rights and interests of individuals and when a business operator handling personal information who has received a recommendation fails to take measures pertaining to the recommendation without justifiable grounds. Additionally, if the business operator handling personal information that has received the recommendation fails to take measures pertaining to the recommendation without a justifiable reason, and it is found that a serious infringement of the rights and interests of individuals is imminent, an order (Article 148, paragraph 2) may be issued as a measure following the recommendation. Finally, when it is urgently necessary to take measures, an emergency order can be issued without first sending a recommendation (Article 148, paragraph 3).

642. With regard to the collection of reports and on-site inspections, a system of indirect penalties has been adopted, and a fine of not more than JPY 500,000 may be imposed on a person who makes a false response when the PPC requests a report or conducts an on-site inspection or who refuses a report or inspection (Article 182).

643. Based on the collection of these reports and on-site inspections, guidance and advice will be given and, if necessary, recommendations and orders will be issued. The effectiveness of the Final Order (and emergency order) is ensured by a system of criminal penalties, which, if violated, can result in imprisonment of up to one year or a fine of up to JPY 1 million (Article 178).

II. Limitations on the Powers of the Personal Information Protection Commission (Article 149 of the Act)

644. Article 149 confirms, in particular, in relation to the exclusionary provisions of Article 57(1), which should be clearly interpreted, that the PPC shall not interfere with freedom of expression, academic research, religion, and political activity when it collects reports, requires the submission of materials, conducts on-site inspections, and gives guidance, advice, recommendations, or orders. In light of the purport of the provisions of Article 149(1), paragraph (2) of this article provides that the PPC does not exercise authority in regard to a personal information handling business operator's act of providing personal information to a person set forth in each item of Article 57, paragraph (1), and it is limited to those cases where each person handles personal information, etc., for a respective purpose stipulated in each said item.

III. Competent Ministers (Related to Article 150 of the Act)

645. Article 150 also establishes the competent ministers of business under the APPI. In the 2015 amendment to the Act, to ensure the appropriate protection of personal information through the centralisation of expertise and prompt and appropriate cross-sectoral law enforcement, the amendment centralised the powers previously dispersed to the competent minister for each business sector into the PPC. In accordance with Article 150(1), the PPC may request necessary assistance from the minister having jurisdiction over the business.

646. The minister having jurisdiction over the business is the minister who requests the PPC's assistance in the investigation of the facts concerning business operators' handling of personal information.

IV. Cross-Border Cooperation in the Enforcement of Laws

647. Article 172(1) provides that the PPC may provide the foreign DPA enforcing those foreign laws and regulations equivalent to this Act with information recognised as contributory to fulfilling their duties.

648. The provisions of this Act may be applied in certain cases to business operators who provide services for the Japanese market without having an office, place of business, or other base of activity in Japan (known as 'foreign business operators'). However, even if the act of a foreign business operator is considered to be an illegal act in violation of the provisions of the Act, Japanese administrative organs cannot physically enter the territory of a foreign country to conduct an investigation due to the risk of infringement of sovereignty; even if a document such as a recommendation or an order is mailed within Japan, such a document will still be deemed to be 'foreign-based'. Therefore, from the viewpoint of ensuring effective enforcement, a mechanism has been established to address such cases by way of cooperation to ensure enforcement by foreign data protection authorities.

649. Therefore, the Commission will provide the enforcement authorities of the country concerned with information about the illegal acts in question and request that they enforce disciplinary action against this foreign operator to rectify any processes that have been determined to be illegal due to the extraterritorial application of the Act. It is expected that the information to be provided by the PPC will include personal information (e.g., personal information confirmed to have been leaked).

650. However, as described below, the provision of information may be restricted in some cases, such as when the information is used in a foreign country for the investigation of criminal cases or when the information is deemed likely to infringe the interests of Japan.

651. Under this article, the provision of information necessary for a foreign enforcement agency to carry out a disposition is possible, and it is left to the discretion of the foreign data protection authority whether or not to actually execute upon receiving this information.

652. The PPC may, per DPA laws and regulations relating to the protection of personal information in a foreign country, provide information that the PPC believes will contribute to the performance of the duties of the enforcement authorities concerned. For example, the PPC may inform the enforcement authority of a foreign country about the misuse or leakage abroad of the personal information of a Japanese national. This section also has the effect of generally removing the obligation of confidentiality under Article 100 of the National Public Service Act.

§2. Law Enforcement Cases

I. Examples of Enforcement Against Foreign Business Operators

653. On 22 October 2018, the PPC issued guidance to Facebook under former Articles 41 and 75 of the APPI as the first case of guidance to a foreign business operator. The content of this guidance was as follows:

(1) regarding social plug-ins (systems for adding Facebook functions to external websites), when users comment on a website using a 'Like' button provided by Facebook, user ID and access history will be sent to Facebook even if the principals do not press the buttons. Accordingly, it is the PPC's opinion that the company must provide such users with clear explanations and obtain

their consent. Additionally, the company should recognise its responsibility as a platform provider and thoroughly monitor the activities of applications on the platform;

(2) with regard to the issue of part of the personal information obtained through the personality assessment application available on Facebook having been illegally provided to Cambridge Analytica (a UK-based election-related consulting business), the information was not shared until as late as 2015. Regarding the problem that the information was provided to a related consulting firm and that the information had not been shared until 2015, the provision for the extraterritorial application did not apply retroactively because this was a case of misuse that occurred before the enforcement of the revised APPI.

654. In the case of the leakage of the personal data of 29 million people due to unauthorised access announced at the end of September 2018, it was found that user account authentication information (access tokens) was stolen through hacking by exploiting 'vulnerability in the system'. The company was required to notify the individuals concerned, investigate the cause of the problem, formulate measures to prevent recurrence and continue to report to the PPC. This was the first case where a foreign business was given guidance based on the APPI.

II. Guidance on the Distribution of Advertisements Using Captured Facial Images

655. On 30 November 2018 and 12 September 2019, the PPC issued guidance[90] to JapanTaxi Corporation under Article 41 of the APPI in relation to the issue of using a camera attached to a tablet device installed on the back of the passenger seat of the taxis to capture facial images of taxi users and then using a gender estimation function to show advertisements, including video advertisement, accordingly.

656. In relation to the use of personal information in the delivery of advertisements and the capture of facial images of passengers seated in front of tablets in taxis, the fact that a camera was used to photograph passengers and automatically determine their gender in order to select the content of advertisements displayed on the tablets in the taxis, the existence of the camera for acquiring facial images, and

90. The Personal Information Protection Commission 'Guidance based on the Act on the Protection of Personal Information' (17 Sep. 2019) states that the reason for the renewed guidance is that 'the Personal Information Protection Commission has decided to implement the guidance again, taking into account the degree of impact on the rights and interests of taxi users and the importance of the customer perspective in the business, as well as the problems with the organisational structure which took time to respond to the PPC guidance. In addition to the degree of impact on the rights and interests of taxi users and the importance of the customer perspective of the operators, the PPC has also taken into account the problems with the organisational structure that took time to respond to the guidance, and has now decided to implement it again.' In addition, the company has also received reports on other improvement measures and will continue to follow up on the policy.

the purpose of the use of the images and gender information as personal information were notified. However, it was considered that there was insufficient notification and explanation to passengers about the fact that the camera existed to acquire facial images as well as insufficient notification regarding the purpose for which the collected personal information was to be used.

657. This guidance was re-issued after the issuance of the 30 November 2018 guidance on providing taxi users with thorough and easy-to-understand explanations, as the company did not implement improvement measures until April 2019.

658. With regard to this guidance, JapanTaxi Corporation stated that 'the images used for this determination were immediately deleted in the terminal without being sent to the server after the gender determination and were not stored in any terminal or server and have not been used for any other purpose'. For this reason, the company insisted that they were not aware of the obligations to acquire personal information subject to the APPI[91] and follow the guidance of the PPC. The company has asserted that the existence of the camera and the purpose of its use are indicated and that the personal information is properly acquired and used. The notification and publication of the purpose of use have been implemented.

III. Two Separate Recommendations on the Provision of Job Offer Rejection Rates

659. On 1 August 2019,[92] *Nikkei* newspaper reported that the company Recruit Career (Chiyoda-ward, Tokyo), operator of the employment information website Riku Navi, which 800,000 job hunters use per year, had predicted job-hunting students' 'internal dismissal rate with respect to job offer[s]' without their consent and provided this information to companies conducting recruitment activities for a fee. Consequently, the PPC issued two recommendations to Recruit Career. The Ministry of Health, Labour and Welfare also issued administrative guidance to the company on 6 September 2019 under the Employment Security Act.

660. The first of the PPC's recommendations, on 26 August 2019, was based on an investigation into Recruit Career's Recruit Navi DMP Follow, which provided a 'job offer rejection rate'. The investigation resulted in recommendations based on Articles 42[93] and 41 of the APPI regarding the company's failure to take appropriate safety management measures as required under Article 20 of the Act and its provision of personal data to a third party without obtaining the necessary consent as required under Article 23(1) of the Act.

---

91. JapanTaxi Corporation (now Mobility Technologies Corporation), 'Guidance from the Personal Information Protection Commission' https://japantaxi.co.jp/news/info/2019/09/17/0110/ (17 Sep. 2019).
92. Nikkei newspaper, 'Job hunter 'decline prediction' information provided without explanation, Rikunabi [Evening Scoop]' (1 Aug. 2019).
93. Personal Information Protection Commission, 'Recommendations, etc., based on Art. 42(1) of the Act on the Protection of Personal Information' (26 Aug. 2019).

661. The facts that gave rise to the recommendation were that, together with the company's acquisition of personal information, its failure to take necessary and appropriate measures for the secure management of personal data in respect of personal information handled on commission from a number of personal information handling business operators constitutes a violation of Article 20 of the Act. Further, it was deemed unacceptable that the company did not have the necessary procedures in place to obtain consent for the provision of personal data to third parties and that the company violated Article 23(1) of the Act in that the personal data of 7,983 persons were provided to client companies without obtaining consent for the provision of personal data to third parties, together with the state of not obtaining the necessary consent from some of its members. As a matter of guidance, it was considered that the content of the privacy policy was not sufficiently clear as an explanation for the provision of personal data to third parties.

662. A second recommendation was issued on 4 December 2019.[94] The reason for the issuing of this second recommendation in December, subsequent to the aforementioned recommendation in August, was that other serious facts relating to the violation of the law were found, in addition to the facts that caused the original recommendation.

663. The fact that led to the second recommendation was that the company calculated the job offer rejection rate using cookies instead of names, which constitute personal information, and using a method that did not identify specific individuals, and provided this information to companies that used it, without obtaining consent to provide it to a third party. Recruit Career knew that the companies that received the job offer rejection rates could identify specific individuals. However, the company providing the data claimed that specific individuals could not be identified and avoided acquiring consent for the provision of personal data to third parties, thereby circumventing the purpose of the law and providing an extremely inappropriate service.

664. Additionally, due to the erroneous understanding that hashing does not constitute personal information, and despite the fact that Recruit Career could identify specific individuals, in order to avoid the obligation to acquire the consent of the individual, the companies using the service interpreted the hashed information as not constituting personal information and provided the information to Recruit Career in a manner that was not in accordance with the Act.

665. As diagramming this problem is somewhat confusing, I will summarise the structure of the illegal provision of job offer rejection rates. (1) Recruit Career receives unique IDs and cookie information from the companies that use the service, which the company cannot use to identify individuals. (2) The information Recruit Career acquired from the companies that use the service comprises unique

94. Personal Information Protection Commission, 'Administrative Measures under the Act on the Protection of Personal Information' (4 Dec. 2019).

IDs and cookie information as mentioned in (1) above, so it is non-personal information that does not fall under the category of personal information at the company. (3) Recruit Career calculates the rejection rate for each of the IDs concerned in a form that does not identify individuals and provides this information to the companies using the service as non-personal information. (4) The companies that were provided with the personal data were able to ascertain the rejection rate of job offers for specific individuals by comparing the rejection rate provided in (3) with the names associated with the IDs retained by the companies.

666. Using this system, Recruit Career provided the information as non-personal data, knowing in advance that the companies to which the information was provided would link the job offer rejection rates to specific individuals.

667. In response to this problem, the 2020 amendment to the APPI stipulated new rules on 'personally referable information', requiring that, for the third-party provision of information that does not constitute personal data at the source but is expected to become personal data at the recipient, it is necessary to confirm that the consent of the individual(s) concerned has been obtained.

IV. Order Against Illegal Posting of Personal Data on Websites

668. On 29 July 2020, the PPC issued an order under Article 42(2) of the APPI to two businesses that illegally posted the personal information of a large number of bankrupt persons on their website, ordering the businesses to immediately cease the dissemination of such information.[95]

669. The concerned website was Bankruptcy Map, where the names and addresses of bankrupt persons notified in the *Official Gazette* were made available on Google Maps, along with a link to a list of the bankrupt persons' names and addresses.

670. The facts giving rise to the order were that, in acquiring the personal information of bankrupt persons published in the *Official Gazette* as a public notice of the decision to initiate bankruptcy proceedings, the purpose of use of such personal information was not notified or announced (Article 18 of the Act), and such personal data were compiled into a database and posted on a website, constituting the provision of personal data to third parties without the consent of the individual (Article 23(1) of the Act).

671. The handling of personal information by Bankruptcy Map not only violated the provisions on notification and publication of the purpose of use of personal information and the provision of personal data to third parties but also, in view of the protection of the rights and interests of individuals, the essential problem is

95. Personal Information Protection Commission, 'Administrative Measures under the Act on the Protection of Personal Information' (29 Jul. 2020).

the use of the information by an unspecified number of recipients for a purpose that deviates significantly from the purpose for which the information on bankrupt persons was published in the *Official Gazette*. In other words, discrimination against bankrupt persons is encouraged, with the effect amplified by the provision of the information to an unspecified number of recipients (publication on the Internet). Further, the provider (operating entity) did not take sufficient measures to protect the rights and interests of the individuals concerned (measures to deter malicious use by an unspecified number of recipients).

672. In light of this, the 2020 amendment to the APPI established a new obligation to prohibit the use of personal information in a manner that may harm the rights and interests of the individual (Article 16-2 of the 2020 amended Act).

V. Guidance on Supervision of Contractors and Provision to Third Parties in Foreign Countries

673. In the current situation where personal information is handled and exchanged across national borders on a daily basis, problems arise when the management of such information is carried out across national borders. On 19 March 2021, the PPC issued a report to LINE Corporation in accordance with Article 40(1) of the APPI and conducted an on-site inspection beginning on 31 March of the same year, followed by the issuance of guidance based on Article 41 of the APPI.[96]

674. The facts giving rise to the guidance were the status of compliance with Article 22 (supervision of contractors) of the Act in relation to the outsourcing of data management to contractor operators located in China and Article 24 (restriction on provision to third parties located in foreign countries). Procedural issues were raised.

675. Many Japanese SNS users rely on LINE as a means of daily communication; hence, LINE is positioned as a substantial part of the communication infrastructure.

96. Personal Information Protection Commission, 'Administrative Measures Based on the Act on the Protection of Personal Information (LINE Corporation, 23 Apr. 2021)'; Personal Information Protection Commission, 'Handling of Personal Information at LINE Corporation' (26 Mar. 2021).

Chapter 4. Remedies

676. There has been some debate as to whether the provisions of the APPI enacted in 2003 regarding requests for disclosure are effective as a basis for exercising the right to request disclosure, as well as whether those provisions are effective as a basis for exercising the right to make a judicial request. Some judgments have denied the position of the right to request in court (Tokyo District Court, 27 June 2007, 1978, p. 27).

677. In recent years, as information dissemination and data utilisation have become popular, concern has arisen about the spread of anxiety regarding the use of personal information without the intention of the person concerned, as well as about the instantaneous and widespread diffusion of a huge amount of information. Against this backdrop, the 2015 amendments to the Personal DPA have clarified that the individual can exercise his or her right of judicial recourse if he or she so wishes, rather than leaving the matter to administrative regulations. In the 2015 amendments to the Act, a new amendment has clarified that the provisions are grounds for judicial claims.

Chapter 5. Liabilities

678. The liabilities under the APPI are provided as Obligations of a Personal Information Handling Business Operator.

Chapter 6. Penalties

679. The penal provisions of the APPI comprise the following penalties:

(i) Provision of a personal information file in which confidential information is recorded by administrative organ officials and related persons (Article 171).
(ii) Obligation to maintain confidentiality at the PPC (Article 172; for violation of Article 140, imprisonment for up to one year or a fine of up to JPY 1 million).
(iii) Violation of an order or emergency order issued by the PPC (Article 173; for violation of Article 145(2) or (3), imprisonment for up to one year or a fine of up to JPY 1 million; Article 179: a fine of up to JPY 100 million for corporations).
(iv) Offences of providing personal information databases (Article 174: imprisonment for up to one year or a fine of up to JPY 1 million; Article 179: a fine of up to JPY 100 million in the case of a juridical person).
(v) Provision or theft of retained personal information by administrative organ officials and related persons for the purpose of making illicit gains (violation of Article 175: imprisonment for up to one year or a fine of up to JPY 500,000).
(vi) Collection of information in which personal secret information is recorded by administrative organ officials through abuse of authority (violation of Article 176: imprisonment for up to one year or a fine of up to JPY 500,000).
(vii) Failure to report or false reporting to the PPC by Personal Information Handling Business Operators, Pseudonymously Processed Information Handling Business Operators, Anonymous Processed Information Handling Business Operators, Personal Information Handling Business Operators, or Accredited Personal Information Protection Organisations (Article 177; for violation of Articles 143(1) and 150: fine of up to JPY 500,000).
(viii) Falsifying confirmation items when receiving personal data from a third party (Article 180(1); for violation of Article 30(2), a fine of up to JPY 100,000).
(ix) Misuse of the name of an Accredited Personal Information Protection Organisation (Article 180(i); for violation of Article 56, a non-penal fine of up to JPY 100,000).
(x) Violation of the obligation to notify an Accredited Personal Information Protection Organisation (Article 180(2); for violation of Article 51, a non-penal fine of up to JPY 100,000).
(xi) Unauthorised disclosure of retained personal information (Article 180(iii); for violation of Article 85(3), a non-penal fine of up to JPY 100,000).

(i), (ii), (iv), (v), and (vi) have foreign criminal provisions, while (iii), (iv), and (vii) have dual punishment provisions where both legal entities and individuals are punished.

680. The application of the penal provisions of the APPI is based on a system whereby penalties are imposed for violations of the law through the step-by-step involvement of the PPC, with the final step being the imposition of an order. The reason for this system is that when the APPI was legislated in 2003, it was considered necessary to improve violations through voluntary measures on the part of the business operator handling the personal information that originally caused the problem.

681. Furthermore, as a direct punishment, the 2015 amendment to the Act established the 'crime of unauthorised provision of personal information databases' (Article 174 of the Act). This provision punishes the mere violation of certain prohibited acts without an administrative order and applies to the act of providing or stealing personal information databases for the purpose of gaining an unfair profit.

682. The personal information handling business operator (or, in the case of a natural or legal person, an officer, representative, or manager) or employee is subject to the Personal Information Database Provision Offence, which applies in the event of personal data leakage. This penal provision also applies to persons who were personal information handling business operators or employees in the past. With regard to employees, not only employees with whom there is an employment relationship, but also persons engaged in work who are in a command-and-order relationship are included.

683. The acts covered include the provision of personal information databases (including those that have been reproduced or processed in whole or in part) handled in connection with the business. The act of providing personal information and personal data that are not searchable or systematic is not covered.

684. It is also limited to provision or theft for the purpose of illicit gain for oneself or a third party. Illicit interests include cases where personal information obtained using one's professional authority or position for personal gain is sold to another entity for financial gain.

685. Around the same time as the amendment of the APPI, the Unfair Competition Prevention Act was amended (Act No. 54 of 2015) to improve the scope of punishment for trade secret infringement, adding as punishable offences (1) those who acquire trade secrets and resell them with the knowledge that unauthorised disclosure has intervened (under the former Act, the scope of punishment was limited to those who have unlawfully acquired trade secrets); (2) punishment of acts of acquiring trade secrets overseas; and (3) punishment of attempted infringement of trade secrets.

686. With regard to the leakage of personal data from within a business entity, it is assumed that personal information databases may contain national identification numbers (My Number). The Number Act provides for a statutory penalty of up to four years imprisonment or a fine of up to JPY 2 million for the act of providing a specified personal information file containing personal secrets handled in the course of business without a justifiable reason.

Part IX. Specific Processing Situations

Chapter 1. Journalistic, Academic, Artistic, or Literary Expression

687. The APPI provides for exemptions to the Obligations of a Personal Information Handling Business Operator; that is, not all obligations apply to the press, literary profession, religion, and politics, and some part of obligations do not apply to academic research institutions. The provisions relating to the Obligations of a Personal Information Handling Business Operator set out in Chapter 4 of the Act are not applicable because of consideration for the fundamental human rights guaranteed by the Constitution. However, they must take the necessary measures themselves to ensure the proper handling of personal information, such as safety control measures and complaint handling, and endeavour to make public the details of such measures.

688. When a broadcasting institution, newspaper publisher, communication agency, or other press organisation (including an individual engaged in the press business) handles personal information for the purpose of providing it to the press, the obligations of the operator do not apply from the perspective of respecting the guarantees of freedom of expression provided for in the Constitution. The term 'press' refers to the widespread dissemination of information on social events through newspapers, radio, television, and other media, while the term 'media organisation' refers to an establishment or organisational body whose purpose is to provide the press with information. The concept of 'press' also includes individuals such as freelance journalists who are engaged in the business of reporting.[97]

689. With regard to the exemption for the literary profession such as novelists and other writers who handle personal information for the purpose of writing, the term 'writing' includes the creation of literary works, literary criticism, and reviews, as well as the writing of academic and practical books and other works that can be regarded as the outcome of human intellectual activity. On the other hand, items that are merely a list of data, such as a list of names, etc., do not fall under the category of 'writing'.[98]

690. With regard to cases where a religious organisation handles personal information for the purpose of using it for religious activities, a 'religious organisation'

97. General Guidelines, p. 155.
98. *Ibid.*

means (i) an organisation with facilities for worship (shrines, temples, churches, monasteries, and other similar organisations); (ii) an organisation that encompasses unitary religious organisations, whose main purposes are to spread religious doctrine, hold ceremonial events, and educate and train believers; (iii) an organisation encompassing unitary religious organisations (denominations, sects, orders, churches, congregations, bishoprics, and other similar organisations). The term 'religious activities' means spreading religious doctrines, conducting ceremonial events, and indoctrinating and fostering believers, while the phrase 'activities incidental to religious activities' means activities such as the management of cemeteries and lodgings and the operation of funeral services for people of other faiths, which are not necessarily religious activities in terms of their main purpose, but which are conducted with the expectation that they will have a secondary effect of activities carried out with the expectation that they will have the effect of spreading doctrines.[99]

691. With regard to cases where a political organisation handles personal information for the purpose of using it for political activities, a 'political organisation' means (i) an organisation whose original purpose is to promote, support, or oppose political principles or measures; (ii) an organisation whose original purpose is to recommend, support, or oppose a particular candidate for public office; (iii) any other organisation which promotes, supports, or opposes political principles or measures, or organisations that systematically and continuously carry out as their main activity the promotion, support, or opposition of a particular principle or measure or the recommendation, support, or opposition of a candidate for a particular public office. Organisations that are closely related to the activities of such organisations and whose purpose is to research political principles or measures or to provide financial support for political parties are also included in the term 'political organisation' in this article.[100]

692. The term 'academic research institution' means a university or other institution or organisation for the purpose of academic research or a person belonging to such an institution or organisation. The term 'universities and other academic research institutions or organisations' refers to national and private universities, research institutes of public interest corporations and other institutions, and 'academic societies' whose main purpose is academic research, and 'persons belonging to them' refers to teachers of national and private universities, researchers of research institutes of public interest corporations, members of academic societies, and others. Research activities at research institutions attached to private organisations also fall under the category of 'academic research institutions' if the main purpose of such institutions is academic research.[101]

693. Academic institutions were exempted from the same obligations of a personal information handling business operator as the press, writing, religion, and

99. *Ibid.*
100. General Guidelines, pp. 155–156.
101. General Guidelines, p. 30.

politics. However, the 2021 amendment to the Act stipulates that academic research institutions are not uniformly exempted from certain obligations and that some duties do not apply to them. Article 59 of the Act stipulates that:

> Academic research institutions which are Personal Information Handling Business Operators must comply with the provisions of this Act with regard to the handling of personal information for academic research purposes, take the necessary measures to ensure the appropriateness of such personal information, and endeavour to make public the details of such measures.

694. Among the regulations concerning academic institutions' use, acquisition, and provision of personal information, with regard to restrictions on the use of personal information for other purposes (Article 18 of the Act), the acquisition of special care-required personal information (Article 20, paragraph 2 of the Act), and the provision of personal information to third parties (Article 27 of the Act), when an academic research institution needs to handle personal information for academic research purposes, regarding the rights and interests of the individual or third parties, special exceptions are made where prior consent of the individual is not required, provided that there is no risk of unjustified infringement of the rights and interests of the individual or a third party.

695. On the other hand, even with regard to the regulations on the use, acquisition, and provision of personal information, the following are not required: specifying the purpose of use (Article 17 of the Act), prohibiting inappropriate use (Article 19 of the Act), proper acquisition (Article 20(1) of the Act), notification of the purpose of use (Article 21 of the Act), and ensuring the accuracy of data content (Article 22 of the Act). The same disciplines as for other personal information handling business operators will apply to academic research institutions that are personal information handling operators.

Chapter 2. Public Access to Official Documents

§1. Act on Access to Information Held by Administrative Organs

696. The Japanese information disclosure (freedom of information) legal system comprises the Act on Access to Information Held by Administrative Organs (Act No. 42 of 1999, promulgated on 14 May 1999 and enforced on 1 April 2001) and the Act on Access to Information Held by Incorporated Administrative Agencies (Act No. 140 of 2001, promulgated on 5 December 2001 and entered into force on 1 October 2002).

697. The information disclosure system is designed to enable administrative organs and incorporated administrative agencies to request disclosure of information held by these organisations. The purpose of this system is to ensure fair and democratic administrative activities by making information held by public organisations publicly available so that the public can understand the activities of these organisations.

698. The bodies subject to public access to information are administrative organs, all incorporated administrative agencies, and other bodies prescribed by law. The documents covered are administrative and corporate documents, which are documents, drawings, and data created or acquired by employees and others in the course of their duties and held by these bodies for organisational use.

699. Anyone can request the disclosure of administrative and corporate documents. When a request for disclosure is made, it is obligatory to disclose the administrative or corporate document to the person making the request. However, they may not be disclosed if they constitute non-disclosable information. The status of non-disclosable information is not determined at the discretion of these bodies; rather, it is the law that defines when information is non-disclosable.

§2. Public Access to Official Documents and Protection of Personal Information

700. The relationship between disclosure of information and protection of personal information is defined by the Act on Access to Information Held by Administrative Organs.

701. Non-disclosable information is the information listed below. If it falls under any of these categories, it may not be disclosed even if a request for disclosure is made:

(i) Personal information (information which has been made public by legal provisions or practice and information relating to positions such as those held by public officials or officers and employees of incorporated administrative agencies are excluded).

(ii) Corporate information (information which, if made public, may prejudice the legitimate interests of a legal entity or information voluntarily provided under non-disclosure conditions and which is not normally made public).
(iii) Defence and foreign affairs information (information which, if made public, may harm national security or damage relations of trust with other countries).
(iv) Public security information (information that, if made public, could hinder the maintenance of public safety and order, such as the prevention and investigation of crimes).
(v) Information on decision-making processes (information on internal or mutual deliberations, examinations, etc., of state organs, incorporated administrative agencies, etc., and local government agencies, which, if made public, may unreasonably impair the frank exchange of opinions).
(vi) Administrative and business information (information concerning the administration or business of a state organ, incorporated administrative agency, or local government agency, which, if made public, may impede the proper execution of such administration or business).

§3. Disclosure Procedures

702. Once a disclosure request is made, a disclosure decision is made within thirty days. However, there are times when an extension of thirty days may be granted.

703. If non-disclosable information is recorded, the requested information will not be disclosed, but the head of an administrative organ or an incorporated administrative agency may, at their discretion, disclose the information if they consider it particularly necessary in the public interest (discretionary disclosure).

704. If there are parts that can be disclosed and parts that cannot be disclosed, the parts that can be disclosed are to be disclosed (partial disclosure).

705. Otherwise, a request for disclosure may be refused without disclosing the existence or non-existence of the document, when the disclosure of the non-disclosable information would result from the fact that the existence of the document is publicly known in the first place (existence or non-existence response refused).

§4. Public Records Management Act

706. The management of administrative documents has been conducted in accordance with Article 22 of the abovementioned Act. Furthermore, the Thorough Management of Administrative Documents (14 December 2007) was published as a liaison conference proposal by the relevant ministries and agencies, and administrative organs have been thoroughly managing administrative documents based on these guidelines. Subsequently, the Act on the Management of Public Records (Act

No. 66 of 2009) was enacted on 24 June 2009 and came into force on 1 April 2011 as a law stipulating how to manage public records in administrative organs and incorporated administrative agencies.

707. This Act stipulates uniform document management rules by law. Specifically, the same law regulates the management of current documents in administrative organs and the management of non-current documents in the National Archives, etc., and establishes statutory unified management rules for administrative documents. Specific standards were stipulated in a Cabinet order and guidelines after study and deliberation by the Public Records Management Committee.

708. To improve the transfer system, a mechanism has been introduced to facilitate smooth transfer, with the support of experts, to assess and select important historical documents as early as possible. A preservation system in the interim archives established and operated by the incorporated administrative agency National Archives of Japan is newly established, which stipulates that all administrative document files, etc., that are important as historical materials must be transferred and that the prior consent of the prime minister is required for the disposal of administrative document files.

709. As a mechanism for checking document management, it requires regular reports from the heads of administrative organs to the prime minister on the state of management of administrative documents and stipulates an on-site inspection system and a recommendation system involving the prime minister.

710. To utilise the knowledge of external experts and specialists, a new Public Records Management Committee consisting of external experts has been established. The Committee investigates and deliberates on government ordinances, appeals concerning the use of specific historical archives, disposal of specific historical archives, and recommendations on the management of official documents and has established a system of on-site inspections conducted by the incorporated administrative agency National Archives of Japan, a preservation system in the interim archives, and an expert technical advice system on the preservation and use of historical archives.

711. To promote the use of specific historical archives, etc., it provides for the establishment of a new right of request for use and an appeal system, the promotion of active public use, and the transfer of all important historical documents, including incorporated administrative agencies' corporate document files.

Chapter 3. Processing National Identification Numbers

§1. National Identification Number System

712. In Japan, a unique number is assigned to each citizen and legal entity, and the number is used in various administrative procedures to increase the efficiency and transparency of administrative affairs and realise a fair and just society that is highly convenient for citizens in order to establish a 'social security and tax number system'.

713. The Act on the Use of Numbers to Identify a Specific Individual in Administrative Procedures (Act No. 27 of 31 May 2013) (hereinafter referred to as the 'Number Act') was enacted on 31 May 2013.

714. The 'National Identification Number' under the Number Law is called 'My Number'. This Number (consisting of an 11-digit number and one digit for inspection) must be (1) complete (assigned to everyone with a certificate of residence), (2) unique (assigned to each person with one number and no duplicates), (3) circulated in a 'private–public' relationship, and (4) available and visible (visibility). The number has the characteristics of usable visibility (visible number). It is used for the purpose of accurate identification in order to implement appropriate income redistribution based on accurate income information and protect the right to receive adequate social security benefits.

§2. My Number Legal System

715. The My Number legal system in Japan consists of (i) the Number Act, (ii) the Act for Establishment of the Number Act (Act on the Establishment of Relevant Acts in Connection with the Enforcement of the Act on the Use of Numbers to Identify Specific Individuals in Administrative Procedures (Act No. 28 of 31 May 2013), (iii) the Local Public Entities Information System Organisation Act (Act No. 29), and (iv) the Government CIO Act (Act to Amend Part of the Cabinet Act).

716. Based on these Acts, (a) the Cabinet Order on the Date for Enforcement of Part of the Act on the Use of Numbers to Identify Specific Individuals in Administrative Procedures (Cabinet Order No. 299 of 2013), (b) the relevant Cabinet Order for the Enforcement of Part of the Act on the Use of Numbers to Identify Specific Individuals in Administrative Procedures (Cabinet Order No. 300 of 2013), (c) the Order on the Organisation of the Secretariat of the Act on the Protection of Personal Information Protection Commission (Cabinet Order No. 301 of 17 October 2013), and (d) the Order for Enforcement of the Act on the Use of a Number to Identify a Specific Individual in Administrative Procedures (Cabinet Order No. 155 of 31 March 2016) have been enacted.

717. The Number Act enables administrative organs, local government agencies, and other persons who handle administrative affairs to utilise the functionality of personal numbers and corporate numbers to identify specific individuals, corporations, and other organisations for the efficient management and use of information and the prompt exchange of information with other persons who handle other administrative affairs. The Act also provides for matters necessary to enable citizens who make applications or notifications and other procedures involving these persons to reduce their burden by simplifying the procedures and obtaining a simple means of identification.

718. The Act on the Local Authorities Information System Organisation provides that, as an organisation jointly operated by local authorities, the local authorities information system organisation is responsible for the administration of the Basic Resident Registration Act, the Act on Certification Services of Local Authorities for Electronic Signatures, and the Act on the Use of Numbers to Identify Specific Individuals in Administrative Procedures, and other local authorities' information. The Government Chief Information Officer (CIO) Act establishes the local authorities' information system organisation for the purpose of carrying out affairs related to local authority information systems on behalf of local authorities and specifies matters related to the organisation and scope of its operations.

719. The Government CIO Act establishes the Cabinet Information and Communications Policy Directorate (Government CIO: Chief Information Officer) as a special national public officer in the Cabinet Secretariat in order to strengthen the general coordination function of the Cabinet Secretariat in relation to the use of ICT. The Government CIO is also a member of the IT Strategic Headquarters (Strategic Headquarters for the Promotion of an Advanced Information and Telecommunications Network Society), and the law stipulates, among other things, that the Headquarters may have the Government CIO carry out some of its administrative tasks.

720. The development of the number system is based on the decision to introduce a 'number system for social security and tax', in which each citizen is allocated a number, as part of the integrated reform of social security and taxation in the Outline of Social Security and Tax Number System compiled on 28 June 2003.

721. The study on personal information protection in this system was mainly conducted by the Working Group on Personal Information Protection, which was established under the Practical Study Group on the Number System for Social Security and Taxation and the Planning Committee of the IT Strategic Headquarters. The study focused on the institutional issues necessary for the protection of personal information and privacy. Additionally, the Working Group on Information Linkage Infrastructure Technology examined matters relating to technology among matters common to the numbering system. Furthermore, to specifically examine the implementation framework for information protection assessment in the numbering system, an Information Protection Assessment Sub-Working Group was established under the Personal Information Protection Working Group to examine the assessment of the protection of specified personal information.

§3. Measures to Protect Personal Information and Privacy under the Number Act

722. Measures to protect personal information and privacy under the numbering system include (i) the number must be changeable, (ii) the scope of use must be limited (in the fields of social security, taxation, and disaster prevention), (iii) requests to provide personal numbers must be prohibited, and (iv) identification must be carried out when personal numbers are provided.

723. With regard to (i), the mayor of the municipality defines the personal number obtained by converting the resident registration code as a legally entrusted task, notifies the person in writing, and allows the number to be changed in case of theft, leakage, or other damage. Foreign residents such as mid- to long-term residents and special permanent residents are also covered.

724. The Number Act stipulates the scope of use of the number, specifically (1) use by national and local institutions in administrative work in the field of social security, levy and collection of national and local taxes, and disaster prevention; (2) use by persons (including agents and trustees) who make applications or notifications for relevant administrative work; and (3) use at financial institutions in the event of a disaster.

725. It is prohibited to ask others to provide personal numbers except in cases provided for in the Number Act, and when a person provides an individual number, the identity of the person must be verified.

§4. Institutional Measures to Protect Personal Information

726. In addition to the proper handling and protection of personal information under the APPI, the APPI requires that measures for the protection of personal information necessary in connection with the handling of numbers must be taken, as follows:

(i) Restrictions on the handling of specified personal information (collection, storage, creation, and provision of specified personal information files) prohibit the collection and storage of specified personal information (personal information with a personal number) and the creation of specified personal information files, except in accordance with the provisions of the Number Act. The provision of specified personal information is also prohibited in principle. However, it is possible for administrative organs to handle such information only in accordance with the provisions of the Number Act, such as the provision of information through the information provision network system.

(ii) Regarding mechanisms that prevent the centralised management of personal information, such as not using the number as a linkage key when providing information through the information provision network system.

(iii) As for the mechanism to confirm one's own information, a system (MynaPortal)[102] is provided to enable citizens to confirm records of information provision from their home computers.

(iv) The Specified Personal Information Protection Commission has been established and began operating on 1 January 2004, and its scope of supervision was since expanded to include the PPC. Based on the rules established by the Commission, a specific personal information protection assessment, which falls under the category of PIA, has also been carried out.

102. This term is the Japanese abbreviation for the My Number Portal website.

Selected Bibliography

Asia Pacific Privacy Authorities, *Welcome New Member Japan*, 29 June 2016 http://www.appaforum.org/resources/media_release/asia-pacific-privacy-authorities-welcome-new-member-japan/.

Agreement between Japan and the United States of America on Digital Trade (abbreviated as US-Japan Digital Trade Agreement), 1 January 2020.

Administrative Guide to the Act on the Protection of Personal Information (for administrative organs, etc.) (effective 1 April 2023).

Cabinet Office, Government of Japan, *Quarterly Estimates of GDP October-December 2022* (The 2nd preliminary) https://www.esri.cao.go.jp/en/sna/menu.html.

Commentary for Guidelines for Protection of Personal Information in Telecommunications Business (MIC Public Notice No. 297 of 14 September 2017 (Updated in February 2021)) https://www.soumu.go.jp/main_content/000744055.pdf.

Ministry of Foreign Affairs, *The 27th EU-Japan Summit* (27 May 2021) https://www.mofa.go.jp/mofaj/erp/ep/page6_000563.html.

Foreign Countries which have Systems for the Protection of Personal Information which are Recognised as Being at the Same Level as Japan in Protecting the Rights and Interests of Individuals (Personal Information Protection Commission Notice No. 1 of 2019).

Geospatial Information Authority of Japan, *Number of islands in Japan* https://www.gsi.go.jp/kihonjohochousa/pressrelease20230228.html (accessed 1 March 2023).

G7 Leaders' Communique, G7 Summit (Cornwall, 11–13 June 2021).

Guidelines for Protection of Personal Information in Telecommunications Business (MIC Public Notice No. 152 of 18 April 2017) https://www.soumu.go.jp/main_content/000744054.pdf. In details of this guideline.

Guidelines and Q&As for Personal Information Handling Business Operators (relating to the General Provisions of the Act on the Protection of Personal Information, Chapter 4, etc.

Guidelines on the Act on the Protection of Personal Information (General Guidelines) (updated 8 September 2022).

Guidelines on the Act of the Protection of Personal Information (Provision to Third Parties in Foreign Countries) (updated 17 November 2021).

Guidelines on the Act on the Protection of Personal Information (Obligation to Verify and Record regarding Third Party Provision) (updated 17 November 2021).

Guidelines on the Act on the Protection of Personal Information (Pseudonymously Processed Information and Anonymously Processed Information) (updated 17 November 2021).

Guidelines on the Act on the Protection of Personal Information (Accredited Personal Information Protection Organisations) (29 October 2021).

Guidelines Pertaining to Administrative Organs (related to Chapter 5, etc., of the Act on the Protection of Personal Information).

Guidelines on the Act on the Protection of Personal Information (administrative organs, etc.) (effective 1 April 2023).

Ministry of Justice, *On Judicial System Reform,* https://www.moj.go.jp/housei/servicer/kanbou_housei_chousa18.html.

Notice for Handling Health Information among Personal Information in the Field of Employment Management.

Personal Information Protection Commission, *International Relations* https://www.ppc.go.jp/enforcement/cooperation/international_conference/.

Q&As on the Guidelines to the Act on the Protection of Personal Information (Q&As added and updated May 2022).

Q&A on the Act of the Protection of Personal Information (for administrative organs, etc.) (addition to and update of Q&A, effective 1 April 2023) (enacted on 1 April 2023).

Statistics Bureau of the Ministry of Internal Affairs and Communications (MIC), *Population Estimates* (finalised October 2022) (published 20 March 2023) https://www.stat.go.jp/data/jinsui/new.html.

Supreme Court, *Overview of the Courts* https://www.courts.go.jp/about/sosiki/gaiyo/index.html.

Supreme Court, 'Judicial System Reform: the Judicial System in the 21st Century' https://www.courts.go.jp/about/sihou/kaikaku_sihou_21/index.html.

Supreme Court, 'The Government's Plan to Promote Reform of the Judicial System' https://www.courts.go.jp/about/sihou/kaikaku_keikaku/seihu_suisin/index.html.

Koji Sato, *A Constitutional Theory of the Right to Privacy* (Its Public Law Aspects), 86(5) KYOTO L. REV.(1970).

Fumio Shimpo, *Big Data as Cliche*, EIP, 2012-EIP-55(7) (2012), pp. 1–6.

TPP11 Agreement (Comprehensive and Progressive Agreement on Trans-Pacific Partnership), signed by twelve countries in February 2016.

The UK-Japan Comprehensive Economic Partnership Agreement (EPA) (26 March 2021).

Samuel D. Warren & Louis D. Brandeis, *The Right to Privacy*, 4 HARV. L. REV.193, 1890.

Index

The numbers here refer to paragraph numbers.

Index

www.ingramcontent.com/pod-product-compliance
Lightning Source LLC
Chambersburg PA
CBHW071437230926
51846CB00001B/265
9789403528670